The Indian Metropolis

The Indian Metropolis
A View Toward the West

Norma Evenson

Yale University Press
New Haven and London

Designed by Ken Botnick
and set in Perpetua type at Brevis Press.
Printed in Hong Kong by South Sea Int'l Press Ltd.

Library of Congress Cataloging-in-Publication Data

Evenson, Norma.
    The Indian metropolis.
    Bibliography: p.
    Includes index.
    1. Architecture—India—Foreign influences.
2. Architecture, British—India.   3. Architecture and
society—India.   I. Title.
NA1502.E94   1989   720'.954   88–27953
ISBN 0–300–04333–3

The paper in this book meets the guidelines for
permanence and durability of the Committee on
Production Guidelines for Book Longevity of the
Council on Library Resources.

10   9   8   7   6   5   4   3   2   1

Contents

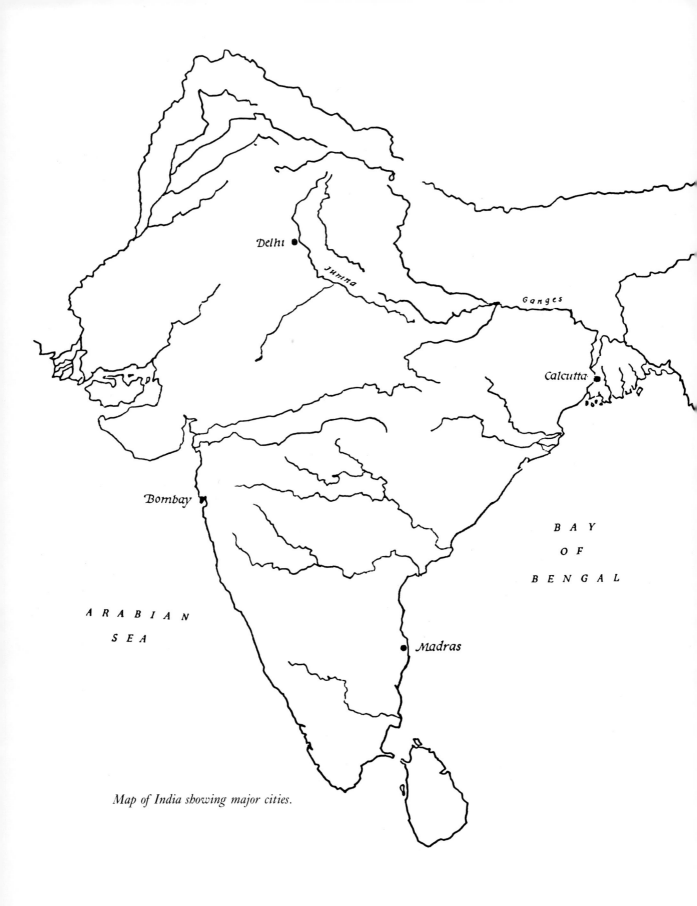

Delhi

Jumna

Ganges

Calcutta

Bombay

BAY

OF

BENGAL

ARABIAN

SEA

Madras

Map of India showing major cities.

Preface

My first sojourn in India was in 1961–62, when I was a Fulbright student posted at the School of Planning and Architecture in Delhi and doing research on the planning of Chandigarh, the post-independence capital of Punjab. The investigation of this controversial city, designed by foreigners, inevitably inspired questions about the applicability of Western planning and architectural concepts to the Indian context. Chandigarh, of course, was by no means unique, but reflected the continuation of a long history of foreign influence on Indian architecture and urban planning. The professional school where I lived had been inspired by British prototypes, with English as its medium of instruction, and was housed in a building clearly derived from the International Style. The Indian architects and planners of my acquaintance were well traveled and cosmopolitan in outlook, and most had studied abroad. While respectful of tradition, all were well versed in the ideology of Western modernism, and seemed to acknowledge a certain universality in its precepts. They belonged to professional organizations modeled on those of Britain, and read professional journals reflective of international opinion. While much of India remained rural, the work of architects and planners seemed to lie primarily within the great metropolis, a hybrid setting that had long provided a fusion of East and West.

This book is based on research begun in 1981–82, twenty years after my first stay in India. In the intervening time, I had continued to study the planning and architecture of major cities, with extensive work done in Brazil and France. My interest in India remained, however, and I found the major cities particularly fascinating because of their varied architectural imagery and cultural juxtapositions. I have attempted a broad survey of the architecture and planning of Bombay, Calcutta, Madras, and New Delhi from their inception until the present time. Created by the British, these cities served in themselves as instruments of cultural change in India, providing a theater for the demonstration of European architectural and planning concepts. (In some respects this study forms part of the history of Western architecture and urbanism.) Yet the cities in question were always predominantly Indian in population, reflecting many aspects of traditional Indian settlements. As intellectual and artistic centers, the metropolises have provided a focus for continuing debate on Western in-

fluence in India. Over the years, the evolution of the built environment has been accompanied by a mixed chorus of praise and condemnation, with points of dispute
ranging from the appropriateness of foreign building styles to the very nature of the
modern metropolis.

Present-day opinion does not always lend itself to easy definitions of East and
West, and many issues currently raised by Indian critics regarding the urban environment are matters of universal concern. Apprehension about the destructive winds of
change, and concern for the viability of tradition in the contemporary context can be
encountered throughout the world. What some may view as a troubling residue of
colonialism may appear to others as the inevitable outgrowth of an international culture, and the reflection of forces that, once set in motion, are unlikely to diminish.
The new motorways and suburbs, the high-rise apartments and office blocks breaking
the city skyline may be seen as evidence of India's progress and prosperity, or as an
alien imposition antithetical to Indian realities. In its juxtaposition of contradictory
images, the contemporary Indian metropolis both enthralls and dismays, and, like its
counterparts elsewhere, raises many unanswerable questions.

Acknowledgments

Field work in India in 1981–82 was supported by the Indo-U.S. Subcommission for Education and Culture and the University Grants Commission, supplemented by a grant from the American Institute of Indian studies in 1986. Archival work in London during the summer of 1984 was assisted by the American Philosophical Society.

In addition to having access to libraries and archives in India, I was fortunate to receive substantial personal assistance. In Calcutta, Dr. N. R. Ray of the Institute for Historical Studies provided an introduction to Calcutta's scholarly community. Dr. B. N. Mukherjee of the University of Calcutta generously gave me access to an important body of research material on Calcutta architecture compiled by an interdisciplinary group at the university. I am particularly indebted to Dr. Somnath Mukhopadhyay, and also to Anit Ghose and Arindam Chakraborty for guiding me to Calcutta buildings. My thanks go also to Harish Gupta of the National Library, and to Lt. Colonel Chitranjan Sawant, who enabled me to view Fort William.

In Delhi, Nalini Thakur and Dr. Narayani Gupta were generous in both time and effort in guiding me throughout the city. Unusual assistance was also provided in Madras by Bennett Pithavadian. While I was in Bombay, Kisan Mehta gave knowledgeable guidance to the buildings of the old Indian settlement, and Prafulla Dahanukar was particularly helpful in taking me to visit Bombay chawls.

I am also grateful to Melvin Webber, Randolph Langenbach, Tata Industries, and Jagdish Mistry for their contributions of photographs.

I.

Three Hybrid Cities

Reflecting on the evolving fortunes of Madras, Rudyard Kipling wrote in 1893:

> Clive kissed me on the mouth and eyes and brow,
>   Wonderful kisses, so that I became
> Crowned above Queens—a withered beldame now,
>   Brooding on ancient fame.[1]

These often quoted lines are somewhat misleading in their evocation of a glorious past and melancholy decline. Madras had never been "crowned above Queens," and was no "withered beldame." Far from reflecting the romantic image of a once-glorious metropolis fallen upon evil days, turn-of-the-century Madras was a prosaically thriving modern settlement of over half a million that had grown steadily from its beginnings two centuries before. It was true, of course, that Madras had failed to match the phenomenal growth and prosperity of Bombay and Calcutta, and it might have seemed backward by comparison. In addition, Madras simply did not look like a city. Rather than a city in decay, visitors found virtually no urban fabric at all.

Like other British colonial cities of India, Madras owed its existence to the trading activities of the British East India Company, founded in 1599. As the Mogul Empire declined, Britain, in competition with the Portuguese, Dutch, and French, established a series of commercial ports in India. The first had been created on the west coast at Surat. A similar settlement on the eastern coast, Madras, was founded in 1639, when negotiations with local rulers permitted construction of a trading center in Vijayanagar south of the fishing village of Madiraspatam. British commerce on the Coromandel coast was largely based on the purchase and export of textiles, and the surrounding territory provided a source of high-quality, yet inexpensive cloth.

The site of the future city consisted of a tract of flat land two miles wide extending five miles along a beach. Opening to the sea at the southern edge was a shallow, winding river known as the Triplicane, now called the Cooum. Another river, then called the North of Elambore, extended on a north-south axis parallel to the ocean about a mile inland. It curved eastward to join the Cooum where it emptied into the sea. Farther inland, the two rivers were joined by a canal.

There was no natural harbor, however, and a visitor noted that it "would probably have been difficult to find a worse place for a capital than that chosen for Madras, on the extreme point of a coast, where the current is most rapid, and where a tremendous surf breaks, even in the finest weather." Ships were compelled to anchor offshore, while cargo and passengers were carried through the surf to the beach in small boats (fig. 1). Transfer from the ship was far from easy in a swell that often ran as high as twenty-five feet, and landing at Madras became a memorable experience for travelers. An Englishwoman arriving in 1780 reported that "nothing is more terrible at Madras than the surf which . . . is not only alarming but dangerous. . . . notwithstanding every care, many lives are lost."[2]

The nucleus of the town was Fort St. George, the first British fortification in India, established adjacent to the beach in April 1640. Consisting of a walled square with pointed corner bastions, the fort included the "factory" or mercantile office, where business was transacted by the agents, or "factors" of the company. The fort was soon surrounded by a walled European settlement called White Town. As viewed in 1699 by Thomas Salmon, an ensign in the Madras garrison,

> the buildings are of brick, several of the houses two stories high, . . . Their roofs are flat and . . . being secured with battlements, they take the fresh air upon them morning and evening. . . . By the dimensions I have given of this place, it may be very well concluded there are no gardens or very large court yards before their houses; and indeed they stand pretty close to the street; but the Governor and people of condition have gardens at a little distance from the town [fig. 2].[3]

Like other colonial cities, Madras attracted Indian settlers and became predominantly Indian in population. As the old Muslim aristocracy declined, a new focus of power evolved within the largely Hindu merchant classes. Like the British, the Indians were creating an aristocracy of trade, and the colonial cities provided many Indians a counterpart to the social mobility and rapid access to wealth that had lured the British to India in the first place.

The separation of British and Indian populations that characterized all the colonial cities was particularly noticeable in Madras, where the Indian settlement, called Black Town (renamed Georgetown in 1906), took the form of a walled enclave directly north of Fort St. George. Although the physical isolation of the British might be seen as a conscious enhancement of their position as rulers, it also reflected prevailing local patterns of urbanization. According to long-standing Indian tradition, religious communities inhabited separate areas, with Hindu districts further subdivided into caste quarters. In the view of orthodox Hindus, the British, for all their wealth and power, were outcastes, and physical contact threatened spiritual pollution. In 1765, it was noted that the Indian servants employed by the British, "are such strict observers of their religion . . . that they will neither eat nor drink, and are even unwilling to sleep in their masters' houses."[4]

Reflecting a regularity in planning similar to that of the British town, Black Town embodied a pattern of straight streets within a rectangular boundary. Thomas Salmon described the settlement as "better than a mile and a half in circumference;

1. *Beach of Madras by William Simpson, 1867.*

2. *A view of part of St. Thome Street, Fort St. George, 1804.*

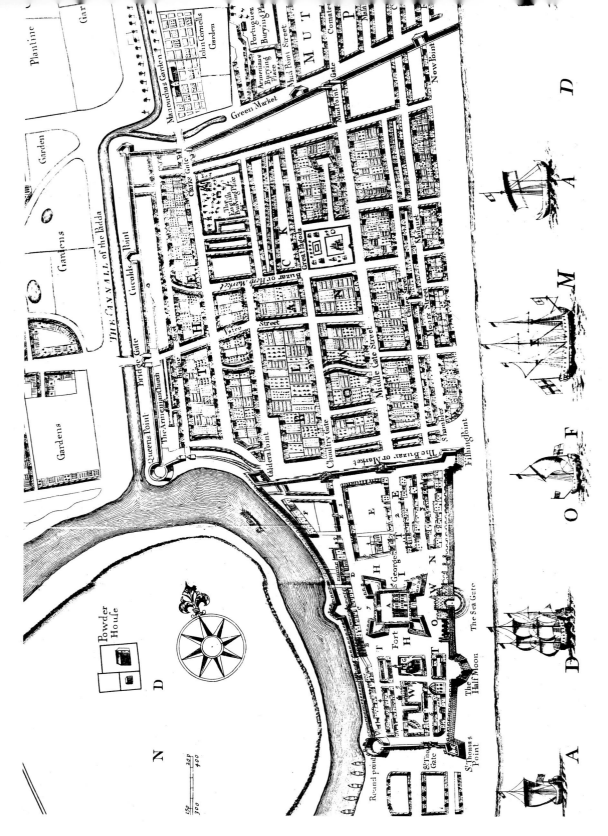

3. Map of Madras by Thomas Pitt, c. 1710. At this time, Fort St. George and Black Town were directly adjacent. Clearance in Black Town to provide defensible space around the fort was begun by the French, who occupied the city in 1746, and continued by the British after 1749.

. . . The streets of the Black Town are wide, and trees planted in some of them; and having the sea on one side and a river on the other, there are few towns so pleasantly situated or better supplied." Beyond the Black Town, he reported, "are gardens for half a mile together planted with mangoes, coconuts, guavoes, orange trees, etc., where everybody has the liberty of walking and may purchase the most delicious fruits for a trifle" (fig. 3).[5]

Politically unstable conditions in eighteenth-century India created a state of more or less continual internal warfare. These conditions were exacerbated by the presence of European powers fighting among themselves and becoming involved in local disputes. Responding to the European war between France and England, the French attacked and captured Madras in 1746, occupying Fort St. George until it was returned to the British in 1749 by the Treaty of Aix-la-Chapelle. Both the French and the British sought to augment the defenses of the fort, with reconstruction culminating in 1783 in a semi-circular ring of pointed bastions. As the closely packed buildings of Black Town were considered a potential shelter for an approaching enemy, the Indian settlement was razed and rebuilt to the north, leaving a protective zone of unbuilt land adjacent to the fort.

Hazardous times seemed to make a compact fortified town the only feasible form of settlement. The French attacked Madras again in 1758, with extensive destruction of outlying buildings, and there were repeated raids by local chieftains. Yet in spite of the continual threat of invasion, Madras evolved in a widely dispersed pattern.

Although the British attempted to duplicate many aspects of European life in India, they made no attempt to recreate the British city. Yet the establishment of colonial settlements in India coincided with what is often judged the golden age of British urban design. Dominated by precepts of Renaissance classicism, large-scale development of such cities as London and Edinburgh was characterized by a regular street pattern, unified terrace housing, and planned sequences of open space or "squares." The great urban estates in Britain were conceived as long-term investments, with land remaining in single ownership, and with a single source of developmental control. Individuality was subordinated to the overriding concept of a unified environment.

The founders of Madras and other colonial cities were temporary sojourners—adventurers in search of wealth. City planning involves an investment in the future, and the future, for those lucky enough to survive and make their fortunes, lay in Britain. Although the initial settlement pattern of Madras embodied compactness and regularity, the overall development of the city reflected a semi-rural type of building. While the London merchant, confined in a narrow terrace house, dreamed of the day when he might retire to a country estate, his counterpart in India enjoyed the life of a country gentleman while still engaged in urban commerce. In spite of the opposition of British East India Company officials to "the folly and vanity of merchants in having the parade of country houses and gardens,"[6] and attempts by the Madras Council to restrict land grants to the upper ranks of employees, a general movement outward proved irresistible.

In the early days of Madras, company employees had often sought release from urban life beyond the walls of the fort, where an eight-acre tract, called the Company's Garden, was developed for recreational use. The more prosperous soon began to create their own gardens, many of which contained pavilions and houses intended for weekend use. Before long the "garden house" became the preferred full-time dwelling (figs. 4 and 5). By the nineteenth century, the fort had been completely abandoned as a place of residence, and a traveler noted, "In appearance, Madras differs widely from Calcutta, having no European town. . . . The gentlemen of the settlement live entirely in their garden houses, as they very properly call them; for these are all surrounded by gardens, so closely planted, that the neighboring house is rarely visible."[7] While admiring the verdant scene, he also noted that the dispersed pattern of dwelling had "certainly increased the labour of paying visits, for, owing to the large extent of ground that is occupied by each house, the distance to be passed is frequently full three miles" (389).

Although the garden house was characteristically a British form of residence, some well-to-do Indians also began to adopt this type of dwelling. For Indians, the most prestigious locations were in the vicinity of the oldest temples of the district, and two favored sites were the villages of Mylapore and Komaleswaranpet. By the end of the nineteenth century, it had become common for Indians to acquire European garden houses, sometimes subdividing the properties into smaller house lots.

For the carriage-owning classes, traversing the verdant expanses of Madras presented a pleasant prospect. One visitor described the city as "ornamented with gentlemen's houses. . . . As they are almost surrounded by trees, when you see one of these superb dwellings encompassed by a grove, a distant view of Madras with the sea and shipping so disposed as to form a perfect landscape, it is beyond comparison the most charming picture I ever beheld or could have imagined." Carriage drives in the evening were to remain a favored recreation in Madras. Another observed that, "one can ride and drive as one will, the roads are excellent, one flies one's way, the air we breathe is balsamic, invigorating. We drive past one villa after the other. All are situated in beautifully laid out and well-kept parks and gardens" (fig. 6).[8]

The evolution of Madras as the "city of magnificent distances" reflected a continual accretion of territory beyond the initial grant of 1639. From this compact settlement, the city spread westward, but primarily toward the south, absorbing a number of existing villages whose names continued to identify neighborhoods in Madras. Although the population of Madras was only 55 thousand in 1750 and 125 thousand in 1800, the geographic area of the city was extensive, encompassing an amorphous patchwork of villages, rice paddys, and low-density residential areas. Many of the villages absorbed by the city would continue their self-contained existence relatively independent of the commercial center. In the absence of any comprehensive plan, major urban thoroughfares evolved from military roads extending outward from the fort. One artery was Mount Road, which led southwest to the outlying settlement of St. Thomas Mount and was destined to become a major commercial street. Another important spine of urban development evolved along Poonamalee Road leading westward from the fort (fig. 7).

Within the sprawling city, Black Town persisted as a focus of high density. A description of Black Town in 1855 noted that

the minor streets, occupied by the natives, are numerous, irregular, and of various dimensions. Many of them are extremely narrow and ill-ventilated. . . . [A typical house took the form of] a hollow square, the rooms opening into a

4. *Madras garden house by Justinian Gantz, 1832.*

5. *Garden house on Poonamalee Road.*

6. Mobrays Road, Madras.

courtyard in the center which is entered by one door from the street. This effectually secures the privacy so much desiderated by the Natives, but at the same time prevents proper ventilation and is the source of many diseases. The streets, with few exceptions, have drains on both side which are deep and narrow, and besides there are three common sewers running from the eastern part of the town towards the sea. The system of drainage, however, is far from perfect, and the fall to the sea is slight [fig. 8].[9]

In the early days of Madras, all company business was transacted within the fort. In 1798, however, the second Lord Clive established the Collectorate of Customs on a site along the beach north of the Fort. This provided the nucleus for a district of mercantile development along the water on what came to be called First Line Beach (later North Beach Road) just east of Black Town. In future years the port would lie adjacent, giving further impetus to commercial development.

In India, as in Europe, the nineteenth century marked a time of extensive public works and improvements in municipal services. In Madras, however, limited budgets tended to keep such projects at relatively modest levels. The spread-out form of the city, moreover, made adequate provision of roads, utilities, and sewers a heavy drain on the city's resources. And while extensive attention was given to amenities in the fash-

7. *Map of Madras published in 1859.*

8. Black Town, c. 1860.

ionable districts, peripheral villages were often neglected, as were the squatter colonies that emerged on the outskirts of the city.

British administrators perennially complained about the resistance of the Indians to taxation for civic improvements. The Indians, for their part, were not always in accord with the British as to the nature of improvements, and they entertained chronic doubts as to the benefits they would derive from British public works. In Madras, as in other colonial cities, Indian participation in municipal government tended to be limited to an elite, westernized class, and many were convinced that tax revenues were employed primarily for the benefit of the British.

Given the semi-rural nature of Madras, proposals for planned open space and "beautification" might have seemed superfluous. Nevertheless, in 1860, a 116-acre "People's Park" was created when the west wall of Black Town was removed. The most beautiful natural feature of the city, the oceanfront beach, was made accessible in 1884 through the addition of a broad boulevard. Governor Grant Duff, sponsor of the project, boasted that "we have greatly benefited Madras by turning the rather dismal beach of five years ago into one of the most beautiful promenades in the world. From old Sicilian recollections, I gave . . . to our new creation the name of the Marina" (fig. 9).[10] From the marina, the beach stretched southward without interruption for more than seven miles. Embellishing the beach, however, did nothing to alleviate the lack of port facilities, and in spite of the progress of modern engineering, nature continually thwarted efforts to create an artificial harbor. Piers constructed during the second half of the nineteenth century were repeatedly destroyed by storms, and it was not until 1895 that a man-made harbor was successfully completed.

Although the nineteenth century reflected a period of growth, and new commercial activity appeared in the form of tanneries, railroad workshops, and textile mills, Madras was bypassed by the great industrial boom that was transforming the rival

9. View of the Marina.

cities of Bombay and Calcutta. Madras did not have a region of natural resources upon which to base a strong industrial economy, and by 1900, one-quarter of the city's 505 thousand people were supported by employment in government, professional, and personal services. The great Indian fortunes of Calcutta and Bombay had no counterparts in Madras. An English visitor noted in 1879 that "they say the town is very poor, and indeed it does present a rather tumble-down, dilapidated appearance; . . . There are no rich native houses such as one sees at Bombay and, I am told, Calcutta; neither are there many rich natives in Madras, as little business is done there."[11]

Having been spared both the blessings and the curses of rapid industrialization, Madras remained remarkably stable in physical character. Sprawling nine miles along the coast, with an average depth of about three-and-one-half miles, the city as a whole never achieved a truly urban image. At the turn of the century, the *Imperial Gazetteer* reported that "the city presents a disappointing appearance and possesses not a single handsome street."[12]

A similar account declared that

> strangers to the city find it difficult to realize that they are in a place as populous as Manchester. Approached from the sea, little of Madras is visible except the first row of its houses . . . and the European quarter is anything but typically urban in appearance. Most of the roads in this part run between avenues, and are flanked by frequent groves of palms and other trees; the shops in the principal thoroughfare, the wide Mount Road, though many of them are imposing erections, often stand back from the street with gardens in front of them; the better European residences are built in the midst of compounds which almost attain the dignity of parks; and rice-fields frequently wind in and out between these in almost rural fashion. Even in the most thickly peopled native quarters,

such as Black Town and Triplicane, there is little of the crowding found in many other Indian towns, and houses of more than one storey are the exception rather than the rule.[13]

Public buildings were judged "more than usually handsome; but this again is a fact which the stranger is not likely to perceive immediately, for they are scattered about in a manner that robs them of all collective effect." It was noted that, "although large parts are strictly urban in their characteristics, the City as a whole is, in fact, rather a fortuitous collection of villages, separated from the surrounding country by an arbitrary boundary line, than a town in the usual sense of the word (figs. 10 and 11).

The failure of Madras to achieve metropolitan grandeur seems to have disturbed none of its inhabitants. If it was a backwater, it was an agreeable backwater, and well into the twentieth century the British of Madras were able to enjoy a style of living that pressures of population and high land values had made impossible in Calcutta and Bombay. It was noted that "compounds are the largest in India, so that quite insignificant official personages or private individuals have their three or four acres of ground, and many have small estates, like miniature parks, with lawns and groves and kitchen gardens and pastureland."[14]

In its decentralization, Madras might, in some ways, be viewed as ahead of its time. In form the city was essentially an urbanized region based on low-density housing, with scattered commercial and institutional facilities and a notable absence of traditional urban structure. Such unfocused agglomerations have become commonplace in our own time, and while we tend to associate amorphous growth with the evolution of motor transportation, in Madras the essential ingredient seems rather to have been a consistent preference for a particular type of housing combined with the abundance of land.

It was British living patterns that determined the overall form of Madras, and it was primarily the British who experienced the city as a whole, traveling throughout its far-flung fabric from home to clubs, churches, and employment. Private transportation was essential. So while the carriage-owning British enjoyed the decentralized aspects of Madras, most of the Indian population continued to inhabit a traditional urban ambient, in which housing, employment, and religious institutions were not separately zoned but interwoven within a single entity (fig. 12). By 1900 one-third of the Madras population lived in Black Town on 9 percent of the total urban area. As a city within a city, Black Town provided both self-containment and reasonable access to the city as a whole. At the same time, existing villages scattered throughout Madras could pursue an essentially rural way of life without regard to the surrounding city. Madras thus provided within a single municipality three distinct styles of living, the essentially suburban ambient favored by the British, the high-density urban core of Black Town, and the intimate village.

Although Madras could be derided for its lack of urbanity, it may have provided a more humane environment for immigrants than the other colonial cities. In contrast to Bombay and Calcutta, largely dominated by male industrial workers, Madras attracted men and women in approximately equal numbers, and the population has been described as "really the ordinary population of an Indian village multiplied many

10. General Hospital Road, Madras.

11. Pycrofts Road in Triplicane, Madras. A villagelike atmosphere persisted even in this relatively central district.

12. *Georgetown continues as a lively, mixed-use district.*

times."[15] For those indifferent to the excitement of the great metropolis, Madras may have seemed a pleasant compromise. And if it lacked the glamor of Calcutta, it also lacked many of the horrors.

Just as Kipling made condescending references to Madras in his verse, he derided the pretensions of Calcutta in a poem containing the following lines:

> Thus the midday halt of Charnock—more's the pity!
>   Grew a City.
> As the fungus sprouts chaotic from its bed,
>   So it spread—
> Chance-directed, chance-erected, laid and built
>   On the silt—
> Palace, byre, hovel—poverty and pride—
>   Side by Side;
> And, above the packed and pestilential town,
>   Death looked down.[16]

The city destined to eclipse Madras was established on the banks of the Hooghly River in Bengal in 1656 (fig. 13). This waterway, flowing southward to the sea, gave access to the rich trade of the Ganges valley and had attracted a number of European trading centers. Approximately ninety-six miles from the Bay of Bengal, the site selected by the British East India Company agent Job Charnock marked the farthest point inland accessible by ocean-going ships. Creation of a permanent settlement was delayed, and it was only following a lengthy period of military action and political maneuvering that, in 1690, Prince Azim Ooshan granted the British the riverside villages of Calcutta, Gobindapur, and Sutanuti for the sum of one thousand rupees. This grant was supplemented in 1716 by the addition of thirty-eight villages, giving Calcutta a territory that extended about three miles along the river and one mile inland.

Although the company agents praised the acquisition of Calcutta as "the Best Money that Ever was spent," the swampy, low-lying terrain was far from ideal. An eighteenth-century visitor observed that Charnock "could not have chosen a more unhealthy place."[17] While the sites of Madras and Calcutta were similar in that they were flat and bordered on one side by water, they were in other ways notably different. Madras was considered a healthy district of dry soil cleansed by refreshing sea breezes. Calcutta was hacked out of jungle swamp. Before the discovery that malaria was transmitted by mosquitoes, common observation had associated swamps with fever-laden "bad air." In Calcutta, the prevailing stench of stagnant water, of decaying flesh and vegetation seemed redolent of death. Even trees were viewed as a menace; their foliage was thought to hamper the circulation of air, and their discarded leaves were feared as a source of rot.

The British of Calcutta became virtually obsessed with "ventilation" as a condition of urban salubrity, and the removal of vegetation would continue to be urged as a health measure. Even though the urbanized area was gradually drained and denuded of trees, the surrounding swamp and jungle were considered a persistent threat. The monsoon season was recognized as the most hazardous time of year, and it was reportedly the custom for those citizens still alive in the autumn to hold a banquet to celebrate their survival.

14. Looking north toward Dalhousie Square from Wellesley Place.

Political conditions in eighteenth-century Bengal remained unsettled, and, as in Madras, the British attempted to enhance the security of the settlement by constructing a fort. The first fort of Calcutta, named for the reigning king, William III, took the form of an irregular tetragon bordering the river. Completed in 1702, it initially contained the governor's residence as well as workshops, warehouses, and lodgings for company employees.

As in Madras, a town soon took form outside the walls of the fort, extending about one-half mile to the north and to the south, and six hundred yards to the east. According to contemporary account, "the town, rising about this old Fort, like one about a baronial castle in the medieval times, was built without order, as the builders thought most convenient for their own affairs."[18] The taste for garden houses was to influence the form of Calcutta as it had that of Madras. In this same account it was noted that people took "what ground best pleased them for gardening, so that in most houses you must pass through a garden into the house" (8).

Adjacent to the fort on the east was a rectangular open space called Tank Square because it contained a large water reservoir (fig. 14). (Such "tanks" were spread throughout Calcutta and provided a major means of water storage.) Tank Square, later named Dalhousie Square, marked the commercial and administrative center of Calcutta, with the extended facade of the British East India Company offices defining its northern edge.

Opposite
13. Map of Calcutta from a survey taken in 1792–93 by A. Upjohn. A. Old fort. B. Tank Square (Dalhousie Square). C. Esplanade Row (after intersecting Chowringhee, this street continued as Dharamtola Road). D. Circular Road. E. Chowringhee Road. F. Fort William. G. Maidan. The Indian districts lay primarily to the north of Tank Square, and the British primarily to the south.

15. View on the Chitpore Road, Calcutta, by Thomas Daniell, 1797.

The commercial opportunities of Calcutta attracted a sizable Indian population in addition to other non-British immigrants. As in Madras, the settlement pattern reflected a separation of communities. The Indian district developed primarily in the northern part of the city, with the British to the south, and an intermediate area between them inhabited by Portuguese, Jews, Greeks, and Armenians. The social divisions of the city were not altogether rigid, however, and were subject to modifications as the city evolved. Well-to-do Indians owned property, sometimes including extensive gardens, throughout the city.

Among the threats to the security of Calcutta were marauding bands of Mahratta tribesmen. Seeking to increase the protection of the city on the eastern side, the leaders of the Indian community proposed, in 1742, to construct a defensive ditch at their own expense. This protective line, called the Mahratta Ditch, was designed to follow a seven-mile, curving path, meeting the river at both its north and south ends. After three miles of the ditch were completed, the project was abandoned as hopelessly ambitious, and the emplacement was eventually filled in to create a street marking the city boundary and known as the Circular Road.

The street pattern of Calcutta evolved in a piecemeal fashion, with some of the major thoroughfares developed from existing roads. The oldest was Chitpore Road, an artery leading northward from the British settlement toward the village of Chitpore, the site of a temple to the Goddess Chtteswari (fig. 15). This street was to become the primary commercial street of the Indian district. Extending southward on the same line as Chitpore Road was a road called Chowringhee leading toward the village of Kalighat, where a shrine to the goddess Kali was located. Although Calcutta never had a geometric street grid, mid-eighteenth-century maps show an informal pattern in which streets take a generally north-south or east-west direction.

The middle of the eighteenth century was to mark a period of crisis for Calcutta, underlining the defensive weaknesses of the city. A period of deteriorating relations between the British and Sirajud-daulah, the Nawab of Bengal, culminated in an attack on Calcutta by his army in 1756. The Company Court of Directors in London had complained in 1713 that the fort made "a very pompous show to the waterside by high turrets of lofty buildings," but had "no real strength of power of defense."[19] The truth of this statement became all too evident as the defenders of the city met with overwhelming defeat. Not only had the fort itself proved inadequate to withstand attack, but the closely surrounding buildings gave protection to the approaching troops.

The disastrous events of 1756 were compensated the following year by resounding victories for the British. Calcutta was retaken, and a series of successful military actions transformed the British into the dominant power in India. The subsequent enhancement of the role of Calcutta accompanied the consolidation of British rule. Following an act of parliament in 1773, the chief of the Bengal Presidency was declared the Governor-General of India, and Calcutta thus attained the status of a capital.

Having regained control of the city, and haunted by the rapid capitulation of Fort William, the British were determined to create a new fort that would be virtually impregnable. The new Fort William, completed in 1773, was situated on the river bank south of the existing British settlement. Polygonal in form, it was surrounded by an elaborate system of projecting bastions and earthworks and protected at its outer edge by a moat.

To provide a clear field of fire, the fort was surrounded by a thirteen-hundred-acre space, which came to be called the Maidan. It was two miles long and about one mile wide, with Chowringhee road defining its eastern edge. Although never destined to fulfill its military function, the expansive clearing did provide Calcutta with a welcome recreational area. Within the Maidan was a road called the Course which became a favored route for evening carriage drives, even though it was noted that one "swallowed ten mouthfuls of dust for one mouthful of air." Possession of a carriage, a costly luxury in Britain, was deemed a virtual necessity. In 1823 an Englishwoman remarked that "to walk is impossible; even the most petty Europe shop-keeper in Calcutta has his buggy, to enable him to drive out in the cool of the evening."[20]

So sizable was the new fort that permission was granted to all British inhabitants of Calcutta to build houses within its walls. Company writers [clerks], moreover, were initially required to live there. Instructions from London in 1767 specified that no writer be "permitted to reside out of the new Fort without the express permission of the Governor," and it was added that "no writer shall be permitted either for himself or jointly with others to keep a country house."[21] British preferences in dwellings, however, soon prevailed over company policies, and no amount of persuasion could keep the British within the confines of the fort.

The increasing security of British India, moreover, made a dispersed settlement relatively feasible. The perimeter of the Maidan provided attractive sites for houses, and Chowringhee Road, marking its eastern boundary, was soon ornamented with mansions set in spacious compounds. An admiring visitor in the early years of the nineteenth century described Chowringhee as "an entire village of palaces," declaring that it "forms the finest view I ever beheld in any city" (fig. 16).[22]

Travelers approaching Calcutta from the sea passed up the river through a district called Garden Reach. Viewing the scene in 1780, an Englishwoman noted that "the banks of the river are as one may say absolutely studded with elegant mansions, called here as at Madras, garden-houses" (fig. 18). She was also favorably impressed with the city itself, reporting that "as you come up past Fort William and the Esplanade it has a beautiful appearance. Esplanade-row, as it is called, which fronts the Fort, seems to be composed of palaces; the whole range, except what is taken up by the Government and Council houses, is occupied by the principal gentlemen in the settlement" (fig. 17).[23]

In spite of the pretentiousness of many individual buildings, the overall townscape of British Calcutta attracted frequent derision. Those schooled in eighteenth-century aesthetics had learned to prize regularity and order, and in this respect Calcutta seemed to violate all rules of urban design. One visitor noted in 1768 that "although it is large, with a great many good houses in it, it is as awkward a place as can be conceived, and so irregular that it looks as if all the houses had been thrown up in the air and fallen down again by accident as they now stand. People keep constantly building; and everyone who can procure a piece of ground to build a house upon consults his own taste and convenience without any regard to the beauty or regularity of the town." Another observer declared that "there is not a spot where judgement, taste, decency, and conveniency are so grossly insulted as in that scattered and confused chaos of houses, huts, sheds, streets, lanes, alleys, windings, gutters, sinks, and tanks, which . . . compose the capital of the English Company's Government in India."[24]

Although the British of Calcutta became legendary for their opulent style of living, not all were affluent. Occasionally, sailors would desert their ships and set themselves up as small shopkeepers or as tradesmen such as smiths, carpenters, and tailors. While the upper levels of British colonial society sought expansive quarters to the south, the less prosperous settled in central Calcutta on the edges of the Indian districts. Such streets as Lal Bazar and Dharamtola attracted a strip development of English taverns and so-called "Europe" shops selling imported goods. One account of Calcutta in 1860 observed that as one proceeded northward "the stable three-storied buildings with spacious verandas and large compounds disappear by degrees, and smaller buildings, on narrow plots of ground and in greater proximity to each other line the streets, until at last they form an almost uninterrupted range of all description of houses and huts, inhabited by a mixed Christian and native population" (figs. 19 and 20).[25]

Beyond this intermediate zone lay the Indian city, to British eyes an impenetrable warren of crowded lanes and squalid buildings. The extremely low population densities of the British areas made the Indian city appear all the more congested. Having observed the Chowringhee district, a British visitor declared that the "Black Town is as complete a contrast to this as can well be conceived. Its streets are narrow and dirty; the houses, of two stories, occasionally brick, but generally mud, and thatched, perfectly resembling the cabins of the poorest class in Ireland." To the British in Cal-

16. *View of Chowringhee Road by Thomas Daniell, 1798.*

17. *A nineteenth-century view of Esplanade Row as seen from Chowringhee Road. The Governor's Palace is at the far left.*

18. View of Garden Reach by J. B. Fraser.

19. A view of the bazaar leading to the Chitpore Road by J. B. Fraser, 1824–26. (The street appears to be Lal Bazaar.)

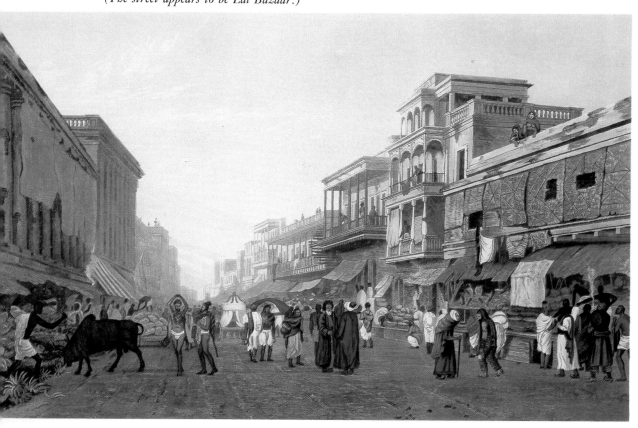

cutta a wholesome environment was equated with abundant "ventilation," and the native city was, in one view, a place where, "ventilation can hardly be said to exist." Another Englishman dryly observed that "it would somewhat extenuate the atrocity of the Black Hole to think it was but a slight exaggeration of the condition of the natives in their daily lives."[26]

The dramatic visual contrast between the British and Indian districts of Calcutta involved not only architectural preferences, but also social and economic factors. The British were few in number, were employed almost exclusively at the upper levels of international commerce and government administration, and therefore embodied a very narrow social and occupational range. The upper-class imagery of the British neighborhoods was emphasized, moreover, by a consistent desire to display wealth through building; the Briton wanted his house to proclaim his lordly status through its spacious grounds and palatial facade. A preference for functional zoning, in which residential areas were separated from commercial districts, had begun to characterize cities in Britain, and this was reflected in British Calcutta, with its residential areas dispersed beyond the compact business and administrative center surrounding Tank Square.

Within the Indian community was a highly varied population, ranging from laborers, craftsmen, and peddlers to wealthy merchants and bankers. The bazaar economy that dominated Indian Calcutta was fragmented into a system of many direct transactions that often supported vast numbers of people at marginal levels of subsistence. The complexity of the social structure was reflected in the physical structure of the city, and although certain areas might be homogenous in terms of occupational caste or religious group, the urban fabric was generally characterized by an intermixture of manufacturing, commerce, and housing, as well as a juxtaposition of social levels (fig. 21).

Great wealth existed within the Indian community, but it was not always conspicuous from the street. Indifferent to functional zoning, rich Indians felt no concern for living in a "good" neighborhood, in the sense of an area dominated by a single class. Great mansions, built to focus on private courtyards, were scattered throughout the city, intermingled with lesser building and even slums. Describing the residence of a hypothetical Bengali, a British writer noted that

> this worthy did not care for what we consider the advantages of open frontage. He was not anxious to erect his mansion in a wide street or open compound, where his women would not be secluded, where the dacoits would find him out, and where his employer would remark, "you must be growing rich. Your mansion is twice as fine as mine." He, therefore, faced his property with mean huts occupied by artisans who paid remarkably well; and you can still only approach his double quadrangle by a lane almost as narrow and tortuous as a rabbit burrow, but which is cool, damp, shaded in the hottest weather, and which could be barricaded at the shortest notice.[27]

As the pressures of an expanding population grew, owners of large properties discovered that they could rent land very profitably by leasing space for small huts. Such tracts were called *bustees* and became a permanent characteristic of the city (fig. 22). Frequently the land was leased to an intermediary, or *thika* tenant, who built

20. *Dharamtola Street looking east from its intersection with Chowringhee. The mosque on the left was built by Prince Gholam Mohammad in 1842.*

21. *Armenian Street in the Indian quarter.*

22. *Calcutta bustees.*

23. *Burra Bazaar at the turn of the century.*

and rented the huts. Indian Calcutta thus evolved as an interweaving of permanent masonry buildings with tracts of mud and thatch. British officials often deplored the bustees as centers of disease "inhabited by people who apparently delight in filth and dirt."[28] With their closely packed masses of thatched buildings, the bustees were also deplored as a municipal fire hazard. In an effort to control the spread of fire, elevated lookout posts were erected throughout the city, enabling watchmen employed by the police to sound the alarm.

The descriptive literature of colonial Calcutta is based heavily on British sources, and it often reflects both national and professional biases. Among the British with extensive exposure to the Indian districts were medical officers, sanitation inspectors, policemen, and missionaries, whose occupational concerns directed their attention primarily to problems and deficiencies. The picture they portrayed laid emphasis on overbuilding and dilapidation, on disease, dirt, and stench. Even so, it is uncertain just why Calcutta achieved its reputation as the ultimate urban horror. Appalling living conditions characterized many nineteenth-century metropolises, and even in the richest and most industrially advanced nations, cities were marked by primitive municipal services, recurrent epidemics, inadequate housing, and widespread poverty. Certain problems may even have been mitigated in India; if you had to sleep in the street, at least you wouldn't freeze to death.

One of the few aspects of Indian Calcutta to intrigue British observers was the spectacle of the bazaar. One Englishman regretted that few of his compatriots

> have ever taken the trouble of exploring the inmost recesses of the Babel-like regions of the Burra Bazar [fig. 23]. . . . Here above and below, may be seen the jewels of Golconda and Bundelkund, the shawls of Cashmere, the broad cloths of England, silks of Moorshedabad and Benares, muslins of Dacca, calicoes, gingh-

ams, chintzes, brocade of Persia, spicery and myrrh and frankincense from Ceylon, the Spice Islands, and Arabia, shells from the eastern coast and straits, iron ware and cutlery in abundance, as well from Europe as Monghyr, coffee, drugs, dried fruits and sweetmeats from Arabia and Turkey, cows' tails from Thibet, and ivory from Ceylon. . . . [The variety of the goods was matched by the variety of the buyers and sellers, who included] Persians, Arabs, Jews, Marwarrees, Armenians, Mundrazees, Cashmeerees, Malabars, Goojratees, Goorkhas, Affghans, Seiks, Turks, Parsees, Chinese, Burmese and Bengalis.[29]

As is always the case in expanding cities, efforts to promote civic improvements remained relatively ineffectual in respect to the magnitude of civic problems. In 1749, a survey of streets and drains had been ordered, with a view to rendering, the settlement "sweet and wholesome," and, two years later, attempts were made to improve the site by cutting down "the old trees and underwood in and around the town." The responsibility for keeping the town in order rested with the police commissioner, and conditions remained notoriously unsanitary. Viewing Calcutta in 1780, a visitor declared the city a "mass of filth and corruption," pointing out that "the very small portion of cleanliness which it enjoys is owing to the familiar intercourse of the hungry jackals by night, and ravenous vultures, kites and crows by day."[30]

Notable civic reform took place under the governorship of Lord Wellesley, who held office between 1797 and 1805. By this time, the population of Calcutta had risen to two-hundred thousand, and it seemed clear that the development of the city could no longer be left to chance. In a minute issued in 1803, Wellesley insisted that "the Capital of the British empire in India, and the seat of Supreme Authority require the serious attention of Government." The swampy terrain of Calcutta made improvements in drains and watercourses a matter of particular urgency. The annual monsoon rains produced periodic flooding, and Wellesley noted that "during the last week, a great part of the town has remained under water."[31] In addition to improved street drainage, he proposed regulation of public markets, burial places and slaughterhouses, suggesting that the locations of new streets be studied with a view to facilitating north-south and east-west movement through the city. To carry out his reforms, Wellesley appointed a Town Improvement Committee of thirty members.

This committee was supplanted in 1817 by the Lottery Committee, which continued to direct civic improvement for the next twenty years.[32] During the tenure of the Lottery Committee, a number of public works were achieved, including construction of a new town hall (fig. 24) and the creation of the Beliaghata Canal. Circulation was enhanced through the construction of a series of broad streets, including Strand Road, a wide thoroughfare bordering the riverfront, and providing access to the dock areas. An expansive north-south artery was created to the west of Chitpore Road, comprising a sequence of four streets—Cornwallis, College, Wellington, and Wellesley (fig. 25)—and it became the site of large institutions such as the university, medical college, and hospitals. A broad east-west axis through the Indian districts was created by the opening of Kolutola and Mirzapore streets. While the Lottery Committee members agreed as to the need to create more new streets and open spaces in the Indian districts, they hesitated in view of the difficulties of expropriating and demolishing existing buildings in this dense part of the city.

24. *Town Hall designed by Colonel John Garstin. It was begun in 1807 and completed in 1815.*

25. *College Street.*

By 1850, the population of Calcutta exceeded four-hundred thousand, with the city sprawling along the river for about six miles. It was becoming a major world trading center and held a virtual monopoly on the jute industry. In terms of civic improvement, however, an 1860 report judged the city to be "half a century behind the spirit and requirements of the age." Not only had Calcutta failed to keep pace with large cities in Europe and America, but it also lagged behind certain Eastern metropolises. This report also noted that, "whilst Constantinople, Alexandria, Cairo, and other cities under Mohamedan rulers are gradually assuming the character of modern European towns, the city of Palaces, the seat of a Christian Government forms an exception to the general advance of civilization. The native part of the town, with trifling exceptions, retains its primitive oriental character, with the usual appurtenances of narrow filthy streets and crooked lanes." At the same time, the European quarter was considered to have developed "totally regardless of any considerations for the health and real comfort of its residents."[33]

Even British neighborhoods were becoming crowded, and residential compounds were no longer as large as in former times. An architectural journal reported that "drawing rooms, rich in every luxury, receive the perfumes of the stable and kitchen, . . . Almost everywhere the houses are just sufficiently detached to render privacy and ventilation alike impossible. . . . Properly built markets do not exist. With a population of 11,000 Europeans crowded about Chowringhee and in the Fort, exclusive of the suburbs, Calcutta possesses neither theatre, concert-rows, walks nor gardens." All in all, the city was judged to be "part Belgravia, part Cairo; combining the expenses of the former, with the dirt and discomfort of the latter."[34]

As to the contributions of Calcutta's citizens toward the betterment of their city, a British observer declared that "private enterprise can hardly be said to exist in India, and in the absence of such, Government is expected to do everything."[35] This was deemed inevitable in a city where the British inhabitants were concerned only with making money and returning home. The Englishman could not "be expected to take a very lively interest in undertakings which can only be carried out by a subsequent generation, and from which he will individually derive no benefits. His primary object is to be off as soon as he can" (3–4). Although the Indian inhabitants would presumably have had a greater incentive toward long-term civic improvement, he insisted that "the natives have done absolutely nothing for their own city" (3–4). Many Indians, like the British, viewed Calcutta as a place of temporary residence, and it remained common to return to the ancestral village for important family functions like weddings and pujas.

Changes continued in municipal administration, with a new corporation created in 1876. Although government reorganization involved increased franchise, powers of decision remained in the hands of the British and members of the Indian upper classes. As in Madras the British often blamed defects in the city on the reluctance of the Indians to support civic improvements. At the same time, Indians maintained that the revenues of the entire city were used principally on improvements in the districts occupied by the British. A report of the Commissioners for the Improvement of the Town of Calcutta declared in 1857 that funds were employed "to the open prejudice of the native town."[36]

26. *Old Court House Street looking north toward Dalhousie Square, c. 1863.*
The building on the right is the Great Eastern Hotel.

A similar view was reflected in an article by Grish Chunder Ghose, published in the journal *Bengalee* in 1863. He noted that

> the traveller who lands at Chandpal Ghat fresh from the atmosphere of European civilization is regaled with the view of a splendid metropolis, with church steeples reaching up to the clouds, rows of palaces on each hand, streets smooth as bowling greens—wide, dustless, and dry—the very perfection of macadamization. He drives into Chowringhee, . . . and his heart cannot wish for higher displays of Municipal talent and conservancy genius and activity than those before him. . . . But should business or curiosity call him to the native Town, . . . he would observe a change in the landscape as violent as any that can be conceived by the imagination. He will see or rather feel, by the jolt of his carriage, streets than which the natural paths of the forest are better fitted for travelling. He will have his nose assailed by the stench of drains which have not felt the ministering hand of man ever since the last rains, his affrighted horse will obstinately back from pits in the thoroughfares wide enough to bury all the rubbish in the adjoining houses, his carriage wheels will stick resolutely into ruts from which release is possible only by the aid of half a dozen men and as many bamboo props. . . . After a heavy shower of rain he will in some places deem it more pleasant and advantageous to hire a boat than swim his horse.[37]

Visitors from Madras were always struck by the comparative density of Calcutta. Madras had retained its character of unfocused sprawl, but Calcutta had a real "downtown" in the area surrounding Tank Square, where business houses and government offices formed continuous street facades. In spite of the city's defects, a traveler in 1871 concluded that "Calcutta is in every respect worthy of being the capital of British India. No other Eastern city can be compared with it. . . . Unlike Bombay and Madras, too, it has, among other good streets a quite European, one, Old Court House Street, so fine and wide, and with shops so brilliant, that no part of London would be ashamed of it" (fig. 26). In contrast to the scattered dwellings of Madras, the mansions of Calcutta were seen to "form a noble line of street."[38]

Turn-of-the-century visitors approaching Madras from the sea saw little evidence that they were in the vicinity of a large city. At the same period, a visitor sailing up the river to Calcutta noted that "brick-kilns and the smoky, tall chimneys of civilization appear along the banks, and soon we find ourselves among docks and wharfs, and a forest of shipping alongside of a modern-looking city."[39] By this time, the population had risen to over one million, making Calcutta the fourteenth largest city in the world. In spite of an apparent prosperity, however, there were portents that the city's days of glory were passing. Its economic primacy in India had already been effectively challenged by Bombay. The Hooghly was changing course and beginning to silt up, and there was disturbing talk of moving the capital elsewhere. The imperial administration, now embodied in the office of the viceroy, had become migratory, and during the hottest months, shifted headquarters from the steamy plains to the clear mountain air of Simla.

Applauding the wisdom of such a course, Kipling pointed out:

> That the Merchant risks the perils of the Plain
>   For his gain.
> Nor can Rulers rule a house that men grow rich in,
>   From its kitchen.
> Let the Babu drop inflammatory hints
>   In his prints;
> And mature—consistent soul—his plan for stealing
>   To Darjeeling:
> Let the Merchant seek, who makes his silver pile,
>   England's isle;
> Let the City Charnock pitched on—evil day!—
>   Go Her way.[40]

Kipling's view of Madras as a "withered beldame" and Calcutta as "packed and pestilential" can be contrasted with his not-unnatural sentiment for the city of his birth, Bombay.

> Surely in toil or fray
>   Under an alien sky,
> Comfort it is to say:
>   "Of no mean city am I!"
> [Neither by service nor fee
>   Come I to mine estate—
> Mother of Cities to me,
>   For I was born in her gate,
> Between the palms and the sea,
>   Where the world-end steamers wait.][41]

Although Calcutta remained the capital of British India, the motto of Bombay, *Urbs Prima in Indis,* would, in many ways, appear justified. Possessed of the only natural deep-water harbor on the west coast of India, and with access to a rich hinterland, Bombay was destined to become India's window toward Europe.

A Portuguese possession in 1652, Bombay was bequeathed to the British in 1661 as part of the marriage treaty between Catherina of Portugal and Charles II. Keenly aware of the value of the site, the Portuguese viceroy in Bombay had been reluctant to submit to the agreement, warning his king that "India will be lost on the same day in which the English nation is settled in Bombay."[42]

At that time the territory of Bombay consisted of seven islands separated by swampy, low-lying areas, and continuous reclamation accompanied the creation of the city. In its final form, Bombay consisted of a trapezoidal island about eleven-and-one-half miles long and from three to four miles wide. On its western, or seaward, side a peninsula called Malabar Hill rose 180 feet above the sea, while a narrow headland, originally the island of Colaba, formed the southernmost extension of the city (fig. 27).

In contrast to Madras and Calcutta, Bombay had a visually dramatic site. As described by a nineteenth-century visitor, "Bombay harbour presents one of the most splendid landscapes imaginable. The voyager visiting India for the first time, on nearing the superb amphitheatre, whose wood-crowned heights and rocky terraces, bright promontories and gem-like islands are reflected in the broad blue sea, experiences none of the disappointment which is felt by all lovers of the picturesque on approaching the low, flat coast of Bengal, with its stunted jungle" (fig. 28).[43]

The nucleus of the settlement was a walled town built on the eastern side of the island adjacent to a quadrangular stronghold called the castle. The term *fort* was used to describe the entire town, which was accessible by means of three gates: Apollo Gate, facing the harbor to the south; Church Gate on the west; Bazaar Gate to the north. Describing the fort in 1775, a traveler reported that "the town of Bombay is near a mile in length from Apollo gate to that of the Bazar and about a quarter of a mile broad in the broadest part. . . . [In the center of the town was] a spacious Green, capable of containing several regiments exercising at the same time. The streets are well laid out and the buildings (namely, gentlemen's houses) so numerous and handsome as to make it an elegant town" (figs. 29 and 30).[44] Although the town lacked a regular plan the principal arteries tended to lead north-south or east-west, and, as in any walled town, the principal thoroughfares were those leading from the gates. The East India Company Court in London had been pleased to see the town attracting Indian immigrants, and indicated that "whatever regulations are made for the encouragement of the people in general and of the richer sort in particular, will always meet with our approbation."[45]

As in Madras and Calcutta, the expansion of the city was left largely to the forces of spontaneous growth. A visitor early in the nineteenth century observed that "Bombay appears for many years to have been left to itself, and individuals were permitted to occupy what land they pleased."[46] It had apparently pleased a number of individuals to scatter houses throughout the land outside the fort walls. Such building was deemed to hamper the defensive role of the fortifications, and the area surrounding the fort was subject to repeated efforts at regulation and clearance.

In addition to the problem of unregulated construction outside the fort, there was by the middle of the eighteenth century a problem of overbuilding within fort itself. Tall buildings were judged a threat to the castle, inspiring reminders of the easy conquest of the similarly encumbered Calcutta fort. Although Indians had initially been encouraged to settle inside the fort, competition for land promoted increasing

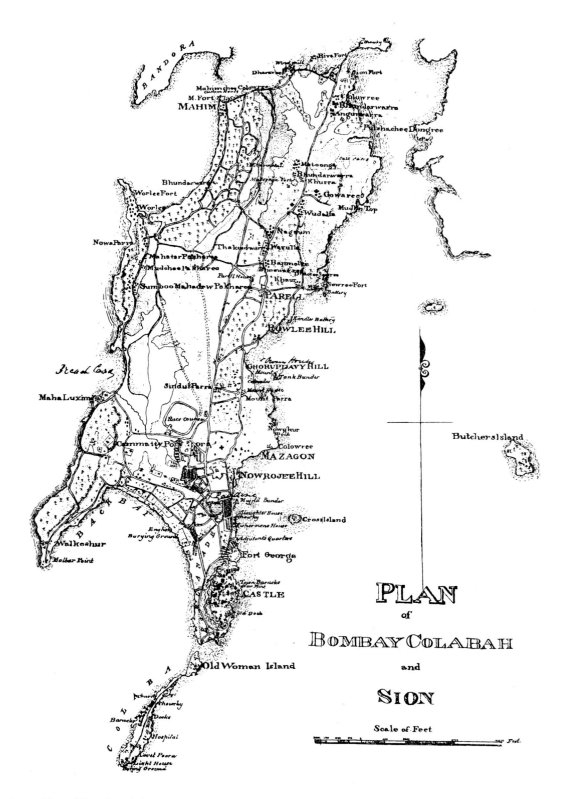

PLAN

of

BOMBAY COLABAH

and

SION

Scale of Feet

27. *Map of Bombay. The castle and adjacent fortified town occupy the southernmost
tip of the land mass, with additional forts studding the shoreline. Colaba was not connected to the
main island until 1838.*

28. *Robert Grindlay*, Approach of the Monsoon, Bombay, *1826. The city is viewed from Malabar Hill.*

29. *Bombay Fort. The walls remained intact until the middle of the nineteenth century.*

30. Scene in Bombay by Robert Grindlay, 1826. The boxlike conveyances are palankeens. *The gentleman with the black hat is a Parsee, a member of a community noted for leadership in Bombay commerce and ship-building.*

attempts by the British to reserve the town for themselves. Indian building was restricted to the northern half, where population pressures promoted a pattern of tall narrow structures. In 1787 a government committee regretted that the "absence of any restriction respecting the height of houses ... has led many of the black inhabitants in their part of the town to raise their houses to so great a height as may be injurious to the healthiness of the town."[47] A limit of thirty-two feet was recommended.

The hazards of building congestion were dramatized when a great fire broke out in the fort on February 17, 1803. The origin was never ascertained, but, according to an observer, "so great and violent was the conflagration that at sunset the destruction of every house in the Fort was apprehended. ... nor did it visibly abate till nearly a third part of the town within the walls had been consumed."[48] To some among the British, the fire provided an excellent pretext to expel the Indian residents from the fort. Included in government instructions to a committee formed to direct reconstruction was the hope "that you will be able to convince the natives in question of the unadvisability of their residing in a garrison crowded with lofty structures ... and

31. The Fort. A view of Apollo Street.

intersected by such narrow streets as existed before the late fire."[49] Although the redevelopment of the fort following the fire did not remove all the Indian population,
the instructions went on to acknowledge that "the poorer sort cannot afford to build
houses upon the new system. . . . Thus the accommodations within the fort will be
left to the more respectable and wealthy merchants who have the best claim to its
protection" (495–500).

A flourishing Indian district began to develop beyond the esplanade opposite Bazaar Gate and became the focus of a northward-spreading pattern of urbanization. As
described in 1838, "the Black Town, as it is called, spreads its innumerable habita-
tions, amidst a wood of coco-nut trees—a curious, busy, bustling, but dirty quarter,
swarming with men and the inferior animals, and presenting every variety of character
that the whole of Asia can produce."[50]

Although the fort had been subject to replanning following the fire, by the middle of the nineteenth century it had apparently regained its old image of disorderly
congestion. In 1855, it was described as "crowded with houses" and "so irregularly
built, as to give it any thing but an agreeable appearance. Efforts have at divers times
been made to induce the native owners of ground to surrender such small patches as
may interfere with the symmetry of the streets, but they have manifested very great
reluctance to yield."[51] The southern half of the fort included European residences,
public offices and buildings, military barracks, shops for the sale of European goods,
offices and warehouses, the docks, and law courts (fig. 31). The northern half continued to be occupied by Indian houses, offices and shops, belonging primarily to the
Parsee, Borah and Banian communities (fig. 32).

Paradoxically, while the British sought to expel the Indians from the fort, they
also had been abandoning it as a place of residence. Like their counterparts in Madras
and Calcutta, the British in Bombay had a strong preference for low-density housing.

32. Borah Bazaar in the fort, 1885.

Recalling his days in Bombay, one Englishman observed that "since I left India [1784] the town houses have been almost deserted by the English, who reside entirely in their country villas."[52] Some found respite from the congestion of the fort by occupying temporary dwellings on the esplanade during the hot dry season. "Some of these," it was noted, "are exceedingly fantastic. . . . Other persons pitch tents, which are often extensive and commodious . . . covering them over with a 'chupper' or thatched roof, supported on slender pillars, and forming a veranda all around."[53] The esplanade was noted especially as a resort of the military, and all regiments stationed in Bombay were allotted lines for their tents there.

As in Madras and Calcutta, outlying weekend houses soon evolved into permanent dwellings. The governor established official residence in the northern district of Parel, and this became the nucleus of a fashionable settlement, as did nearby Byculla. Another outlying area destined to attract residential building was the peninsula of Malabar Hill, where a few British dwellings existed as early as 1780. A house on Malabar Point became the hot-weather retreat of the governor, and by the mid-nineteenth century, Malabar had become the choicest residential district of the city (fig. 33). Houses were reportedly erected "upon every available spot of ground which commands the prospect beneath; and it is almost impossible to conceive a scene of more varied beauty, than is exhibited from the verandas of some of these abodes."[54]

Because of its restricted land mass, Bombay was not adaptable to the extensive sprawl characterizing Calcutta and Madras. As population grew, land values rose, and complaints about both the cost and scarcity of housing became frequent among the British. Predominantly renters rather than property owners, the British often felt themselves exploited by native landlords. A British observer noted in 1852 that "the

33. Malabar Hill. Lord Curzon shown in Walkeshur Road, 1900.

principal dwelling-houses in the island are now owned by Parsee landlords, and are either inhabited by themselves, or let out at high rents to the English residents, who are rarely inclined to involve themselves in the troubles and responsibilities of land proprietorship, in a country where their stay is supposed to be merely of temporary duration."[55]

Settlement of outlying districts was made possible through continual efforts at reclamation. The most important of these involved closing what was called the Great Breach to the west. Through this separation in the land mass between Mahalakshmi and Worli, the sea poured in, and it was observed in 1772 that "the sea had so gained upon the land with its irruption that it almost divided the island in two and made the roads impassable."[56] Completion of an effective barrier was finally achieved in 1784, making the central portions of the island available for reclamation and settlement. The last of the original seven islands to be joined to the rest was Colaba, which was connected by a causeway in 1838.

A system of road construction and widening during the first half of the nineteenth century provided a framework for the settlement of the island. Many roads that were begun as elevated causeways built through open country to connect outlying areas evolved into the principal traffic arteries of populous districts. The first such causeway had been Bellasis Road, built in 1793, followed in 1805 by the Sion Causeway. Grant Road, leading to Girgaum, was opened in 1839; it required a parapet wall on either side because of its considerable elevation above the adjoining lands. In 1830, it was declared that the previously separated districts of Bombay "may be considered as one town,"[57] and by the middle of the century numerous tracts of land in the interior had been raised in level and given over to habitation.

34. *Bendhi Bazaar Road.*

Observing the expanding native city, an Englishwoman noted in 1841 that "the indications shown of wealth and industry are exceedingly gratifying to an eye delighting in the sight of a happy and flourishing population. . . . The processes of widening, draining, pulling down, and rebuilding, appear to have been carried on very extensively; and though much, perhaps, remains to be done . . . the eye is seldom offended, or the other senses disagreeably assailed, in passing through this populous district."[58] Bhendi Bazaar, one of the principal streets, was described in 1857 as follows:

> a long, tolerably wide, irregular street, with high irregular houses on either side, containing many windows, built principally of wood, some of the projecting parts rudely, yet rather richly carved, some painted, all full of dirt and darkness, and crowded with inhabitants. The lower story is usually devoted to the goods to be sold, where the vendor sits, cross-legged, on the same shelf as his bread, cakes, flour, grains, oil, stuffs, calicos, earthenware, wine, or whatever other article he has for sale. [fig. 34].[59]

In spite of reclamation efforts, the Bombay shoreline remained relatively undeveloped before the 1860s, and it was noted that "all round the Island of Bombay was one foul cesspool, sewers discharging on the sands, rocks used only for the purposes of nature. To ride home to Malabar Hill along the sands of Back Bay was to encounter sights and odours too horrible to describe."[60] Mud flats provided the site for some of the most pestilential slums—huts raised only a few inches above the fetid slime.

Strong impetus to urban redevelopment was provided by Lord Elphinstone, who served as governor between 1853 and 1860. Among his achievements was initiating efforts toward the removal of the wall surrounding the fort. By the mid-nineteenth century, the fort was deemed "a costly and filthy nuisance." It was obsolete as a military device, and the massive outworks seemed a waste of valuable urban land. Movement to and from the fort was hampered by a network of "embattled walls, sally-ports, and moats with two great gates strangling the traffic." The surrounding esplan-

35. Looking south along Esplanade Road, built on the site of the demolished fortifications. The monument in the center, Flora Fountain, marks the intersection with Churchgate Street. Since independence, the space has been renamed Hutatma Chowk, and the street Mahatma Gandhi Road.

ade, moreover, presented a "dreary, treeless, sunburnt wilderness."[61] Demolition was completed during the governorship of Sir Bartle Frere, who ordered the total removal of the fortifications in 1862. The land made available to the city through the razing of the fortifications provided scope for new roadways and recreational open space, together with extensive government and commercial building (fig. 35).

Although Bombay had grown steadily from the time of its founding, the events of the 1860s would dramatically enhance the city's fortunes and inspire a period of rapid transformation. The Bombay economy was heavily dependent on cotton; the city was not only a leading exporter of raw material, but had also become a center for cloth production. In 1854, the Bombay Spinning and Weaving Company had been established, and by 1860 six additional mills had been created. It was proudly declared that "Bombay has long been the Liverpool of the East, and she is now become the Manchester also. Factory chimney-stacks already meet the eye on every side." The outbreak of the American Civil War in 1861 produced a blockade of Confederate ports, and Bombay suddenly acquired a virtual monopoly of the cotton trade. In the resulting boom, the possessors of newly-made fortunes were caught up in a frenzy of speculation and land gambling. Journals predicted with alarm, "There is a gambling saturnalia going on!" "This must end in a fearful smash, and we warn the Bombay public to beware!"[62]

As recounted in a Bombay Chamber of Commerce report for 1864–65, "the unexpected wealth poured into the lap of Western India by the terrible incident of the American Civil War . . . was not used wisely. . . . A mania for share speculation broke out which continued to grow in intensity till it seemed to absorb the time and attention of the community. . . . Bombay was flooded with 'Financial Associations' and doubtful schemes of reclamation. . . . [Following the] unexpected termination of the American Civil War, gambling speculation suddenly collapsed, and insolvency and bankruptcy followed on a scale of magnitude unknown in any other crisis of modern share speculation."[63]

The most ambitious of the many schemes spawned during the heady days of the boom was that of the Back Bay Reclamation Company. The Back Bay lay to the west of the island, stretching from Malabar Hill to Colaba. Extension of its curving shoreline would have added land to the city in an area of concentrated population and high land values. Anticipating astronomical profits, the Back Bay Reclamation Company, formed in 1863, had proposed to reclaim fifteen hundred acres through landfill along the shoreline. By the time their financing institution, the Asiatic Banking Corporation, collapsed, they had succeeded in creating a narrow strip of land that would subsequently provide space for a street and a railroad line. Although the financial crisis resulted in suspension of the reclamation scheme, the Back Bay would continue to be considered by the Bombay government as a logical area of urban extension.

The opening of the Suez canal in 1869 greatly enhanced Bombay's status as a port, and the development of railroads made the city a transportation hub for all of India. Control of harbor activity was vested in the Port Trust, created in 1873 and modeled on the Mersey Board in England. Extensive reclamation work was undertaken, and among the new docks completed toward the end of the century were Princes Dock, opened in 1880, and the Victoria Dock and Merewether Dry Dock between 1883 and 1893. By this time more than half the imports and exports of India passed through Bombay.

The period following the American Civil War reflected a time of municipal reform for Bombay. Administrative changes in 1865 provided for a municipal commissioner appointed by the government, and for a municipal corporation empowered to levy taxes. The ambitious programs of this administration, however, drew accusations of extravagance, and public pressure brought about the creation of a new municipal corporation in 1872. This governing body was more directly representative of the taxpayers, and Bombay was regarded as the first city in India to develop a true measure of municipal self-government.

Although at the beginning of the nineteenth century Bombay had lagged behind Calcutta, by the end of the century, it had clearly surpassed its rival. Industry was flourishing, and visitors to "cottonopolis" were advised to "stand on some eminence looking north, and mark the scores of tall chimneys belching forth smoke, then descend into the industrial quarter, and listen to the roar of machinery that is bound some day to drive Lancashire textiles out of India" (fig. 36). In Bombay, as in European cities, industrial prosperity was accompanied by chronic housing shortages. A health officer writing to the municipal commissioners in 1872 called attention to "the desirability of erecting artisans' and labourers' dwellings. It is extremely difficult for European mechanics and others to get respectable lodgings at a reasonable rate; and the filthy dens in which the laboring classes of the city live are among the chief causes of the very high death rate."[64]

Even though many parts of Bombay were densely populated, the distribution of

36. Bombay factory landscape.

settlement was highly uneven. In 1887 it was noted that 37 percent of the population lived on 3.5 percent of the land, and while densities as high as 254 people per acre were found in some districts, over half of the city had a density of only 8 per acre.

In the populous areas, overcrowded dwellings were common, with every inch of space, including verandas, rented out as sleeping space for laborers. Additional storeys were hastily added to existing houses, often resulting in the collapse of buildings. The slums of Madras and Calcutta took the form of villagelike clusters of huts, whereas the multistorey tenement became characteristic of Bombay. A physician observed that "what has been said of Scotland may with equal truth be applied to Bombay, that families instead of living on the earth in the pure air with the sky over their dwellings, in many instances prefer lying stratum over stratum in flats opening into a common staircase, a 'continuation of the street,' as it has been called, which receives the organic emanations of the families on each floor."[65]

As the peasants of Europe were being transformed into industrial workers, so migrants to the colonial cities adapted to a wholly new way of life. It was observed in 1887 that "there is growing up in our population a class which can be distinguished from their own race, engaged in other work, and from every other class, by a pallid look, which may be called a factory countenance" (fig. 37).[66]

Like other industrialized cities, Bombay encompassed dramatic contrasts of wealth and poverty, opulence and squalor. Particularly impressive was the physical transformation of the city center on land resulting from the removal of the fortifications. Some of the land had been sold by the government, and the profits were combined with government grants to provide a special fund for new public building. Replacing the line of the ramparts was a broad avenue called Esplanade Road, providing the site for substantial commercial structures. Parallel to this street was a row of government and institutional buildings facing the Oval Maidan, a landscaped park adjacent to the beachfront of the Arabian Ocean (fig. 38).

37. Bombay textile-mill workers.

The redevelopment of the fortifications embodied the first planned architectural ensemble to be found in an Indian colonial city, and the results brought immediate approbation. "The long and magnificent series of public buildings" was described as "one of the finest sights of its kind in the world. The buildings are in themselves grand, but other cities may have structures as grand, though probably separate. Bombay, however, has all her structures in one long line of array, as if on parade before the spectator."[67]

38. The High Court, one of a group of new buildings constructed during the 1870s along the Oval Maidan. The High Court was designed by Colonel J. A. Fuller and built between 1871 and 1878.

Within the renovated fort, the old Cotton Green was redesigned as a circular park enclosed by an ensemble of architecturally unified commercial buildings, for which the cornerstone was laid in 1864. Named to commemorate the former governor, Elphinstone Circle, with its disciplined balance of open space and ordered facades, reflected a type of urban design that had become fashionable in eighteenth-century Britain, but had been previously ignored in British India (fig. 39). The project was an immediate success, and the municipality, having assembled the property, was able to sell plots quite profitably to leading mercantile houses. In addition to its architectural unity, the new complex was notable for the provision of a covered arcade at ground level, a device that came to characterize the Bombay commercial center. The arcade is such a welcome feature in the tropics, giving protection from both the intense summer sun and the driving monsoon rain, that it is surprising that it had never been used before in Indian colonial cities (figs. 40 and 41).

Revisiting India in 1886, Sir Edwin Arnold considered "the Bombay of to-day hardly recognisable to one who knew the place in the time of the Mutiny and in those years which followed it. Augustus said of Rome, 'I found it mud; I leave it marble,' and the visitor to India who traverses the Fort and the Esplanade-road after so long an absence as mine might justly exclaim, 'I left Bombay a town of warehouses and offices; I find her a city of parks and palaces'."[68]

Among the differences observed between Bombay and other Indian colonial cities was a lessening of the physical isolation of the British. An increasing intermixture was also becoming apparent within the Indian community. The census of 1906 indicated that while the Hindus dominated in most districts of the city, it was impossible to localize definitely any one community. Not only was the population physically juxtaposed, but Bombay was deemed to encompass a degree of social interaction unique in colonial cities. It was observed that

> in most parts of India the line of demarcation between the Englishman and the Indian is sharply drawn . . . In Bombay the line is so faint that it must soon be extinguished. Englishman and Indian, Parsi and Mohomedan, Jew and Hindu, meet in daily and intimate commercial dealing. They sit side by side in the Hall

39. *Elphinstone Circle, begun in 1864. (Renamed Horniman Circle after independence.) The idea for creating the circle came from the police commissioner, Mr. Charles Forjett. The facades were designed by James Scott, chief engineer of the Elphinstone Land Reclamation Company.*

40. *Arcades on Dadabhoy Naoroji Road, formerly Hornby Road.*

41. Arcades on Rampart Row.

of the Municipality and the Senate of the University, they foregather nightly at the Orient Club, and interdine frequently. . . . In all these respects Bombay is nearly a generation ahead of any other part of India.[69]

The British often invoked the prosperity of the colonial cities to demonstrate the benefits of British rule, pointing out the abundant commercial advantages for the native populace. In Bombay, however, the Indians seemed to have become a bit too pushing and thriving. The Indians were reputed to own "the finest houses; they are monopolising the choicest residential sites; they drive the most expensive horses, ride in the showiest carriages, elect the majority of the municipality, run the best of the cotton-mills, and every day they are getting more of the profitable business of the town into their hands."[70]

By the close of the nineteenth century the days in which a British merchant might rapidly amass a great fortune had long passed. The Englishman was far more likely to be a civil servant, military man, or salaried employee. It aroused particular self-pity among the British of Bombay that they could not compete with wealthy Indians for the most desirable housing, and although, in the eyes of outsiders, they seemed well off, it was noted that "the Englishman complains bitterly that he has no room to live. . . . [On Malabar Hill] nearly all the finest houses are occupied by natives, who live there in great style." In what was deemed the ultimate indignity, many an Englishman was compelled to inhabit an apartment. "For him," it was said, "the Parsi land speculator builds blocks of flats down near the sea-front, and he has to pay a relatively high rent for his three or four stuffy rooms, and be glad to get them, while his landlord looks down upon him from his eyrie three miles away."[71]

Although some might have regretted the apparent decline of the lordly Englishman, others admired the cosmopolitan richness of Bombay. All the colonial cities contained mixed populations, but it was only in Bombay that a truly hybrid society seemed to have been formed. To those among the British who saw their mission as the transformation of India toward Western ideals, Bombay had become "the connecting link between Europe and Asia, the point where two civilizations meet and mingle." Seeking precedent in the past, one writer declared that "Bombay is becoming to all Asia what Alexandria was during the earliest cultures of the Christian era. . . . It is at Bombay that Western civilization is now first confronted with and seeks to engraft itself upon that of the East."[72]

42. *Remnant of the Raj, Calcutta.*

2.

The Architecture of Empire

The British liked to make an analogy between building construction and human character. Old Fort William in Calcutta had been described as "an irregular tetragon of brick and mortar, called *puckah,* which is a composition of brick dust, some molasses and cut hemp, and when it comes to be dry is as hard, and tougher, than firm stone."[1] The term *puckah* or *pukka* came into general use to describe permanent masonry construction, as distinguished from *cutcha* building of temporary materials such as bamboo, mud, and thatch. In popular terminology, the ideal Briton was the *pukka sahib,* stiff of upper lip, unshakably firm, impervious and indestructible as stone itself, and the creator and embodiment, one assumed, of an equally *pukka* empire.

The imagery of building may, of course, be interpreted according to taste. It is possible to see colonial architecture as a visual embodiment of British confidence and power, as a conscious and effective attempt to commemorate British rule with monuments of permanence and grandeur. One may choose to see the remnants of colonial building still standing solid and true, reminders of the Western power that so long dominated India, and of the Western ideas that continue to make themselves felt. But, of course, nothing is really permanent, and even *pukka* building decays and crumbles. Depending on one's perspective, British dominance might be judged but a passing incident in India's long and varied history. Viewing the architectural remains of colonial India, a British writer, Jan Morris, recently chose to emphasize the ephemeral, commenting that "somehow the British in India generally failed to achieve that sense of rootedness which is the hallmark of most good architecture" (fig. 42).[2]

British building in India was initially dominated by Renaissance classicism, a tradition that, in various permutations, had been adopted throughout Europe and exported wherever European settlements existed. Presumed to reflect fundamental and eternal principles, classicism was deemed an architecture of universality; it was based on rules, and these rules could be learned and applied by anyone anywhere.

Classical building had originated under the brilliant Mediterranean sun, and some observers found its crisp sculptural forms well suited to the Indian ambient (figs. 43–45). It was not unusual for travelers in India to describe the architecture of Madras and Calcutta as an evocation of ancient Greece. In spite of the overall impression of grandeur it gave, however, colonial building did not always strictly apply classical precepts. Few trained architects found their way to the eighteenth-century colonial cities, and much building was adapted from pattern books. Particularly influential in Britain at this time was a new edition of the works of Palladio that included prototypes for a large number of country mansions. And it was the Palladian country house, rather than the Georgian town house, that provided the model for British dwellings in Madras and Calcutta.

In the burgeoning colonial cities, military engineers assumed charge of major building. During the Napoleonic wars, a British army officer, Charles William Pasley, had been impressed by the efficient organization of French military works, and with Wellington's support, in 1812, he created a school of military engineering at Chatham. Knowing that officers, when sent to the colonies, were often "required to perform duties analogous to those of architects and civil engineers without having had any previous opportunity of acquiring a practical knowledge of the details of those duties," Pasley introduced a course in architecture for junior officers.[3] Beginning in 1854, government construction was administered by the Public Works Department (PWD) established under the central government. Offices of this department were placed under the control of military engineers and included civil engineers on their staffs. In Britain, the Royal Engineering College at Cooper's Hill was created in 1871 specifically to train civil engineers for the Indian PWD. Engineering colleges also were developed in India, one of the most notable being the Thomason Civil Engineering College at Roorkee. But British training was generally thought to be superior to that in India, so those educated at Cooper's Hill were employed in the elite "imperial service," while the Indian-trained went into the "provincial service."

The dominance of engineers in government architecture became a source of repeated criticism as the architectural profession evolved during the nineteenth century. Although the PWD occasionally engaged consulting architects for limited appointments in India, supervisory powers remained in the hands of engineers. The professional pride of architects was affronted by their lack of recognition in official India, and opposition to the policies of the Indian PWD provided a frequent theme for the British architectural press. With the founding of the *Bombay Builder* in 1865, architectural journalism existed in India as well. Denouncing the quality of government design in 1868, the *Bombay Builder* demanded, "who is there in the Public Works Department who has the smallest artistic power? Or who even knows anything at all about architecture? . . . If Engineers are such good architects, why doesn't Government in Britain employ them to do new law courts, national gallery etc.?"[4]

Although the design of colonial architecture was British, its construction was dependent on local materials and craftsmanship. Just as Indian craftsmen, at the time of the Mogul invasion, had adapted their techniques to Islamic arches and domes, they accommodated as best they could to demands for classical columns and pediments. Observing the efforts of local workmen to cope with new and alien aesthetic concepts, one British traveler early in the nineteenth century reported that

in their execution the native will display great ingenuity, consummate patience, and often great delicacy: but in design, taste, composition, perspective, consistency, and harmony, he will prove himself to be completely ignorant. As an apol-

43. *St. John's Church, Calcutta, designed by James Agg, and built in 1784–87.*

44. *Entrance to the Governor's Palace, Calcutta. It was designed by Captain Charles Wyatt and built between 1799 and 1803.*

45. *The Town Hall, Bombay, designed by Colonel Thomas Cowper and opened in 1833.*

46. Indian wood carver.

ogy it may again be justly pleaded, that in every branch the Indian mechanic is called upon after, perhaps, only a few days of observation . . . to perform that which we judge to be unattainable, except by the application of several years. . . . Instead, therefore, of condemning, we should rather admire their operations.[5]

Construction was usually under the direction of a *mistree,* equivalent to a master builder. Discussing local building trades in 1873, Julius George Medley, an engineer with extensive experience in India reported that "the mistrees, or native head-masons and carpenters, are generally intelligent and good men, quick to learn and easily managed, but few have any theoretical knowledge. [The native bricklayers] require close watching, and often systematic instruction in the all-important subject of bond." He judged the native carpenters to be "generally very fair, and sometimes very clever workmen, though they *do* squat on the ground, and hold a piece of wood with their toes while they work the drill by means of a bow and string with their hands" (fig. 46). Building methods were governed by long tradition and hereditary caste, and, in general, Indians seemed disinclined "to be driven out of their own customs, and to try experiments."[6]

When Europeans first arrived in India, the industrial revolution lay in the future, and they encountered a society in which methods of work were not radically different from their own. During the nineteenth century, however, European technology evolved at a rapid pace, creating an expanding gulf between the unmechanized East and the industrialized West. British engineers working in India often encountered craft methods long supplanted at home. Hand labor remained relatively cheap, and it was noted in 1873 that "steam engines, steam cranes, steam pumps, steam pile-drivers, . . . even such things as hand-pumps, horses, carts, and wheelbarrows are rarely used." The absence of machinery did not, however, prevent sizable works from being undertaken. "Earthwork, for instance, is constructed almost entirely with wicker baskets as the sole means of carriage; yet few countries have had so many massive embankments thrown up." Caution was advised in introducing European devices into India, for "if your fine carts or pumps get broken, who is to repair them?"[7]

The building material most readily available in Madras and Calcutta was brick, but a surface comparable to the stone of European classical prototypes was obtainable through the use of a lime plaster made from sea shells, called *chunam*. Chunam was of particularly high quality in Madras; it produced a lustrous sheen so diaphanous as to be likened to polished glass, providing an effective substitute for marble.

Contemplating Calcutta in 1870, Sir Bartle Frere predicted that "a hundred years hence, possibly, the English people would not look with great pride on the 'City of Palaces' because the materials employed are not such as any architect would use for architecture of a high order or intended for posterity."[8] In this respect Calcutta was sometimes contrasted with Bombay, where stone was sufficiently abundant to permit its use in all major building. Bombay might thus be destined to convey the image of Western civilization long after Calcutta had crumbled to dust. The governor's residence in Calcutta was modeled on Kedleston Hall in Derbyshire, an estate belonging to the Curzon family. When Lord Curzon, serving as Governor-General, was asked to comment on the resemblance of the two dwellings, he pointed out that "the columns here are only lath and plaster: at Kedleston they are, of course, alabaster."[9]

Building in Calcutta suffered from more problems than a shortage of stone. At a depth of forty feet, the soil became a semi-fluid quicksand, making it difficult to build heavy structures or to keep them vertical and safe from cracking. Indeed, most large buildings tended to suffer from unequal sinking. In addition, brick and plaster work were subject to "rapid disintegration" owing to "a saline nitrogenous miasma rising, chiefly at night, about 16 ft. or 20 ft. above the ground, which affects injuriously every building in the town."[10]

The annual monsoon season, moreover, produced periodic water damage. Wooden elements were constantly threatened by rot and by the depredations of termites, or "white ants." The removal and replacement of beams was a frequent occurrence. In buildings occupied by Indians, structural damage was frequently produced by the wild fig tree (*peepul,* or *ficus religiosa*). This tree grew from seed deposited by birds and was regarded as sacred by Hindus. As the tree could not, without sin, be destroyed or even pruned, it was permitted to embed its roots in the building fabric, causing fissures and eventual collapse. Visiting Bengal in 1824, Bishop Reginald Heber noted that "many powerful agents of destruction are always at work so that no architecture can be durable, and though ruins of buildings of apparently remote date are extremely common, it would perhaps be difficult to find a single edifice 150 years old."[11]

Other climatic conditions made the provision of environmental comfort a continual challenge. An Englishman, commenting on the dangerous effects of sun, was of the opinion that Europeans "must conform to the habits of the natives to a certain extent, if they would retain health or comfort. Yet too many walk about without *chattahs* [umbrellas] during the greatest heats, endeavouring by such a display of indifference,

47. House on Chowringhee Road, Calcutta.   *48. House on Park Street, Calcutta.*

to shew their great reliance on strength of constitution." While avoiding comparisons with mad dogs, he pointed out that during the time of greatest heat "the peaceful Hindoo confines himself to an apartment from which light is generally excluded. There he sits among his family, enjoying his pipe, refreshing himself occasionally by bathing, drinking the pure beverage from some adjacent spring or well; and in general avoiding to eat, except of ripe fruits . . . till the cool of the evening."[12]

British buildings tended to include large external openings that were shaded or screened when necessary to deflect glare and heat. Visiting the governor's mansion in Calcutta in 1780, a newly arrived Englishwoman noted that the windows were "hermetically closed; sashes, blinds, and every opening, except where tatties were placed to exclude the hot wind. This surprised me very much: but I understand no method is so effectual for that purpose."[13] The *tattie* was a cooling device that seems to have been in use among the British by the 1760s. It consisted of a split bamboo frame placed in a door or window opening and filled with a screen woven of a grass fiber called *khuss-khuss*. A servant would keep the screen soaked with water, and as the breeze passed through, evaporation might cool the air as much as ten degrees below the external temperature. Although the tatties darkened the interior considerably, newcomers were assured that "should these *tatties* not be used, the air that you breathe would be of a feverish nature, dry and parching to the skin, and almost impossible to be borne."[14] The tattie was useless, of course, if there was no breeze or during the rainy season, when the air was already saturated with moisture.

Normally windows were fitted with solid shutters or venetian blinds, and sometimes with wooden awnings. The classical mansion was usually graced by a columned portico or veranda. This provided a measure of shade for the interior, but the columns were usually too tall to allow shelter from horizontal rays. In order to provide additional sun protection, slatted screens or latticework were sometimes inserted between the columns (figs. 47 and 48).

49. *House interior with punkah.*   50. *Church interior with punkahs.*

Internal comfort in British building was heavily dependent on a swinging fan called a *punkah*. Although its origins are unclear, it appears to have been in use in Calcutta by the 1780s, and from there it spread to Madras and Bombay. In form it comprised a light wooden frame about fifteen feet long and four feet wide, over which was stretched cloth or canvas, with a loose fringe or border on the lower edge. Suspended from the ceiling, it was swung by means of ropes and pulleys. Often the pulling rope passed through a wall aperture to a veranda where the *punkah-wallah* sat moving the rope up and down with his hands or, occasionally, lay on his back, moving it with his feet (figs. 49 and 50).

After giving the matter serious study in the 1870s, British military engineers projected optimum dimensions for the punkah. The frame was to be twelve to eighteen inches wide, with a heavy fringe eighteen to twenty-four inches deep. If several punkahs were used together, they needed to be rigidly connected so as to swing evenly, and for maximum effect should move through an arc of five feet with a velocity of two-and-one-half feet per second. In spite of advancing technology, it was concluded "that no machine had been brought to their notice equally effective and economical with a man's arm."[15] Although people unaccustomed to punkahs sometimes complained that the device gave them headaches, most of the British found them indispensable. It was observed that "there is a *punkah* over the sleeper in bed; over the preacher . . . in the pulpit; over the party at dinner, whether on land or sea; over every man, woman, or child who wishes to breathe with any degree of ease."[16]

In the evenings, householders frequently escaped from stuffy interiors to the flat balustraded rooftops, which were often also used for entertaining. One Englishman in Calcutta judged the roof to be "the greatest extent of ground trodden, in way of exercise by the European foot."[17] The use of the rooftop was one of the few aspects of domestic living in which British custom resembled that of the Indians.

Essentially the same type of house was preferred in Madras and Calcutta. As

51. Castle Rainey in Ballygunge, Calcutta.

described by a visitor to Madras, houses were generally "square, flat-roofed buildings of two stories, having pillared porticoes, verandas opening into stately rooms, with handsome staircases, broad passages, and entrance halls." Single-storey houses were also common in Madras, as the ground was dry and considered to be relatively free of pestilence. In Calcutta, however, multistorey dwellings were more common because the ground level was considered unhealthy for sleeping. The nocturnal mist was feared as a source of sickness, and one visitor observed that "the deep fogs in Calcutta rise thick and heavy as high as the first floor; from the veranda of the second you may look down on the white fog below your feet."[18] A single-storey house was customarily elevated above a five-to-seven-foot basement that was used as a storage area (fig. 51).

Interior rooms were spacious and lofty, and in the grandest houses the scale was truly palatial. A drawing or dining room might be as long as fifty feet and twenty-five feet tall. High ceilings were necessitated by the use of the punkah. To provide free ventilation, openings were numerous and expansive to the point where "the room assumes the appearance of a bird-cage or a summer house."[19]

When Bishop Heber arrived in Calcutta in 1824, he found his house to include

a lofty and well-proportioned hall, 40 feet by 25, a drawing-room of the same length, and six or seven rooms all on the same floor, one of which served as a Chapel, the lower story being chiefly occupied as offices or lobbies. All these rooms were very lofty, with many doors and windows on every side; the floors of plaister, covered with mats; the ceilings of bricks, plaistered also, flat and supported by massive beams, which were visible from the rooms below, but being painted neatly had not at all a bad effect.[20]

Plaster floors were necessary to foil termites, and roof beams were exposed so that the condition of the wood could be continually open to inspection. To some eyes, the exposed beams produced a barnlike appearance, and those wishing to obtain the semblance of a flat ceiling would stretch a cloth, called a *chandny,* across the top of a room. This was sometimes whitewashed so that the visual result was similar to a plaster surface. Both walls and floors were plastered, and, although Heber describes his as "white and unadorned," they were customarily tinted.

Living in India, the British soon learned that frequent bathing was not a luxury but a necessity. Bathrooms were always provided, and in large houses it was not uncommon for a bathroom to be attached to each bedroom. The floor of the bathroom was usually covered with stone or tile, with the surface sloping toward an outlet connected to a drain. Bathing followed the traditional Indian method of dipping water over oneself from jars.

Meals were prepared in a separate structure that might be forty to fifty yards away from the house. Utensils were rudimentary, the floor was employed as a work surface, and cooking was done on a low brick hearth while smoke drifted out through openings below the roof. Although the British were often unnerved by what they saw in the kitchen, they were usually pleased with the edibles that emerged. Newcomers to Indian housekeeping were generally advised to stay away from the kitchen; there were things it was best not to know too much about.

British houses in Madras and Calcutta reflected a consistent effort at classical grandeur, but those in Bombay were initially more modest. Bombay developed more slowly than the other colonial cities, and as late as 1825, the company directors described the city as "of little importance to the Company."[21] British dwellings in Bombay were often modeled not on the Palladian mansion but on an unpretentious Indian rural dwelling, the bungalow. The term derived from a Hindi and Mahratti word, *bangla,* and was first used to describe a type of Bengali peasant house. The bungalow took various forms, but it was generally a single-storey house with a pitched roof and surrounded by a veranda (fig. 52).

Arriving at his Bombay residence in 1852, one Englishman encountered such a structure "looking for all the world, like a comfortable English cow-house! . . . However, we must admit that the similarity to the cow-house extended no further than the exterior; and our drooping spirits began to revive as we stepped direct, without any intervening hall or passage, into a large and elegant drawing-room, supported upon pillars of faultless proportions, and furnished with every modern luxury that either taste could suggest or wealth command."[22] The veranda of the bungalow, with its relatively low proportions, provided far better sun protection than a classical portico, and it was extensively used as an outdoor living area.

However comfortable a dwelling, the bungalow by this time was being supplanted by the externally more impressive classical mansion. It was reported that the bungalow was "not to be considered as a criterion of the general aspect of English residencies, which are usually lofty and stately-looking mansions, with facades adorned with spacious porticos supported on pillars of sufficient width to admit two carriages abreast." The interiors of such houses were described as being "much the same as in England."[23]

By and large, the British tried to duplicate the type of furnishings to which they were accustomed at home. The houses of the very rich were lavishly appointed with

52. Bungalow in Bombay.

carpets, chandeliers, silk and damask upholstery, mahogony and marble tables, statuary and paintings. Not everyone lived on such a lavish scale, though, and to some eyes British houses in India seemed rather sparsely furnished. A Calcutta resident observed in 1862 that "for, at least, eight months in the year, we cannot appreciate what in England you so much esteem,—a 'snug little room.' . . . we avoid therefore overstocking an apartment with furniture and lumber, as they not only rob us of space for circulation of air, but harbour dust, and afford shelter and encouragement to insects."[24]

In the early years of colonial settlement, most European furniture was imported and, consequently, both scarce and expensive. An Englishwoman visiting Calcutta in 1768 complained that "furniture is so exorbitantly dear and so very difficult to procure, that one seldom sees a room where all the chairs are of one sort."[25] The situation eventually improved as imports increased and local craftsmen became adept at imitating European styles. Describing Calcutta in 1822, another traveler reported that "the most beautiful French furniture was to be bought in Calcutta of M. de Bast, at whose shop marble tables, fine mirrors, and luxurious couches were in abundance. Very excellent furniture was also to be had at the Europe shops, made by native workmen under the superintendence of European cabinet and furniture makers."[26] Of the Indian-made furniture, the most highly prized was that produced in Bombay. The Dutch had provided the initial patronage for highly carved blackwood furniture, and

Indian-made articles of European style were marketed not only in India, but also abroad.

Although the creation of a domestic environment duplicating that of a British house may have been the ideal, most of the British in India found themselves compromising a bit. Woven grass mats were frequently used as floor coverings, in part because of the expensiveness of carpets, but also for the sense of coolness they gave. A thick Indian cloth, called a *satrinje,* was sometimes used for the same purpose. In the Indian climate, the British soon discovered that massive beds and thick bedding were far less practical than simple cots surrounded by mosquito netting. As ubiquitous as the *punkah,* and equally essential to well-being, mosquito netting seems to have come into use during the latter part of the eighteenth century. Initially, it consisted of a fabric called *kabbradool,* a gauze of raw silk, usually dyed light green.

In any event, no matter how one might struggle to create the illusion of British surroundings, nature provided intrusive reminders of the tropics. It was noted that

> bugs, such as infest beds in Europe, are beyond imagination numerous throughout the East. . . . Hence, it is scarcely possible to prevent their infesting the furniture. [While dining] during the rainy season, when insects of every description are beyond credibility numerous, it is often absolutely necessary to remove all lights from the supper-table. Otherwise, moths, flies, bugs etc., would be attracted in such numbers as, if not to extinguish them, to prove extremely obnoxious. . . . lizards . . . frequent the interior of houses, and may often be seen in great numbers crawling about the walls, or on the ceiling. . . . Frogs, toads, and occasionally snakes, patrolling about the skirts of the apartments, even of the best houses in the country, must be put up with as matters of course; as must also the alighting of cock-roaches on the face while at table, or at cards, etc. Nor, indeed, must the resident in India be very squeamish in regard to bats, which freely indulge in aerial circuits over the heads of the company.[27]

Some observers have viewed British building in India as an instrument of power, as one of the devices by which a small ruling group could visually enhance its presence. Yet in terms of policy, the creation of important architecture had been remote from the aims of the British East India Company. Colonialism was a strictly commercial venture, and the company begrudged every penny spent for building. Indifferent to the virtues of imperial image making, the directors grumbled about the cost of even such practical works as fortifications, and they continually fulminated against waste and extravagance in construction. But Britain was far from India, and communications were slow. The company's representatives were generally both ambitious and enterprising, and with or without London's blessing, an impressive body of architecture was created. When the company was deposed in 1857, and India came under the direct rule of the Crown, a more munificent attitude might reasonably have been anticipated. Imperial administration did not necessarily alter policies, however, and critics of the Public Works Department often deplored its parsimony with regard to architectural works.

Not unexpectedly, some of the most lavish buildings were designed to house the colonial governors. In Madras, Government House, designed in 1800, was a spacious two-storey mansion surrounded by colonnaded verandas, and it was accompanied by a large separate banqueting hall in the form of a Tuscan-Doric temple (fig. 53). The following year, the directors pointed out that "it by no means appears to us essential to the well-being of our Government in India that the pomp, magnificence and ostentation of the Native Governments should be adopted by the former." Such expense was deemed "highly injurious to our commercial interests."[28]

Even more costly was the house erected in Calcutta by Lord Wellesley, who served as Governor-General from 1797 until 1805. Keddleston Hall, a Palladian country house designed by Robert Adam and built in Derbyshire between 1759 and 1770, provided the prototype (fig. 54). Lord Curzon, who occupied the house as Viceroy between 1899 and 1905, believed that the design was "admirably adapted to a climate where every breath of air from whatever quarter must be seized. . . . In England the many mansions of the nobility and gentry that were built upon this plan in the Palladian furor . . . were as a rule uncomfortable and inconvenient. . . . But in India . . . where a legion of native servants renders distance and inconvenience of relatively minor importance, no better model could in all probability have been chosen. . . . the many frontages, facing all points of the compass, rendered it possible to cope with every condition of temperature."[29]

Viscount Valentia, who had witnessed the inauguration of Government House in 1803, noted that "the sums expended upon it have been considered as extravagant by those who carry European ideas and European economy into Asia; but they ought to remember, that India is a country of splendor, of extravagance, and of outward appearances. . . . In short, I wish India to be ruled from a palace, not from a counting house; with the ideas of a Prince, not with those of a retail dealer in muslins and indigo."[30] Valentia was generally pleased with Calcutta architecture as worthy of the seat of the eastern outpost of the British government.

The distinctive architectural style of European building underlined the exclusiveness of the colonial rulers, defining a private world where the British could camouflage their exile through reassuringly familiar surroundings. It was observed of central Calcutta that, "an English visitor may come and go almost without realizing that he has been to India at all."[31] Colonial building, however, did more than provide a setting for British private life. It created the stage for a major part of public life, including an urban realm shared by the Indian population.

British policy in India encouraged a process of westernization. Education was strongly influenced by the recommendations of Thomas Babington Macaulay who, in a minute written in 1835, urged the schooling of Indians "to form a class who may be interpreters between us and the millions whom we govern, a class of persons, Indian in blood and colour, but English in taste, in opinions, in morals and in intellect."[32] Within the colonial cities, new educational institutions arose, employing the English language and designed to promote Western knowledge. Emerging from these institutions was an Indian professional class trained along British lines and oriented toward Western ideas. While some of the British disliked and distrusted westernized Indians, many felt pride in the changes they were promoting, and it was boasted that "the few English who have governed India have done more to bring it into harmony with Western civilisation and culture than perhaps all Europe has done for the world south of the Mediterranean."[33]

Western-style buildings provided the setting in which Indians were exposed to

53. *Governor's Banqueting Hall in Madras, by John Goldingham, 1798–1803.*

54. *Government House, Calcutta, completed in 1803. (See also fig. 44)*

55. Central Post Office, Calcutta, by Walter Granville, 1864–68.

European concepts. An urbanized Indian who studied at a university, sat in a local assembly, testified in court, received medical treatment, bought a railway ticket, or mailed a letter did so in European surroundings. Architecture was deemed to have an instructive function, and critics of colonial building often stressed the need for an architecture that would suitably represent Western civilization. Sir Richard Temple complained in 1881 that "the style of many British structures was so erroneous or defective as to exercise a debasing influence on the minds of those Natives, who might be induced to admire or imitate it as being the production of a dominant and presumably a more civilized race."[34]

Classicism remained dominant in Madras and Calcutta until well into the nineteenth century. Particularly distinguished in Calcutta was the work of Walter Granville, who was appointed consulting architect to the Indian government in 1863. His work included a group of buildings for the University of Calcutta and a monumental central post office marked by Corinthian colonnades and a domed corner pavilion (fig. 55). He retained the classical mode for a museum sited on Chowringhee to house a collection of Indian art.

56. Madras Christian College.

Although the classical tradition had a long and pervasive influence in India, nine-teenth-century colonial building reflected a wide range of European revival styles, from the Italianate to the Queen Anne cottage. As in Britain, however, the strongest rival to classicism was the Gothic Revival (figs. 56 and 57). In terms of symbolism, Gothic might have been judged an unlikely style for export. While classicism had been regarded as a universal style based on rationally apprehended principles, Gothic had associations that were peculiarly national and Christian; it was linked to the crafts-manship and intuitive artistry of a particular culture. Unlike classicism, it had origi-nated in northern Europe, and some found its delicate and intricate forms incongruous under glaring tropical skies. It proved, however, to be functionally adaptable to Indian conditions, and its specifically Christian associations were susceptible to symbolic dilu-tion. Like classicism, the style could be reduced to the level of decorative motif.

Although the Gothic Revival made only limited inroads into the architectural scene in Madras and Calcutta, it came to dominate Bombay. The flowering of High Victorian Gothic in Britain coincided with a period of urban renovation in Bombay, and it was perhaps inevitable that this newly fashionable style should be adopted. The

57. St. Paul's Cathedral, Calcutta, designed by Major W. M. Forbes of the Bengal Engineers and consecrated in 1847.

59. Bombay University Senate Hall, built between 1869 and 1874.

government complex resulting from the removal of the fortifications was characterized by variations on the Gothic mode. At the southern end was the secretariat designed in 1865 by Colonel H. St. Clair Wilkins and completed in 1874. Just north of this was the University of Bombay, including a library ornamented by a soaring clock tower, and a Senate Hall for university ceremonies, both based on designs by the noted British architect George Gilbert Scott. In style, the library incorporated Venetian Gothic elements, while the Senate Hall reflected an interpretation of fifteenth-century French Gothic (figs. 58 and 59).

One factor making Gothic building difficult to employ in India was its dependence on sculptural decoration. The relatively simple and standardized forms of classical design could be easily copied by Indian craftsmen, but it would be more difficult for them to duplicate the more spontaneous and individualistic forms of Gothic carving. A Bombay guidebook of 1887 called attention to certain crudities in the decoration on the university buildings, noting that "many bits of the carving . . . have evidently been

58. Bombay University Library, adapted by M. Molency from a design by George Gilbert Scott and built between 1869 and 1878.

taken from well-known sources, illustrated by hard line German prints, and are un-meaning in form and character."[35] The guide suggested that the problem might be remedied by sending plaster casts from England as models for native craftsmen, or by importing English stone carvers.

Beyond the university complex lay the High Court designed by Colonel Fuller (fig. 60), the Public Works Office by Colonel Wilkins, and the General Post Office by government architects J. Trubshawe and W. Paris. By the end of the 1870s an impressive line of buildings faced the seafront, ornamenting the Bombay skyline with the picturesque projections of towers and high pitched roofs. The university clock tower, supposedly inspired by Giotto's campanile in Florence, was the tallest structure in Bombay, and it became a noted landmark.

Not everyone agreed as to the appropriateness of Gothic architecture in India. One observer described Bombay government building as exemplifying "a fine official disregard for all local associations." Another visitor noted that the main features of the secretariat "have been brought from Venice, but all the beauty has vanished in trans-shipment." He added that "the University Hall . . . seems to have been meant for a

60. Bombay High Court, designed by Colonel Fuller and built between 1871 and 1878.

western College Chapel, and is as exotic as the system of education which we have introduced into the land." As to the High Court, it was "a large, imposing, ugly Gothic construction, out of character with the climate; but the building is probably not more out of character with the climate than the mode of administering justice within its walls is out of character with the habits of the people."[36]

Among the ornate Gothic buildings that were added to nineteenth-century Bombay, the most spectacular was undoubtedly the terminus and headquarters of the Great Indian Peninsular Railway, later known as Victoria Terminus. The station, designed in 1878 by Frederick William Stevens, was distinguished not only for its extraordinary size and opulence, but for its employment of what is considered the first masonry dome adapted to a Gothic building (fig. 61). Although the Gothic revival was dominant in Bombay in this period, other European styles were also in evidence. The uniform facades of Elphinstone Circle, for example, were designed in the Italianate mode, a choice that may have reflected a desire to avoid a stylistic clash with the classical town hall bordering one side of the circle.

Bombay's ambitious building program proved a strong impetus to civic pride, and the new government ensemble became a visual symbol of the city. Even though design faults continued to be observed in individual structures, the overall scenic effect was admired as unrivaled by any city in Asia. To some, this comparison was too modest. Bombay buildings could stand comparison "with almost any city in the world. . . . The Briton feels himself a greater man for his first sight of Bombay."[37]

61. Victoria Terminus, designed by Frederick William Stevens and built between 1878 and 1887.

So intent were the British on the creation of a westernized ambient that, to their eyes, the large Indian districts of the colonial cities seemed virtually nonexistent in terms of architecture. The Indian community did, however, contribute extensively to the physical character of the city. Indians controlled large tracts of property, and, in addition to creating expansive areas of housing and commerce, they patronized a wide range of religious and institutional buildings. India possessed a distinguished architectural tradition, and it might have been reasonable to anticipate that the prosperous Indian residents of Madras, Calcutta, and Bombay would foster and enhance a vital local architecture within the fabric of the colonial metropolis. The development of the

62. Calcutta from the Hooghly River: Gentoo Buildings, by Thomas Daniell, 1788.

colonial cities, however, coincided with an apparent decline in the local artistic tradition, and Indian building of the period was generally derided. The dissolution of the Mogul empire had disrupted a system of court patronage, and during the subsequent period of warfare, political and economic insecurity combined to hamper artistic production. Those who sought the beauty of Indian building found it in the monuments of the past, far from the bustling confines of the modern colonial cities.

One Englishman described the Calcutta native quarter in 1888 as consisting of "dusty brick houses, utterly devoid of architectural merit." His views were shared by a compatriot who complained that the houses "have not a single picturesque feature," adding that "the bazaars would be equally uninteresting . . . were it not for the dense crowds who move through them." Concurring, another British writer observed that, "for beauty, regularity, and ornament," Calcutta was "not to be compared with Benares and Delhi, the handsome stone cities of Upper India." As to religious architecture, a turn-of-the-century guidebook advised that "in this city there are no Hindu temples worthy of mention. . . . What pundit in his senses would recommend the tourist, who has Benares and perhaps the stupendous temples of Southern India to visit, to waste even an hour at Kalighat? . . . Calcutta is essentially a place of *English* interest" (fig. 62).[38]

While the British might have been expected to disdain any architecture but their own, the Indians themselves often denigrated the quality of local building. A Parsee discussing nineteenth-century Bombay noted that "a stranger . . . will be irresistibly struck by the total absence of any kind of notable architecture in the places of religious worship of the principal communities." Although the city contained four hundred Hindu temples, in addition to numerous mosques and Parsee fire temples, "there is not one such edifice which can satisfy the artistic eye." Pointing out Bombay's lack of ancient Indian monuments, he observed that "the city is in reality an upstart, a parvenue, and cannot hold comparison beside the ancient Hindu shrines and temples in Northern and Southern India." Although merchant communities have been known to provide enlightened and generous artistic patronage, he blamed the state of Bombay architecture on the city's narrow commercial focus. "Bombay has been intensely shop-keeping, and that is the reason why the temples, the mosques and other places of worship inspire neither reverence nor awe, let alone beauty and joy."[39]

It is difficult to form an accurate picture of the native districts of colonial cities because of the lack of documentation. British building was extensively portrayed by European artists beginning in the eighteenth century. Such artists were also attracted to the Indian landscape and to the great monuments of Indian tradition. They loved to record the sublimity of mountain scenery and the picturesque outlines of ancient temples, mosques, palaces, and tombs. The Indian buildings in colonial cities, however, seemed to provide little inspiration for the European artist.

A British physician, describing Calcutta in 1837, observed that the houses of the rich natives

> are uniformly built in the form of a hollow square, with an area of from 50 to 100 feet each way, which on the occasion of Hindoo festivals, is covered over, and when well lighted up, looks very handsome. The house itself is seldom of more than two stories, the lower portion, on three sides of it, being used only for storerooms, or for domestics; on the remaining side, and that always the northern one, is to be found the Thakoor Ghur, or abode of the Hindoo Gods. This is always furnished with care, and when the owner is wealthy, the lustres contained in this sacred apartment are of considerable value. Above the stairs are the public apartments, with verandas, always [opening] inwards: these are generally long narrow slips, containing a profusion of lustres and wall lights. . . . jutting out from this main building are situated the accommodations allotted to the females and family; they consist of smaller hollow squares, with petty verandas opening inwards, and some houses have two or three sets of these zunnanahs, with one or more tanks attached, but which are generally kept in a very neglected state. Altogether, this form of building, if placed on open ground and made more roomy, would not appear ill-calculated for the climate.[40]

The courtyard form of dwelling was maintained among the Indians for security and also for visual privacy, because nothing could "offend a native more than the erection of an edifice overlooking the interior of that enclosure in which his family resided."[41] The purdah system required the seclusion of women from the eyes of the outside world, and, even within the dwelling itself, separate quarters for men and women were often maintained (fig. 63).

British and Indian houses were similar in providing transitional areas in which outsiders might be received without entering the intimate living quarters. Among the British, the veranda often served as place where visitors were met, where tradesmen might display their wares and tailors do their work. In some parts of India, native houses incorporated a front veranda or entry room for outsiders. A British clergyman

63. Courtyard of an Indian house in Delhi being used for a nautch (a performance of music and dancing) during the 1860s. The audience is entirely male, although the hooded figures watching from the balcony may be women of the household.

visiting a house in Madras reported that "the street-door opens into a small room where all visitors can be received without their having to go into the more private apartments."[42] Houses in Madras were often fronted with an open platform or *pyal*. This was used as a sitting area and also as a place where travelers might sleep. An increase in family size frequently meant that the *pyal* had to be enclosed, with the house then further extended in front, resulting in an encroachment on the street.

The joint family system in which married sons remained in their parents' household tended to produce large domestic establishments, including family members, numerous servants, and various hangers-on. Among the British a single man might occupy a twenty-room mansion, and they often professed amazement at the numbers of people who might inhabit an Indian dwelling. An Indian scholar has noted that "though relatively rich to begin with, the landlord families could decay within one or two generations from the pressure of numbers. An imposing structure might look like a rabbit-warren or be covered with jungle because of the neglect of the co-sharers or the receivers appointed by the law-court. A house might be built on a grand scale with the firm conviction that seven generations would live there," yet fall into disrepair because of "the succeeding generations being too busy quarreling or making ends meet."[43]

Among the three major colonial cities, it was only in Bombay that the British seem to have responded favorably to the aesthetics of native building. The typical Indian dwelling in Bombay was notably different from that found in either Calcutta or Madras, where the house was built to the outer edge of the lot, leaving open space in the center. Land was scarce in Bombay, and houses occupied narrow street frontages. While Calcutta houses seldom went above two storeys, Bombay houses were tall and narrow, with verandas in front and courtyards at the rear of the lot, rather than in the center. The rooftop in Bombay was not employed as a living area. Instead of flat roofs, Bombay houses usually had tiled pitched roofs, and construction was based on a wooden frame, rather than on load-bearing masonry.

In the view of one Englishman, the streets of Bombay "constantly remind you, especially in the woodwork, of the houses of the Ionian Greeks, as the learned have reconstructed them from the remains: and the woodwork is the essential framework, the solid skeleton of native houses in Bombay, and is put up complete before a stone or brick is placed on it." The passage of time often brought rot and decay to older dwellings, and reports of collapse were not infrequent. Pressures on land resulted in "the piling of storeys upon old houses often incapable of supporting their weight, . . . Hardly a year passed, hardly a monsoon set in, without some of these overweighted houses collapsing, and dealing swift death or injury to inmates."[44]

The most striking external feature of Bombay building was its decorative carving, a quality that linked it with traditional Gujarat architecture. In the view of one British visitor, Bombay stood "alone among the modern cities of India" in that it "reproduces the character and charm of the older centres of population. . . . The houses ascend four, five and six storeys, their facades are broken with airy balconies enriched with graceful carving and painted all colours of the rainbow. Indeed, the most populous streets bear a far closer resemblance to those of Amritsar and Lahore than to anything in the other towns that have grown up under British rule." The overhanging stories reminded some of European medieval towns; one visitor even declared that "the wooden houses with their wooden verandas, . . . and heavy sloping roofs," presented a "Swiss rather than an Oriental appearance." Another traveler likened a Bombay house "with projecting storeys and balconies and casements—the top tiers nothing but painted wood and glass" to "the stern of a huge three-decker" (fig. 64).[45]

Although Indians were often obsessed with domestic privacy, every activity of the bazaar was open to view. The British were often amazed to find that

> people do all sorts of things in public which to our thinking should be transacted in privacy, such as dressing, shaving, washing, and sleeping, and, in spite of the caste rules and religious restrictions, even a good deal of eating. . . . As you pass along the streets of the bazaar you can look right into half the houses. The shops are simply boxes, set on end, with the lids off. You can, if you please, stand and watch the baker rolling his flat loaves, the tailor stitching and cutting, the coppersmith hammering at his bowls and dishes, the jeweller drawing out gold and silver wire over his little brazier. The Indian townsman does not mind being looked at. He is accustomed to it. He passes his life in the midst of a crowd.[46]

Usually, the shop was raised above the level of the street, providing a low platform to

64. *House on Kalbadeve Road, Bombay. Although the old houses of central Bombay have been largely destroyed or mutilated, this one gives an approximation of the appearance described by many 19th-century observers.*

65. *Chandni Chowk, the principal bazaar in Delhi.*

serve as a counter for selling or a workbench for craftsmen. Some visitors likened the open shopfront to a miniature stage (fig. 65).

Small craftsmen and wealthy merchants were equally at home in the crowded confines of the bazaar, and even the most affluent often clung to traditional surroundings for doing business. A visitor to Bombay observed an old moneylender who "squatted among cushions, smoking his long pipe. . . . Near him are boys and assistants, totting up accounts or writing letters on their knees. The man is worth thousands of pounds, but his place of business is not bigger than a dining-room table— and there are scores like him."[47]

One of the major differences between British and Indian architecture lay in the realm of interior furnishing. The British equipped their interiors with a variety of bulky objects. They sat on chairs and sofas, ate and worked at tables, slept in beds, and hung pictures on their walls. The Indians had managed for centuries with only minimal domestic equipment. An Englishman once observed that, "if we may judge from the example of India, the great art in furniture is to do without it." Visiting the home of a wealthy Indian, he noted that his host "sits on a grass mat or cotton sattrinji or Cashmere rug with a round pillow at his back." He added that "up country you may pass through a whole palace, and the only furniture in it will be rugs and pillows, and of course the cooking pots and pans, and gold and silver vessels for eating and drinking, and the wardrobes and caskets, and graven images of the gods. But you are simply entranced by the perfect proportions of the rooms, and polish of the ivory-white walls, the frescoes round the dado, and the beautiful shapes and niches in the walls, and of the windows, and by the richness and vigour of the carved work of the doors and projecting beams and pillars of the veranda. You feel that the people of ancient Greece must have lived in something of this way."[48]

An Englishwoman who had been invited to visit the women's quarters of an aristocratic family in 1823 reported:

> The floor of the room was covered with white cloth; several lamps of brass were placed upon the ground, each stand holding, perhaps, one hundred small lamps. In the centre of the room a carpet was spread, and upon that the gaddi and pillows for the Begam; the gaddi or throne of the sovereign is a long round pillow, which is placed behind the back for support, and two smaller at the sides for the knees; they are placed upon a small carpet of velvet, or of cloth of gold. . . . native beds (*charpai*) are about one foot high from the ground; people of rank have the feet of these couches covered with thick plates of gold or silver, which is handsomely embossed with flowers. . . . The seat of the bed is formed of broad cotton tape, skillfully interlaced, drawn up tight as a drum-head, but perfectly elastic. It is the most luxurious couch imaginable, and a person accustomed to the charpai of India will spend many a restless night ere he can sleep with comfort on an English bed.[49]

Occasionally, an interior would be provided with a *tukt-posh,* a low dais covered with a quilt, large enough to accommodate several people reclining on pillows.

To some of the British, the absence of domestic furnishings among the Indians seemed an almost perverse disregard of normal human comfort. One English clergyman, J. E. Padfield, observed that "as a rule, even amongst the better classes, there is a complete absence of most of the domestic conveniences which the poorest Europeans consider indispensable. . . . Taste and wealth are not manifested in grand furniture and costly hangings or any other of the things that go to make up a luxurious home in Europe. Good timber, well-made wooden ceilings, and elaborate carvings are here

66. Indian mansion in Calcutta.

the things most admired." The lack of heavy furniture gave considerable flexibility to the use of interior spaces. People could sleep anywhere, and this same clergyman observed that the men often spread mats on the inner veranda. "No place seems too hard, or, to our ideas, too uncomfortable." Charpoy beds might be shifted from place to place to take advantage of cool breezes or shelter from rain. In addition to the charpoys, the only other furnishings might be a few stools, storage boxes, and cooking pots. While some might have equated the spartan Indian interior with a spiritually enlightened asceticism, Padfield considered that "all Hindu homes have one thing in common, and that is the absence of that comfort, that indescribable something which is the charm of an English home, and which causes us to use the word as a synonym for the eternal happiness beyond."[50]

It was inevitable, of course, that British styles would modify and in some ways replace Indian tradition. European customs embodied prestigious associations with a ruling class. Most of the British took for granted the superiority of their way of life and regarded it as only appropriate that the better class of natives should try to conform to it. To the British view, "the peculiarities and habits of the natives of an Indian city make it impossible for Englishmen to live in their streets. It is not a question of pride or fashion; the dwellings are altogether unfitted for Europeans."[51] It was deemed far from impossible, however, for Indians to adapt to British dwellings.

67. *Raja Manmatha Nati Ghose's house.*

68. *Courtyard of Raja Manmatha Nati Ghose's house. Three sides were surrounded by a classical colonnade.*

Bishop Heber, observing the natives of Calcutta in 1824, noted that "their progress in the imitation of our habits is very apparent, though still the difference is great. None of them adopt our dress. But their houses are adorned with verandas and Corinthian pillars; they have very handsome carriages, often built in England; they speak tolerable English, and they show a considerable liking for European society where (which unfortunately is not always the case) they are encouraged or permitted to frequent it on terms of any thing like equality."[52] In the case of urban houses, Indians usually retained the traditional plan of the courtyard dwelling. A classical portico might face the street, and the internal courtyard be surrounded by colonnaded loggias. In basic form, such houses resembled an Italian palazzo more than any British prototype (figs. 66–70).

For some Indians, foreign styles may have provided no more than a superficial novelty. In many cases, however, the adoption of Western architecture coincided with a sophisticated range of intellectual interests. In some ways, the Indians who favored European design were counterparts to the Englishmen who had first employed Renaissance classicism. The new style was associated with the cosmopolitan views of a cultural avant-garde.

A classical mansion was built in Calcutta around 1795 by the Maharaja Joynarain Ghoshal, a scholar and poet fluent in Sanskrit, Urdu, and Bengali, as well as in English and French. Classical architecture also characterized the eighteenth-century house of Raja Nabakrishna, who became a friend and confidant of Robert Clive, tutoring him in Persian, Urdu, and Sanskrit. The raja was a noted patron of scholars, and his house became a center of cultural and political activity. Raja Digambar Mitra, a

69. Courtyard of Raja Manmatha Nati Ghose's house. As in many such houses, the Thakur Ghur employed traditional styling.

70. Govindra Ram Mitra's house. The courtyard of this house contained a Hindu temple, the Madan Mohan temple, built in the Ionic style.

philanthropist and sportsman who served as sheriff of Calcutta and president of the British India Association was also housed in the classical style. Another patron of westernized architecture was Raja Ram Mohan Roy, the founder of the Brahmo-Samaj, the Society of God. A brilliant linguist, he promoted the Atmiya Sabha, or Society of Friends, and was instrumental in establishing a Unitarian Committee in Calcutta to advance education and religious debate. The distinguished Tagore family also employed classical design in several of their Calcutta houses.

One of the most remarkable classical mansions built by an Indian family in Calcutta was the so-called Marble Palace built by the Raja Rajendra Mullick in 1835–40. Although this house incorporated a traditional courtyard plan, it followed the British fashion of setting the house within a spacious garden. Like many Indian classical houses, the Marble Palace employed architectural motifs with a certain freedom and eclectecism (figs. 71 and 72).

In addition to their residences in town, many wealthy Indians had country houses. Dwarkanath Tagore owned a villa in the English style set in a picturesque garden five miles outside Calcutta. He frequently entertained European guests, and his dinner table was reputed to hold "the richest wines and even roasted joints of the sacred animal." Bishop Heber reported visiting an Indian country house that was "more like an Italian villa, than what one should have expected as the residence of Baboo Hurree Mohun Thakoor. Nor are his carriages, the furniture of his house, or the style of his conversation, of a character less decidedly European."[53]

European architectural motifs could be found in many types of Indian buildings, often juxtaposed to traditional styles. Just as the English, during the Renaissance,

71. *The Mullick house, or Marble Palace.*

72. *Portico of the Mullick house. The family possessed an extensive collection of Western art.*

sometimes made classical additions to medieval buildings, the Indians might incorporate European features when repairing an old structure. Often buildings were designed with a mixture of Western and Indian elements. A striking juxtaposition of styles occurred in the Gopalji Temple built in Calcutta in 1845. The temple compound was designed to be entered through a classical portico. The inner courtyard was surrounded by a Doric colonnade, while the upper levels of the structure embodied traditional forms (figs. 73 and 74).

Institutional buildings often reflected both Western architecture and Indian patronage. This was especially true in Bombay where a rich and philanthropically minded Indian community contributed extensively to the architectural image of the city. The university library was endowed by a Hindu businessman, Premchand Roychand, with the clock tower, called Rajabai Tower, dedicated to the memory of his mother. The university senate hall had been donated by a Parsee, Sir Cowasjee Jehanghier. Indian munificence also sponsored numerous hospitals, schools, and libraries. In many instances, private support and government sponsorship were combined, with design and construction directed by the PWD. For the Indians financing such projects, questions of architectural style seem to have had little importance.

It was sometimes deplored that wealthy Indians whose generosity might otherwise have encouraged local art forms chose to patronize an alien style. One might have argued, however, that many of the institutions being housed had no traditional roots, but reflected instead the growing westernization of urban society. The new schools and universities had been created to promote European learning, the hospitals facilitated Western medical practice, and the libraries contained English works. Yet even in buildings with uniquely Indian functions, Western styles were often used. The headquarters of the Parsee community in Bombay, for example, was housed in an Italianate structure designed by Dinshaw Dorabjee Mistry in 1871 (fig. 75). In the colonial cities, Macaulay's hope that Indian education might eventually produce a class of dark-skinned Englishmen seemed in many ways fulfilled.

By the mid-nineteenth century, architecture employing European styles reflected not only Indian patronage, but also Indian participation in design and construction. With the development of professional education based on Western models, Indians began to enter the fields of medicine, law, and engineering. Professional training in architecture, however, was delayed until the twentieth century. Government building continued to be directed by engineers, and it was as civil engineers that Indians became engaged in architectural production. The university senate house, for example, had been completed under the supervision of a Hindu engineer, Muckoond Ramchunder.

Typifying the type of career beginning to open up to Indians was the achievement of M. C. Murzban. Born in 1839 into a Parsee family, he graduated from engineering school in Poona and entered the Public Works Department in 1857. During the building boom of the 1860s, he was transferred to Bombay, becoming assistant to J. Trubshawe. Murzban had no formal architectural training, but he studied informally with one of Trubshawe's colleagues, a British architect, Roger Smith, who was professor of architecture in King's College, London.

Exceptionally gifted as an engineer and administrator, Murzban rose to be executive engineer of the Bombay Municipal Corporation in 1892, the first Indian to be so

73. *Palladian motifs were combined with traditional forms on the Tipu Mosque on Prince Anwar Shah Road.*

74. *Courtyard of the Gopalji Temple, 1845, showing the entrances to the sanctuary. The outer entrance to the courtyard was marked by a classical pedimented portico.*

75. *Parsee Panchayat, Bombay.*

appointed. During his career in the PWD, Murzban was involved with a wide range of engineering and architectural projects, serving as both designer and construction supervisor. In addition, he developed a successful private design practice, and he promoted a suburban housing tract.

Professional life in India emulated that in Britain, and through journals and professional associations, Indians maintained close ties with their British colleagues. In 1874, Murzban became an associate member of the Institute of Civil Engineers of England, and he was made a full member in 1896. He was made a fellow of the Royal Institute of British Architects in 1889, and in 1892 a member of the Society of Arts in London. Membership in such organizations was essential in maintaining professional status in India. It was taken for granted that Britain set the standards for training, licensing, and practice, and that the best education was obtainable only in Britain. According to strict Hindu observance, transoceanic travel was prohibited, but increasing numbers of Indians seemed willing to risk spiritual pollution for the intellectual and material benefits of study abroad. In a further effort to integrate Indians into the British system, the British instituted special titles for distinguished Indians to be included in the annual honors lists. In 1877, the year in which Queen Victoria became Empress of India, M. C. Murzban was titled Kahn Bahadur, and in 1899 he was made Companion of the Most Eminent Order of the Indian Empire.[54]

The adoption of Western architecture among Indians brought with it the adoption of Western interior furnishings and, consequently, changes in living patterns. For some Indians, the creation of a European interior was primarily a concession to foreign guests. The British only felt at ease in familiar surroundings and tended to view chairs as a fundamental base of civilization. A British clergyman describing a visit to a Calcutta family in 1871 observed that one room "looked most comfortable, being furnished in European style; but it was never used except as a show-room to foreigners." On another occasion, he was invited to one of the most opulent mansions of the city and reported that "we were ushered into a splendid drawing-room, furnished in European fashion, and in the most costly manner. . . . It was touching to see the keen desire this native gentleman displayed to do all honour to European tastes by thus expensively furnishing those fine apartments, which neither himself nor his family ever occupied. . . . It was evident, however, from the unnecessary quantity of furniture of every kind—great crystal candelabra, bronzes, busts, timepieces, and such-like— which crowded the rooms, no less than from the quality of much that was there, that the rich native gentleman's kind heart and want of knowledge, as well as his wealth, had been taken advantage of by tradesmen. An English lady or gentleman of taste could have produced infinitely better results with immensely less outlay." Struck by the simplicity of traditional Indian surroundings, he declared that "it would astonish many a European to see the apartments where an Eastern family of rank live, eat, and sleep, as contrasted with what the outside world is permitted on great occasions to see in their palace-home!"[55]

The distinction between the public, or European, part of a house and the private, or Indian, portions represented in some instances the separation between the men's and women's areas of the house. While the purdah tradition remained in force, it was only the men who associated with foreign guests and had occasion to use and develop a taste for Western furnishings.

Among the Indians who became strongly anglicized were those who entered upper levels of civil and military service. Often provided with the same sort of housing as their British counterparts, they inevitably adjusted to the way of living it implied. A Muslim woman whose father had been a government medical officer recalled that Indians like her parents "felt it was their incumbent duty to prove to Englishmen that they could emulate them to perfection. . . . Our house, therefore, was furnished to look exactly like an English house. In the drawing room there were heavy sofas . . . lace curtains, gleaming brass and silver . . . and knicknacks displayed in cabinets. The dining room had a fairly massive sideboard . . . displaying a lot of heavy silver." Particularly assiduous in their attempts to emulate British customs were the Eurasians, or "Anglo-Indians." A British writer once described their houses as "furnished in unconscious caricature of English taste, with even more occasional tables, silk cushions, brassware and potted ferns than in the bungalow of the Collector."[56]

The Parsees were among the most westernized of the Bombay communities, and a visitor to one of their houses declared that "you might well imagine yourself in the drawing room of some wealthy Englishman" (fig. 76). Another English account of a Parsee interior describes "a long drawing-room with its rocking chairs ranged in a straight row, the enormous cut-glass chandelier, the model of the Taj Mahal on a blackwood table, the glass cupboards full of English china, the dark oil-paintingss of ancestors, the highly colored prints of King Edward VII's coronation and of Zoroaster in meditation. On the table a silver teapot even more massive than those commonly seen in European bungalows." Outdoor statuary was also favored, and it was reported that "in the gardens of many of the biggest houses on Malabar Hill were forests of Venuses and Athenes holding up lamps or pointing to clocks in their stomachs, statues that were a source of pride to their owners who would drape mackintoshes round them during the monsoon."[57]

The British often assumed an air of superior amusement as they dwelt on the clumsy efforts of Indians to emulate the elevated canons of European taste. The na-

76. Interior of Esplanade House, belonging to the Parsee, J. N. Tata, and built in 1887.

tives, it seemed, just couldn't get anything right. Happily indifferent to British sneers, however, rich Indians had quite a lot of fun with their newly acquired foreign possessions. A Parsee, describing the days of the nineteenth-century cotton boom, recalled such furnishings as "large mirrors in gilt frames, . . . all shades of chandeliers. The Bohemian or Venetian glassware was the pride of the rich, and he who hung in his hall or *pedhee* the largest number of these decorated by the glittering prismatic drops, was esteemed a man of great riches. There would be also by way of foreign novelty a musical or dramatic clock with soft chimes and other mechanical devices. Mechanical toys, too, of foreign origin would be exhibited with the greatest gusto. . . . As commerce increased the richer classes imported Brussels carpets and many other knick-nacks to adorn their halls."[58]

The adoption of Western artistic fashions in India raised many questions. Was it really progress? Or was the heritage of an ancient civilization being deplorably eroded? In some ways, the cultural cross-currents of colonial India produced remarkable individuals. The cosmopolitan Indian might be seen as a genuine citizen of the world, multilingual, open-minded, flexible, and tolerant. At the same time, the anglicized Indian might be viewed as a species of cultural traitor. Did one adopt a facade of westernization in a craven effort at ingratiation with one's foreign masters? Or was it a lure prompted by expediency, a mask disguising unplumbed and murky depths of Asian deceit? Was adaptability a form of duplicity?

Kylas Chunder Dutt, a Bengali, published an essay in 1836 in which he described a Calcutta entrepreneur with a chameleonlike ability to emulate both Eastern and Western custom, and always to his own benefit:

> Before Europeans veal, jelly, and burgundy are his delights, before Hindus his abominations. "I wonder", says he to Mr. Credulous, "why the Bengalese are averse to taste these." In Indian circles, he declares himself horrified, "when I see the white islanders feast on fowl and beef." He is a member of the Beefsteak club as the Dhurma Shuba. . . . He is considered the richest individual in the city. . . . Besides he is a very clever fellow! He speaks English as if he had been born and bred in London; understands Sanscrit, Hindee, Persian, and the rest of the Oriental Languages; he is an admirable musician and an unrivalled vocalist. The Italian airs are as familiar to him as the Hindee.[59]

His house is revealed through the bedazzled vision of a British guest, Mr. Dupe, a newly appointed judge. Ascending the steps of the mansion, the Englishman admired "as he went along every object that he was fortunate enough to cast his eyes upon. The suite of apartments in this beautiful villa was fitted up with extraordinary taste. The drawing-room was the most splendidly furnished, the carpet was genuine Mirzapore, chairs of mahogany with cushions of sky blue colour, sofas covered with damasks of great brilliancy, pictures the imitations of Raphael and Claude with some originals, which seemed living realities, diamond cut wall shades with brilliant drops were arranged with care, two tables of solid marble, white as morning snow, with two large chiming clocks and other ornaments of the most curious workmanship, were part of the gorgeous furniture." An antechamber was furnished in similar Western style and contained a large collection of splendidly bound books. In the retiring chamber, the bed "was composed of down, with velvet covering; the curtains were of flowered gauze. French prints were hung round the room, and a large portrait of Venus in all her loveliness, [was] placed at the front so as to be visible to a person reclining on the bed."

As the evening progressed, it became clear that the Indian host was gratifyingly free from Hindu prejudice against the use of alcohol: "The cup was introduced which was not likely to be relinquished. Cup after cup was drained of its delicious draught." Warmed with intercultural camaraderie, the two gentlemen exchanged head gear, and as they stood arm and arm before a mirror, Dupe concluded, "the turban sets me off to the best advantage." Unaware of the snare prepared for him, gullible Mr. Dupe was induced to accept a substantial loan from his new chum. Duped indeed, his fate was sealed as the wily Bengali calculated the interest rate and reflected, "I shall have one Civilian more that will dance when I wink."

3.

The Long Debate

Comparing the French settlement of Pondicherry with British colonial cities, a travel writer in the 1880s declared that the French "do not attempt to introduce into India the manners and habits of France." The English, by contrast, "always tread disdainfully a foreign soil; and, whether in China or Kamschatka, still think themselves on British ground. The Englishman, in effect, does not travel: he changes his scene, but always carries with him his home." Responding unperturbably, a Britisher maintained that "when a stronger but less numerous race is called upon to live with the weaker but more numerous race which it has conquered, it is well that it should retain its own individuality. We hold India by virtue of our superiority, and that superiority would soon disappear if we assimilated ourselves to Indian habits and manners."[1] Within their carefully maintained cultural isolation, many of the British remained indifferent and even hostile to Indian civilization.

Toward Indian architecture the British could be actively destructive. Declaring that "the Anglo-Indian Philistine has been a greater enemy to Indian art than either Mahomedan or Mahratta," one army officer recalled occasions when "rich mediaeval pillars were ground down into road material, whilst temple friezes and bas reliefs were converted into targets for rifle practice." According to Lord Curzon, "in the days of Lord William Bentinck the Taj was on the point of being destroyed for the value of its marbles. The same Governor-General sold by auction the marble bath in Shah Je-han's Palace at Agra, which had been torn up by Lord Hastings as a gift to George IV, but had somehow never been despatched. In the same regime, a proposal was made to lease the gardens at Sikandara to the executive engineer at Agra for the purpose of speculative cultivation. In 1857, after the Mutiny, it was solemnly proposed to raze to the ground the Jumna Musjid at Delhi, the noblest ceremonial mosque in the world."[2]

Not all of the British, of course, were indifferent to Indian architecture. Artists like the Daniells were attracted by the monuments of Indian antiquity, and particularly intrigued by picturesque ruins (fig. 77). Contact with Asia had inspired such eighteenth-century European fashions as the fanciful "chinoiserie," and Indian motifs were similarly adopted as a form of playful decor. Travelers in India soon began to seek out monuments of Indian architecture. They were fascinated by the rich carving

77. *Elephanta by Thomas Daniell, 1793. Although the city of Bombay could boast of no ancient monuments, the nearby island of Elephanta was the site of Buddhist rock-cut temples dating from the eighth century* A.D.

of Hindu temples, the elegant clarity of the great mosques, and the picturesque contours of palaces, forts, and tombs. A virtual love affair developed between the British and the Taj Mahal, with its flawless proportions and sentimental associations.

It was essentially through architecture, then, that the British began to be attracted to Indian culture. Although there had always been a handful among the British who read Indian literature, studied Indian philosophy, and collected Indian artifacts, they tended to be isolated eccentrics. Architecture, however, has a universality that makes it one of the most accessible aspects of any culture. India came to be described as the "Italy of Asia" in terms of picturesqueness, "a veritable fairyland of exquisite architecture." One writer, not especially enamored of Indian culture, conceded that "in architecture alone can India put forward a really plausible claim to equality."[3]

Having been initially attracted to Indian architecture as an exotic curiosity, the British of the nineteenth century began to apply the techniques of European scholarship to its study and analysis. Among these early scholars was James Fergusson who attempted to acquaint the British public with Indian design through a series of publications. Fergusson urged that buildings be used as documents for the study of Indian history, for, in his view, "there are no written annals which can be trusted." He believed that the primary importance of Indian building lay in the circumstance that "architecture in India is still a living art." Western influence, he maintained, had continually undermined this art, and he once noted that "whatever may be said of the Renaissance, or revival of classical architecture in Europe in the 16th century, in India it was an unmitigated misfortune."[4]

Gradually, colonial government leaders developed a sense of responsibility toward the study and preservation of Indian architecture. The Archaeological Survey of Northern India was created by Lord Canning in 1860, and local surveys were subsequently established in Madras and Bombay. The work of these bodies included the description of monuments and antiquarian research, with decisions regarding preservation left to local governments. Relatively little was accomplished, however, and in 1878 the central government appointed a special conservator to guide restoration efforts. Policies varied over the years, with long periods of apathy and neglect leading to the extensive deterioration of many monuments. Preservation efforts received strong encouragement from Lord Curzon, who became viceroy in 1898. He strengthened the organization and financing of the archaeological survey, broadened the scope of preservation legislation, and extended government control over the excavation of ancient sites and traffic in antiquities.

European scholars increasingly became the self-appointed guardians of Indian civilization, and so dynamic were their efforts that many Indians came to accept the vocabulary, classification, and aesthetic judgments employed by them. As their investigations of Indian buildings progressed, the British became convinced that they were confronted by one of the world's great architectural traditions. Evidence seemed to indicate, however, that its greatness lay in the past. Although its modern decline might have been attributed to political instability and periodic warfare following the breakup of the Mogul empire, it was more difficult to explain after more than a century of British rule. The British continually assured themselves that they had brought peace and prosperity to India—all that was needed, presumably, for a rich artistic life. Yet something had apparently gone wrong and, perhaps for the first time, the British began to feel uneasy about their influence in India.

In the view of British scholar and educator E. B. Havell, "the history of the art of every country is contained in the history of its architecture. . . . Every national movement in art has first formed expression in building. A decline in architecture means a decline in national taste and thus when architecture decays, the rest of the arts suffer with it. . . . The first and foremost question to be asked is—how has British rule affected the architecture of the country?"[5]

Some contended that the British had consistently set a bad example through their own building. In a London lecture in 1870 Sir Bartle Frere pointed out that

> when the English nation suddenly found itself the possessor of the great empire and of its great works of architecture, architecture in England was at such a low ebb that we could not realise what was essential to the progress of the art in India. . . . We sent forth our representatives to receive and acquire the Indian empire at about the same time as we were building Red-Lion square and the acres and miles of featureless streets, roads, and squares, and the nightmare churches . . . Our ancestors, in consequence, left no good architecture behind them in India. . . . The whole of what the English Government has done for the adornment of the capitals of India may be summed up by saying that very few public buildings have been erected which would be considered in any small seaport town in this country to be above ordinary merit.[6]

A forum for the expression of architectural criticism in India appeared in 1865 with the publication of the *Bombay Builder*. This architectural journal emerged just as the city was undergoing major redevelopment, and considerable attention was given to the new government architectural works. One article declared that "here in Bombay, where lacs upon lacs have been spent within a few years, and within a small radius, there is hardly a building that is not positively ugly to look at, not one that is in the least degree instructive, and not one that does not raise sorrow in the mind that so much wealth should be displayed in so much poverty."[7]

Contrast was often made between the enlightened artistic scene in Britain and that of British India. It was reported that "in all places under the British Government at the present moment there is more doing in the way of building than ever before, and greater trouble and pains are being taken to secure the best artistic talent for the work, e.g., the new Law Courts, the Manchester Assize Courts and Town Hall, the new National Gallery . . . But in India alone . . . no one seems to care what we shall get for our money." Deploring the artistic indifference of Public Works Department engineers, the writer observed that "it is certainly a pity that men placed in such positions do not read some of the numerous good architectural works now available, say either Ruskin or Burges, Street, Butterfield and others."[8]

British attitudes toward architecture in the nineteenth century were strongly influenced by the Gothic Revival and the Arts and Crafts movement, in which an architecture based on classical rule was supplanted by an ideal of creative craftsmanship, as well as a romanticizing of pre-industrial society. Industrialism was seen to have brought not only a debasement in design standards, but also the abolition of the artist-craftsman. Inherent in the movement was a conviction of the importance of art as an expression of the deepest needs of society. To those concerned with artistic matters, British policies in India appeared doubly reprehensible. The British were accused of both introducing an inferior level of European building into India and, at the same time, destroying a vital local tradition.

Europeans had initially been lured to Asia through a desire to buy its products. As colonialism evolved, the trade was reversed, and European wares began to dominate. Local craftsmen were often unable to compete economically with cheap machine-made products. In 1830 the Calcutta Trade Association was formed to popularize European imports in India, and, especially among the urban classes, foreign products became increasingly fashionable. A British engineer observed in 1872 that "some of the once famous Indian manufactures have almost disappeared in modern times," and such crafts as existed "are apt to degenerate at the present day into a grotesque copying of European design."[9]

At the same time, as interest in Indian design developed among the British, efforts were made to acquaint the Western world with its rich tradition. Indian craft products were shown at international expositions, often within pavilions recreating Indian architecture (fig. 78). Examples of architectural detailing became part of the permanent collection of the South Kensington Museum, and increasing information became available through publications. The popularity of certain craft products in the West was destined to have unfortunate side effects in India, however. The East India Company's display at the Crystal Palace exhibition of 1851 inspired a market for Indian carpets. Consequently, the imperial government attempted to increase production by introducing carpet manufacturing into Indian prisons. Cheap materials and aniline dyes were used in conjunction with patterns from books to make a product notably inferior to traditional work. A critic complained that "they handed this great historical craft, this glorious art, over to the Thugs in their jails, and the Thugs strangled it."[10]

Although the so-called jail carpets were intended primarily for export, they were also sold in India. A household guide for British residents in India, published in 1882,

78. *Indian pavilion at the 1889 Paris exposition.*

advised readers that "if, while in India, you chance to light on a carpet of really good old Indian design, unless it is very expensive, and beyond your means, purchase it at once. . . . Unfortunately, we English are spoiling the Indian carpet industry. The old low-toned tints, worked in exquisitely artistic designs, are being superseded by bright glaring colours; aniline dyes are creeping in, and such horrors as magenta, vivid greens, crude blues, etc., appear now in most Indian stuffs. Far from improving on Eastern colours and taste, we are rapidly doing our best to ruin both."[11]

In British artistic circles, a conviction grew that the Indian tradition should be encouraged. The India Society sponsored the *Journal of Indian Art*, which began publication in 1886. The purpose, as stated in the first issue, was "to direct progress in the right groove and to prevent the decline of Indian Art by pointing out when and how to check degradation." A continuing theme was the failure of modern Indians to encourage local art forms. In the view of one British observer, modern, educated Indians were "singularly devoid of artistic culture. . . .and they take little or no interest in the attempts, chiefly inspired by Europeans, to revive the ancient crafts in their own country."[12]

A British official, F. S. Growse, attempting to promote traditional styles in government building, found himself frustrated not only by official policies but by local indifference. He recalled his distress at the application of misunderstood classical elements to the house of a well-to-do Muslim, observing that "the details seem to have come from everywhere and yet to belong to nowhere." In reply to Growse's suggestion that an indigenous style might have been more appropriate, the Indian maintained that the Englishman's "personal predilection for Indian forms is only a weakness or eccentricity; such designs would be out of harmony with my own more advanced views, which are all in favour of English fashions." In a similar spirit, a Rajput chief once assured an Englishman, "You admire what is ours because it is strange; for similar reasons we like the work of Europeans, and, moreover, adopt that which adds to our comfort."[13]

In discussions of the decline of local artistic tradition, the policies of the Public

Works Department were repeatedly denounced. No matter what direction Indian patronage might take, the circumstance remained that an extraordinary amount of building in India was controlled by the colonial government. According to Growse, "in no art is the crying need for generous encouragement more felt than in architecture. But in none is it so difficult to bestow. The influence of our PWD is thoroughly demoralizing."[14] The use of European styles had eliminated the need for many craft skills, and the *mistry* or master builder, with his traditional methods and intuitive designs, could not be fitted into the bureaucratic structure of the PWD.

In one article, John Lockwood Kipling pointed out that all Indians employed in PWD offices had been trained in British engineering colleges and had, "neither knowledge of nor sympathy for indigenous forms." "The best mistries of the old school," he noted, "are often skillful in several crafts, and have a wonderful facility in designing ornament." The engineer, by contrast, could "seldom handle a tool of any kind." Considering the education of the Rourkee engineering school, Kipling declared it a "strange omission that in a college for Indian students there should be no Oriental department. Not a single native draughtsman turned out from this school has been taught the architecture of the country."[15]

Although the educational system in nineteenth-century India provided professional training in law, medicine and engineering, there had been no attempt to introduce degree programs in architecture. Such training had been slow to develop even in Britain. In contrast to France, where institutionalized instruction in architecture was given in the Ecole des Beaux Arts, England long maintained an informal system of tutelage. An aspiring architect would pay a fee to an established designer and serve a period of apprenticeship in his office. Customarily, such pupils would live in the architect's home, taking meals with the family. The scarcity of architects in India, together with the social separation of Indians and British, would make the importation of such a system highly unlikely.

In London, part-time architectural classes began at King's College in 1840 and at University College in 1841. Evening classes also came to be offered by the Architectural Association and the Royal Academy. It was not until 1892, however, that a three-year, full-time architectural course was created at King's College. During the period when Indian universities were being organized there was thus no British model of full-time architectural training that could have been adopted. The dominance of engineers in the Public Works Departments, moreover, tended to denigrate the status of architects and encourage Indians to become engineers instead.

In nineteenth-century India, the British concerned with artistic education were often enamored of tradition. The Arts and Crafts Movement encouraged an idealization of the master builder, and seeking to perpetuate his craft, they made little effort to train a modern Indian architect who might supplant him. They readily condemned the engineering schools, however, for their artistic limitations. E. B. Havell observed that "in the colleges of engineering, where architectural design adapted to official requirements is taught as an extra, the Indian student is supposed to be qualified in the subject when he has copied or learnt by heart a few diagrams of the European classic orders and some Gothic mouldings."[16]

An alternative venue for architectural training might have been developed in the art schools that began to appear during the 1850s. The first of these was the Madras School of Industrial Arts, founded in 1850 by Dr. Alexander Hunter. It had been organized "with the object of improving the taste of the native public as regards the beauty of form and finish in the articles of daily use."[17] Efforts were made to perpetuate local craft traditions, especially that of wood carving, and craftsmen were engaged as teachers. Emphasis was on the decorative arts, with no attempt to expand training to architecture.

Another institution inspired by the Arts and Crafts Movement was the Government College of Art and Craft, initially the School of Industrial Art, founded in Calcutta in 1854. Its organizers had obtained guidance from the Science and Art Department of the South Kensington Museum in London, and instruction was given in a range of art forms, with a class in architectural and mechanical drafting added after 1886. Cultural breadth was to be encouraged, and in his report of 1870–71, the principal, Mr. Locke, noted, "my desire is that while Callimachus and Apollodorus, Ghiberti and Sansovino shall be studied with all reverence, the students of the Bengal school of art shall acquire at the same time a knowledge of the type and details of which belong to the admirable ornamental art of their fathers." Student work included drawing from Indian architectural models and illustrating archaeological work in Orissa, as well as studying fresco painting on the principles of ancient Indian decoration. Most of the students, however, seemed attracted to European art. One teacher, Mr. Ghilardi, believed in the necessity of reinstating Indian decorative art in "its original brilliancy," but he found "in the native students themselves the chief and the strongest opposition to our efforts."[18]

The directorship of the school was taken over in 1896 by E. B. Havell, who had supervised the Madras School of Art from 1884 to 1894. During that period he had conducted a government survey of Indian arts and manufactures and had developed a profound admiration for the local tradition. Deploring British influence, he once declared that "even the Goths and Vandals in their most ferocious iconoclasm did less injury to art than that which we have done and continue to do in the name of European civilization." In the Calcutta school, it was his policy that "Oriental Art will be the basis of all instruction given."[19] The response was a vigorous student protest during which a third-year student, Ranada Prasad Gupta, led some of his fellows to secede and form a new institution based on the teaching of Western art. (This new school, founded in 1897, was named the Jubilee Art Academy to commemorate Queen Victoria's diamond jubilee.)

Observing that the school art collection consisted "almost entirely of copies of the old Italian and early English school,"[20] Havell sought to remedy the cultural imbalance in 1904 by selling the European pictures and replacing them with Indian works. His action was vociferously attacked not only by the students but by the public and press. Among Havell's few supporters was the viceroy, Lord Curzon, who in the same year had promoted the Ancient Monuments Preservation Act.

Contemporary with the art schools of Madras and Calcutta was the Sir J. J. School of Art in Bombay. Its founder, Sir Jamsetji Jeejeebhoy, was a Parsee businessman and philanthropist who had served on a committee selecting Indian products for the 1851 Crystal Palace exhibition. Like many others, he sought to counter the decline in traditional crafts and, having consulted with Dr. Hunter in Madras, endowed a school containing art and craft workshops. The cultural emphasis of the J. J. School varied according to the preferences of the faculty. Much of the training in Bombay was along Western lines, and according to an Indian writer

> when the European teachers in the Sir J. J. School exhorted the students to study Indian manner of work, the students did not like it. They probably thought that the English teachers were afraid of a professional rivalry and were deliberately diverting Indian students from the new progress which showed very prosperous results. The impact of Western sciences, art and life was very powerful and fresh. It blinded the Indians and the art students. . . . Only a few persons who studied ancient Indian traditions suspected that the great admiration which the Europeans expressed towards Indian culture may be genuine.[21]

Although it would not be until the twentieth century that the Sir J. J. School would offer a professional architectural degree, the importance of the field was long recognized, and various proposals were made to introduce such training. For many years, architectural course work focused on the creation of ornament, and students produced the decoration for all major public buildings from the 1870s until 1900. A program in architectural drafting was introduced in 1878, and by 1881 it was reported that "advanced students have been taught examples of building construction comprising of plans, elevations, section and detail."[22]

Among British architects and engineers the question of Western influence continued to be debated. Denying accusations that Public Works Department policies had destroyed the local tradition, a government architect argued that "if it should prove to be true that native Indian architectural art has died under our rule, I think it is very doubtful whether we should be blamed for it. Only art with little vitality could be killed by Government's letting it alone, which is all we are accused of doing." He strongly questioned the expenditure of public money "in providing artificial props to an art that has not sufficient life in it to survive without such official aid." As to the reputed failure of the PWD to appreciate the skills of the master builder, he demanded, "whom have we had to depend on for the carrying out of our work but Indian master builders and craftsmen? If there are more of these to be found and of better quality, we shall be only too glad to hear of it; and if there are higher uses to which they can be put, we shall be only too happy to employ them. Our bitterest complaint is of the poor quality of the class of assistance we are given in the country, both in our drawing offices and on the works."[23]

In contrast, another government architect announced, "I have now completely come round to the view that salvation for India lies in the adoption of some form of Oriental architecture which has grown up in the country, and is most suited to its climatic and other conditions. . . . In fact, no one who really comes in contact with Indian art and architecture in their natural surroundings, and devotes some attention to them, can escape the fascination exercised by them." Countering those who claimed that Indian styles were too costly, he pointed out that "there is no necessity for introducing expensive features such as domes and kiosks in all buildings." Among the devices he favored was the *chujjah,* an overhanging slab cornice, "which protects the walls from rain and sun, and throws a most effective shadow." By and large, he be-

lieved that "it makes practically no difference as regards cost whether a building be designed in an Indian or a European style."[24]

The desire to produce an architectural mode appropriate to India was eventually manifested in a hybrid style termed Indo-Saracenic. Such building reflected the current European fashion for eclecticism, and in most cases combined essentially Western building forms with Indian decorative elements. In Bombay the Gothic Revival, with its pointed arches and sculptural ornament, was readily adapted to Indian motifs, and it was not unusual for a building to exhibit Gothic elements together with bulbous domes and cusped arches (figs. 79 and 80).

Typifying the Indo-Saracenic style was the Prince of Wales Museum by George Wittet. Designed to house a collection of Indian art, the building utilized a variety of Eastern embellishments including a Mogul dome and ogee arches set with carved screens. Providing one of the principal landmarks of the city was Wittet's Gateway to India, a ceremonial arch commemorating the visit of King George and Queen Mary in 1911, and modeled on sixteenth-century Gujerat architecture (figs. 81 and 82).

80. Detail of the Municipal Corporation Building.

Opposite
79. The Municipal Corporation Building, Bombay, by F. W. Stevens, designed in 1888 and opened in 1893. It was praised as successful fusion of Gothic and oriental design.

81. *Prince of Wales Museum by George Wittet. The cornerstone was laid in 1905; the central block completed in 1914.*

82. *Gateway to India by George Wittett.*

84. *University of Madras Senate House, by Robert Fellowes Chisholm, 1874.*

83. *Taj Mahal Hotel by Chambers and Frichley, 1904.*

One of the most conspicuous landmarks on the Bombay waterfront was the Taj Mahal Hotel, built in 1904 by a Parsee businessman, J. N. Tata, to attract both British and Indian clients. His son, who was a student at Oxford and a William Morris enthusiast, hoped the design might reflect Arts and Crafts principles. In discussing the architecture with his son, J. N. Tata pointed out, "taste in this matter keeps so constantly varying that often fashions change every few years; . . . Under the circumstances, we must try to do what we think our customers would like."[25] The lure provided for customers by the architectural firm of Chambers and Frichley was a flamboyant stylistic melange crowned by a ribbed dome (fig. 83).

Some of the most distinguished Indo-Saracenic designs appeared in Madras in the work of Robert Fellowes Chisholm, who served at one time as director of the Madras School of Art. Included in his works were Presidency College of 1864–65, and the Senate House of the university, done in 1874 (fig. 84). Both formed part of an ensemble of new buildings facing the ocean in the marina district. Chisholm also designed additions to Chepauk Palace, a complex of government offices occupying what had once been the residence of the Nawab of Arcot.

The most spectacular building added to Madras was the High Court of 1888–92, designed by J. W. Brassington and revised by Henry Irwin and J. H. Stephens (fig. 85). A picturesque extravaganza of red brick, it embodied a complex interworking of courtyards, arcaded loggias, domes, and minarets. A flamboyant domed tower was sufficiently tall to serve as a lighthouse for the city. Irwin was also the designer of the Victoria Memorial Hall, now the National Art Gallery, built of red sandstone in 1906 and reportedly inspired by the Mogul architecture of Fatehpur Sikri (fig. 86).

Although Indo-Saracenic architecture reflected a well-meaning attempt to counteract the inroads of European design in India, it often inspired critical derision. Created without regard for traditional building plans or patterns of townscape, it was generally no more than a superficial appliqué of Indian motifs on otherwise conventional European buildings. One PWD architect considered this an advantage, and, opposing the contention that Indian design was unsuitable to modern requirements, pointed out that "the style can be successfully applied to any plan whatever."[26]

Indian stylistic elements were employed not only without regard to building type or plan, but also with indifference to regional traditions. Thus northern styles might be used in the south, and eastern styles in the west. The National Gallery of Art in Madras, for example, demonstrated the application of northern Mogul design to a building in the predominantly Hindu south. A British architect studying the city observed that, in terms of appropriateness, "some of the European styles, as the Greek trabeated architecture, are less out of harmony with Dravidian buildings than what is usually termed the Indo-Saracenic style." Indian craftsmen working on Indo-Saracenic buildings were often compelled to follow mechanical patterns fully as foreign to them as classical and Gothic designs. Far from placating the opponents of European architecture, this hybrid style frequently inspired their wrath. E. B. Havell, for example, strongly opposed using the Indian craftsman "as an instrument for creating a make-believe Anglo Indian style."[27]

Some contended that in the colonial cities the issue of Indian design was irrelevant. As British settlements they were seen to have no architectural tradition other than that established by their European founders. This argument was employed by

85. *High Court, Madras, designed by J. W. Brassington, and revised by Henry Irwin and J. H. Stephens. It was built in 1888–92.*

Lord Curzon at the time the construction of the Victoria Memorial was being contemplated in Calcutta. The building was a museum intended to commemorate the period of British rule in India. Although Curzon was an admirer of the Indian tradition and an ardent preservationist, he maintained that "in Calcutta—a city of European origin and construction—where all the main buildings had been erected in a quasi-classical or Palladian style, and which possessed no indigenous architectural type of its own—it was impossible to erect a building in any native style. . . . It was self-evident that a structure in some variety of the classical or Renaissance style was essential, and that a European architect must be employed."[28] The memorial, as designed by Sir William Emerson, was a domed classical structure of white marble located in the southern part of the Maidan (figs. 87 and 88).

The debate over architectural style reached a crescendo at the time New Delhi was being planned. The decision to move the capital from Calcutta was announced at the 1911 Durbar, a ceremonial visit to India of the king-emperor George V. Although there had been rumors of such a move for many years, the sudden announcement provoked vociferous opposition. There was consternation in Calcutta at being deprived of capital status, and some condemned the project as an attempt to separate the government from a center of active public opinion.

86. *National Art Gallery, Madras, by Henry Irwin, 1906.*

87. *Victoria Memorial, Calcutta, by Sir William Emerson. Lord Curzon initiated the project in 1901, and construction began in 1904. It was completed in 1921.*

88. *Victoria Memorial, Calcutta.*

89. Delhi and surrounding country drawn by A. Maclure, 1857. The walled city of Shahjahanabad appears at the left. The Red Fort borders the river, with the wide street of Chandni Chowk leading westward from the fort to the Friday Mosque. The great mosque, or Jama Masjid, occupies an elevated central site. The British settlement, including a military base, or cantonment, occupies the ridge at the right.

The British had assumed control of Delhi in 1803. The then-existing city of about 125 thousand had been founded by Emperor Shah Jahan in 1639, and it had continued as the residence of the Mogul rulers (fig. 89). Shahjahanabad, as it was initially called, was a walled city bordered on one side by the Yamuna River. The monumental focus of the city was a large palace complex, the Red Fort, constructed in 1639–48. Concealed behind its red sandstone walls was an ensemble of exquisite marble pavilions set in formal gardens. To the southwest of the fort lay the great mosque, the Jama Masjid, built between 1644 and 1658. It was sited on a rocky eminence leveled to create a natural platform accommodating a courtyard three-hundred-twenty-five feet square. Delhi was a city based on walled enclosures, ranging in scale from the outer wall of the city, through the walled palace complex, to the courtyards of mosques and houses that made up the fabric of city. Beyond the city walls, dotting the surrounding plain, were the architectural remains of older settlements, including such notable monuments as the Qutb Minar built around 1200 for the first Muslim sultan of Delhi, and Humayun's tomb of 1565.

Bishop Heber, visiting Delhi in the 1820s, reported it to be "a larger and finer city than I expected to see. . . . The houses within are many of them large and high. There are a great number of mosques, with high minarets and gilded domes, and above all are seen the palace, a very high and extensive cluster of gothic towers and battlements, and the Jumna Masjeed, the largest and handsomest place of Mussulman worship in India" (fig. 90).[29]

Delhi had continued to lure British tourists, who found it far more attractive than Indian districts in the colonial metropolises. A visitor in 1871 reported, "although there are many streets as tortuous and narrow as are found in other towns, I did not see anywhere that squalor and tumble-down confusion which arrest the eye in

90. *Looking toward the Jama Masjid in 1858. The foreground buildings were included in the district demolished by the British following the Mutiny.*

91. *Chandnee Chowk, a turn-of-the-century view.*

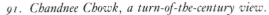

the native quarters of Bombay or Calcutta; while one chief thoroughfare, the Chandnee Chouk, leading direct from the Lahore Gate to the Palace, is really a fine street, being ninety feet wide, about a mile long, with a row of trees and a canal along its centre (now covered, except in a few places), and with comfortable-looking verandah-houses and good shops on either side" (fig. 91).[30]

It had been customary in India for the British, when settling in an existing Indian town, to create their own community outside. The military establishment would occupy a cantonment, while civilians would live in what were called civil lines. Laid out in an orderly formation, and low in density, these settlements were seen by some to provide "magnificent object lessons to the native."[31] In Delhi, the British troops were quartered outside the city in an elevated area called The Ridge. Some British civilians lived within the walls, preferring to settle in Daryaganj, a district south of the fort, or else to the north of the fort just inside Kashmiri Gate. There was also a civil station adjacent to the cantonment where the British occupied bungalows in spacious compounds.

British attitudes toward Delhi were strongly affected by the 1857 mutiny. This widespread uprising, which has sometimes been called the first war of Indian independence, had as its ostensible cause an army protest against the use of cartridges greased with the fat of cows and pigs, and thus unclean for both Muslims and Hindus. The mutiny is believed, however, to have involved much wider issues of British dominance and forced westernization. During the period of fighting, in which the British were besieged on the Ridge outside Delhi, the aged Mogul emperor provided a rallying point for Muslim revivalism.

Following the reconquest of Delhi, the British gave themselves over to a frenzied vengeance of looting and destruction. The population that had not been able to flee the city was driven out and only gradually permitted to return. Meanwhile, the British considered whether to obliterate Delhi completely. Some suggested that razing the city would be suitably "symbolic of the invincibility of British power." Others contended that only major monuments be demolished. It was proposed that the Jama Masjid be destroyed and the ground leveled. The City Magistrate, Philip Egerton, suggested, however, that the great mosque be converted into a Christian church, "and on each of its thousand compartments of the marble floor, the name of one of the Christian martyrs be inscribed." The destruction of the palace complex of the Red Fort was also advocated, together with its replacement by a new British fort called Fort Victoria. It was at this time that the idea of Delhi as the British capital was put forward. As punishment, the people of Delhi might be made to pay for a new capital city intended to symbolize "the living, active, Anglo-Saxon power."[32]

For security, it was decided to keep British troops stationed within the city, and the palace complex was taken over for army use. Its adaptation was pursued without regard to historical or artistic values, and in 1900 Lord Curzon expressed regret at, "the horrors that have been perpetuated in the interests of regimental barracks and messes and canteens in the fairy-like pavilions and courts and gardens of the Shahjahan" (fig. 92).[33]

In order to protect the approaches to the fort, surrounding buildings within a distance of 450 yards were demolished. This quarter had been an aristocratic one, and the destruction included some of the finest houses of Delhi. As a result of building demolition by the British and their expropriation of large areas for the military, the habitable territory of Delhi was reduced by one-third. Sadly viewing the transformation of the city, an Indian writer complained, "where is Delhi? By God, it is not a city now. It is a camp. It is a cantonment" (figs. 93 and 94).[34]

As memories of the mutiny faded, British attitudes toward Old Delhi were inevitably modified. The Jama Masjid and the remaining Mogul buildings within the fort

92. *Coexistence. Mogul garden pavilion and British barrack in the Red Fort.*

94. *View from the Jama Masjid toward the Red Fort, showing the area cleared of building.*

93. *Delhi, 1873. The eastern part of the city has been taken over by the British military establishment, and the city between the Red Fort and the Jama Masjid has been razed. Railroad tracks have been cut through the northern part of the city. Eventually, railroad tracks would also be built along the western boundary.*

95. Old Delhi looking northward from the Jama Masjid.

were eventually classified as historic monuments. Antiquarian interest in Old Delhi increased, and the city as a whole became a focus of study (figs. 95 and 96). A detailed government survey, supervised by Gordon Sanderson, was published in 1916. It comprised a listing of Muslim monuments made by Maulvi Jafar Hasan, together with Hindu buildings selected by Y. R. Gupte. There were 410 structures in all, including mosques, temples, gates, tombs, and houses. According to Sanderson, the exact date of many monuments was a matter of conjecture. A general attempt at dating was based on the reign of the emperor or, if this was doubtful, by style or local tradition. Many structures were classified as "late Mogul," the period between the end of Aurangjeb's reign (1707) and the mutiny of 1857, a time "marked by but few buildings of any architectural excellence."[35]

The monuments listed were divided into three categories. In category one were structures in good condition that were recommended to be maintained because of their archeological and historical value. Category two included those it was possible or desirable to save from further decay by minor measures. In category three were monuments judged to be in an advanced state of decay or of comparative unimportance. Virtually all of the listed monuments were placed in the last category—that is, the one for which no preservation measures were recommended. Almost the only structure suggested for preservation and not already listed as a protected monument was the surrounding wall of the city. Sanderson pointed out that "because a building is put into Class III, on account of its very dilapidated condition, it does not follow that

96. Old Delhi.

there should be any unseemly haste in converting it into road metal. It may still be a monument of interest as long as it keeps together."[36] How long such a building might keep together was apparently to be left to chance. Thus a study that might have been the first step toward preserving the architectural fabric of Old Delhi became almost detrimental in this regard. Anyone consulting the list would have received assurance that Old Delhi had been thoroughly examined and judged largely unworthy of protective efforts.

In symbolic terms, the decision in 1911 to make Delhi the capital of India could be variously interpreted. Some saw it as a means to strengthen the imperial image, placing the government in lofty isolation from the country as a whole. Others saw the selection of Delhi as a conciliatory gesture toward Indian sensibilities. The viceroy, Lord Hardinge, pointed out that the city was "intimately associated in the minds of the Hindus with sacred legends which go back even beyond the dawn of history. . . . To the Mohammedans it would be a source of unbounded gratification to see the ancient capital of the Moguls restored to its proud position as the seat of the Empire."[37] Some pessimists observed, however, that the ancient site of Delhi was known as the graveyard of dynasties, and to settle the government there might be tempting fate.

Just as the transfer of the capital was subject to controversy, the architectural design of the government buildings provoked lively and sometimes acrimonious discussion. Some saw the new construction as an opportunity to revitalize local craft traditions, pointing out the proximity of the Mogul monuments in Delhi, and stressing the need for visual harmony between the Indian and British settlements. E. B. Havell insisted that "the best architects in England are now endeavoring . . . to revive the old system of co-partnership between the architect and the craftsman . . . Unless the British artistic conscience is always to be less sensitive east of Suez, it must also become the new Anglo-Indian way." He recalled the golden age of Mogul rule when, in his view, the arts had served to reconcile racial and religious differences between Hindu and Muslim. This artistic link between cultures, he noted, "is a bridge which we have not yet built. . . . Macaulayism, helped by the archaeological pedant, instead of building a bridge between East and West, has separated them by a high social wall, through which they occasionally shake hands ceremoniously."[38]

The building of the new capital provided an opportunity for the conscious creation of an architectural image for British India, a decision that had political as well as aesthetic implications. What did colonial rule imply in the twentieth century? Public opinion in Britain had become increasingly liberal, and in India there had been steady pressure from the Congress party for greater Indian participation in government. Indians had already been appointed to the Viceroy's council and the Council of India in London, and in 1909 the Indian Councils Act had opened membership in provincial executive councils to Indian members. Imperial rhetoric sometimes portrayed the British role in India as a benevolent guidance toward political democracy, and some might have predicted a future of steady evolution toward home rule and possible dominion status. Concessions had been grudgingly conceded, however, and conservative forces continued to resist strenuously any efforts to erode British paramountcy in India. The continuance of British rule in some form was regarded as a fact of life.

If the political statement of New Delhi were to dramatize the power and permanence of British domination, a purely European style would be most effective. If it were to reflect a more moderate posture of intercultural reconciliation and cooperation, a stylistic compromise might be in order. Curiously, at the time New Delhi was planned, the debate over architectural style seems to have been a purely British affair. Although the Indian press joined the discussion over the decision to move the capital, little concern was demonstrated about how the city would be built.

Indians themselves were not altogether consistent in artistic taste. Many had become strongly anglicized and had enthusiastically adopted European modes. Paradoxically, it was among the anglicized Indians that a sense of national identity was becoming strongest. An Indian scholar, A. K. Coomaraswamy, had noted that "the majority of English-educated Indians who call themselves nationalists do not really love India— they love suburban England, and the comfortable bourgeois prosperity that they hope will one day be established when India has learned enough science and forgotten enough art to successfully compete with Europe in a commercial war conducted on European lines."[39]

Among the advocates of Western design was the chief architect of the city, Sir Edwin Lutyens. To his eyes, European classicism embodied all that was civilized, rational, and humanist, and he strongly resisted pressures to compromise. As to Indian architecture, it did not exist: "I do not believe there is any real Indian architecture or any great tradition. There are just spurts by various mushroom dynasties with as much intellect as there is in any other art nouveau. . . . India has never had any real architecture, and if you may not graft the West out here, she never will have any." "Why," he demanded, "should we throw away the lovely subtlety of a Greek column for uncouth carelessness, unknowing and unseeing?"[40]

The viceroy, Lord Hardinge, was among those advocating an indigenous style for New Delhi, declaring to Lutyens that "it would be a grave political blunder, and in my opinion an absurdity to place a purely western town amidst eastern surroundings."[41] Encouraged by Hardinge to visit some of the famous monuments of India, Lutyens remained resolutely resistant to the seduction of the East. The great medieval rock fortress of Chitorgarh he considered "barbaric ruins," and the Mogul city of Mandu "childish," "with a wonderful made picturesqueness but with no intellect." He considered the palace city of Fahtepur-Sikri and the Taj Mahal impressive as scenery rather than architecture. Describing the Taj, he declared that "it is wonderful, but not architecture, and its beauty begins where architecture ceases to be."[42]

No missionary intent on promulgating the true faith could have been more dedicated than Lutyens was in promoting the principles of classicism. "Architecture," he observed, "more than any other art, represents the intellectual progress of those that are in authority." In India, "they have never had the initial advantage of those intellectual giants the Greeks, who handed the torch to the Romans, they to the great Italians and on to the Frenchmen and to Wren, who made it sane for England. . . . I should have liked to have handed on that torch and made it sane for India, and Indian in its character."[43]

The result of Lutyens's determined effort was a government complex of extraordinary scale and scenic splendor. The overall plan reflected the baroque classicism visible elsewhere in the replanning of Washington, D.C., and in Canberra, Australia. Culminating a long ceremonial axis was the palace of the viceroy, its approach flanked by the symmetrical buildings of the secretariat. These office buildings were designed by Herbert Baker, who collaborated with Lutyens in the creation of the monumental complex (figs. 97 and 98).

Baker advocated a type of architecture that might be called "imperial," rather than specifically European, incorporating "the great elemental qualities and traditions of the Mediterranean lands."[44] Observing the cross-cultural nature of certain architectural forms, Baker pointed out that "the colonnade and arcade . . . the open court of audience, are common features in southern classical architecture. The deep portal arch of Persia and India has its prototype in the classical exedra common in the Roman bath and well known in the Vatican. The pride of Indian architecture, the dome, has its highest manifestation in St. Paul's. And the magnificent ground-planning of the Taj Mahal is but an Eastern example of the 'grand manner' of the West."[45] Although Baker's secretariat buildings, like the viceroy's palace, were essentially classical in form, they incorporated Indian decorative elements such as carved screens, or *jalis,* and small domed kiosks called *chattris* (fig. 99).

In spite of his insistence on the use of Western classicism, Lutyens's design for the viceroy's palace reflected the influence of Indian prototypes in such elements as arches and columns. The upper edge of the building was defined by a *chujja,* a thin projecting cornice found in both Hindu and Mogul architecture, and decorative chattris were also employed along the cornice line. The most dramatic feature of the building was its central dome, the form of which could be linked to classical precedents, but which, in the Indian context, might be likened to a Buddhist stupa. Lutyens also employed "Buddhist railings" reminiscent of those found at Sanchi. Thus although the overall massing of the structure was classical, its detailing embodied a gesture toward local tradition (fig. 100). One side of the palace faced a twelve-acre garden designed to emulate traditional Mogul landscaping.

The cumulative effect of the government complex was a perfect expression of the imperialist spirit, its gigantic scale reflecting the vast reaches of administrative control commanded by the British. The viceroy's palace, providing the focus of the composition, was a masterpiece, grand and austere, with its looming dome and dignified ceremonial portico. Commenting favorably on the symbolism of the palace, a British critic, Robert Byron, wrote that

> in the 18th century, the English had imported into India a severe and rather uncouth classical style which they adapted to the needs of the climate. Subsequently, with the subordination of aesthetics to sentiment and reminiscence, a hideous chaos developed, in which Hindu ornament and Moslem domes fought for the possession of Gothic superstructures. In 1911 English and Indian opinion still demanded a fusion of national motifs. Sir Edwin Lutyens sought the solution of the problem on a less superficial basis. . . . The outcome of it is monumental. Never was so large, so well planned, so arrogant, yet so lovely a palace, so fit a setting for the man who, if power be measured by the number of those subject to it, is the most powerful man that breathes.[46]

In Byron's view Lutyens had achieved a true fusion of East and West, while Baker had succeeded only in alluding to Eastern motifs. In the design of Baker, "the elements have remained separate and allusive: body embryonic; ornament a writing in

97. New Delhi government complex by Sir Edwin Lutyens and Herbert Baker. The design of the city was begun in 1912, and it was dedicated in 1931.

symbols." Lutyens, by contrast, had "combined the gorgeous facade, coloured and dramatic, of Asia, with the solid habit, cubic and intellectual, of European building."[47]

The question of creating a stylistic fusion seems to have concerned only the major monumental complex of New Delhi. In other buildings, an undiluted European classicism dominated. The commercial center, Connaught Place, projected in the form of a circus by W. H. Nicholls, was unified architecturally through the employment of a double colonnade combined with Palladian motifs (fig. 101). Classical colonnades marked the two large legislators' hostels designed by R. T. Russell, who prepared the detailed design of Connaught Place. Government housing consistently carried classical detailing, as did the two major British churches of the city, the Cathedral Church of the Redemption (fig. 102) and the Roman Catholic Cathedral, both by H. A. N. Medd.

The admiration of classicism embodied in Byron's criticism reflected a shift in British artistic fashion. The eclecticism of the nineteenth century and the moralistic ideology that had supported the Gothic Revival were becoming passé. Like Lutyens, Byron expressed contempt for the buildings of Bombay, terming the city an "architectural sodom." Although, in the previous century, the *Bombay Builder* had urged acquaintance with the works of Ruskin and other Gothic revivalists, Byron admiringly judged the "magnificence of New Delhi" to be "characterized by a restraint which cannot appeal to a taste contracted under the spell of Ruskin and Gilbert Scott." While he felt Indian taste had been corrupted by the Gothic Revival, it was Byron's hope that New Delhi would lead the Indian "to discover the true virtue still latent in the West."[48]

Some, of course, had hoped that the construction of New Delhi would provide for the active participation of Indian craftsmen. A British architect, Claude Batley, pointed out, however, that the "surviving craftsmen had sunk to the position of mere mistries, or village master carpenters and masons, and were entirely incompetent to

98. *New Delhi government complex, looking toward Raisina Hill. During construction, the sight lines toward the Viceroy's Palace intended by Lutyens were altered, diminishing its visibility from below the hill.*

tackle such a problem of modern town-planning and building on palatial lines." As to the inclusion of Indian architects, the "only recognized school of architecture on modern lines was just feeling its feet and her rising young architects had neither sufficient prestige nor practice to compete, on anything like equal terms, with the foreign architects of established reputation, who had already 'delivered the goods' in other parts of the Empire, and so the great opportunity was inevitably and forever lost."[49]

Although Indian artists were involved in the decoration of the viceroy's palace, the building of the city followed normal PWD policies, with British architects and engineers in charge, and Indians in subordinate positions. The vast labor force was provided by Indian contractors, with English foremen imported to direct such specialties as joinery, plumbing, and electrical wiring. Lutyens had no romantic notions about Indian craftsmen. He often recounted an incident of an Indian mason who tried to alter a template to fit a badly cut stone, and declared that no one could achieve good work in India "without power of life and death" over the workers.[50]

In retrospect, the air of solidity and permanence conveyed by the New Delhi government complex seems to belie the growing insecurity of British rule in India. C. Northcote Parkinson used New Delhi in his book *Parkinson's Law* to substantiate his claim that "perfection of planned layout is achieved only by institutions on the point of collapse." New Delhi, he claimed, was "a British Versailles, splendid in conception, comprehensive in detail, masterly in design, and overpowering in scale. But the states of its progress toward completion correspond with so many steps in political collapse."[51] Lord Irwin moved into the viceroy's palace in 1929, the year after the Indian Congress had demanded independence, and, appropriately enough, the first official visitor to ascend the great stairs of the palace was Mahatma Gandhi. Clearly, he was not among those likely to be awed by the lofty portico and intimidating dome.

Gandhi, like many leaders of the independence movement, had been touched by Western ideology and culture. A strong influence on his thinking had been the writ-

99. New Delhi Secretariat by Herbert Baker.

ing of John Ruskin, especially a book called *Unto This Last*. He had first read it while on a train traveling from Johannesburg to Durban in 1904. As he recalled it, "the book was impossible to lay aside once I had begun it. It gripped me. . . . I could not get any sleep that night. I determined to change my life in accordance with the ideals of the book."[52] Unlike many of Ruskin's works, this was an essay on social philosophy and had little concern with art. It did, however, contain one statement relating to building. Ruskin urged, "see that your poor are healthily lodged before you try your hand at stately architecture."

New Delhi, in its monumental building, might be seen to embody the image of a benign but masterful rule—British strength, intellect, and order providing the framework for a controlled display of native tradition. Yet as Gandhi mounted the great ceremonial staircase, the architectural dispute became irrelevant. Like Lutyens, Gandhi understood visual symbolism and used it to perfection. His rough sandals and homespun *dhoti* reflected Indian culture in ways that went far beyond chattris and chujjas on British building. That critics might judge New Delhi Eastern or Western was of no importance. The greatest imperial architecture in the world could not have deflected the course of events.

100. Viceroy's Palace by Sir Edwin Lutyens.

101. Connaught Place, planned by W. H. Nicholls,
with architectural design by R. T. Russell.

102. Church of the Redemption by H. A. N. Medd.

103. *Bombay textile mill.*

4.
Modern Planning and the Colonial City

The evolution of the colonial metropolis in India was often likened to that of the industrial-age city of the West. There were obvious similarities of untrammeled growth, of congestion, pollution, inflated land values, and vivid juxtapositions of opulence and squalor. In India, as in Europe, the modern city could be regarded as both a center of progress and a force promoting the disintegration of traditional society. "What," demanded E. B. Havell, "has been the gospel by which we would create a new heaven and a new earth in India? Only the dismal gospel of the nineteenth century—that India must . . . humbly sit at the feet of Europe to learn civilization. . . . Leave your villages, . . . Come into the factories, with your women and your little children; we will show you the magic of the machine. We will build you great cities like Manchester and Birmingham. Progress lies only with capitalism and machinery. Work for us, you poor benighted artisans; we will give you all the blessings of Western civilisation. They are now enjoying a foretaste of these blessings in the purlieus of Bombay and Calcutta!" (fig. 103).[1]

In Britain, the problems of the nineteenth-century city had attracted a variety of reformers, and a growing desire for control over urban development inspired a series of legislative efforts culminating in the Town Planning Act of 1909. Municipal powers brought increasing public dominion over land use, services, transport, and housing, while city planning emerged as a multidisciplinary profession.

As urban renovation increased in scale, opinion was often divided about its aesthetic and social results. In Paris, the sweeping destructiveness of Haussmann's work inspired lasting controversy. Some found the new standards of design mechanical and overscaled, and they deplored the destruction of old buildings. In Britain, the Public Health Act of 1875 had created new regulations for house design and street width. Although the resulting urban pattern reflected hygienic improvements, many architects condemned the resulting monotony of straight, wide streets lined with uniform buildings. In artistic circles, *bylaw streets* became a term of opprobrium frequently used to illustrate the unimaginative eye of the municipal engineer.

Toward the close of the nineteenth century, Britain became a center of innovative thinking among urbanists. The Garden City Movement, founded by Ebenezer

Howard, advocated a program of systematic decentralization and attracted a wide range of supporters. The restricted size envisioned for the Garden City fostered a heightened sensitivity to the aesthetics of the small-scale environment, while its emphasis on social reform encouraged designers to focus on the human aspects of the city.

It was not unexpected that the ideas of British city planners would have an impact in India. Just as evolving fashions in European architecture were reflected in the colonial cities, so attempts were made to import European planning techniques and concepts of urban form. Studies were conducted and planning recommendations made by British urbanists, while legislation was developed to strengthen municipal planning powers. In India, however, no body of information existed comparable to that which had been developed through the study of Western cities. Visiting planners drew on what they knew of the West together with what they could observe in India, and their work inevitably reflected planning theories and design guidelines that had arisen in the Western context.

Highly influential in promoting the study of cities, especially with regard to their social aspects, was Patrick Geddes. A wide-ranging generalist, he had been trained in sociology and had become noted as a planning expert. To publicize the Town Planning Act of 1909, and on the occasion of the London Town Planning Conference in 1910, he had directed a Cities and Town Planning Exhibition in London. One of the admirers of Geddes's work was Lord Pentland, Governor of the Madras Presidency. He invited Geddes to bring his exhibition to India, and he sought to interest the governors of Bombay and Bengal in providing additional patronage.

Geddes arrived in Madras in 1914, and within eight months he had produced twelve studies of towns in the presidency. He made a second visit to India in 1915–18, focusing primarily on the northern plains and making a detailed investigation of the town of Indore. Between 1920 and 1924, Geddes served as professor of civics and sociology at the University of Bombay.

Unlike the British engineers who had directed most municipal public works in India, Geddes had a sympathetic appreciation for Indian townscape. Just as the British in India had ignored the best of their urban achievements when developing cities in eighteenth-century India, they also appeared unaware of progressive developments in modern urbanism. According to Geddes, British planning in India seemed to be drawn from outmoded sanitary bylaws, "with their enormous product of mean streets in our industrial towns, not from contemporary town planning at all."[2] The delicate urban fabric of Indian quarters was often subject to brutal renovation in the name of sanitation and improved circulation, "a matter of doing puja to the straight lines of the drawing board and set squares." With apparent disregard for existing buildings, streets would be cut through "comparable to the rather sweeping operations of Haussmann in Paris fifty years ago."

Geddes believed that the main object of good town planning was "so to plan and build that the local sentiment and even conservation of the Indian home and its quarter . . . may increasingly be recovered and maintained." Pointing out that "we have in a large measure to maintain the populous and gregarious Indian type of village and town" (fig. 104), Geddes advocated what he called "conservative surgery" with regard to clearance. Instead of driving straight streets through congested districts, he favored

104. Street in Georgetown, Madras.

a careful examination of the existing physical fabric so that it could be gradually renovated while conserving what was best.

Even though Geddes was no friend to overbuilding, he deplored the planless
sprawl of British "garden houses." Attempts to achieve romantic gardens were not always successful in Madras, and he called attention to the acres of "desert compounds,
so largely left to weeds and snakes, with ill-planted trees between each one and its
neighbor. . . . We have to mitigate the Crusoe-like individualism of the too-scattered
and almost planless bungalow compounds and endeavor gradually to convert these into
a true Garden City."

Geddes observed that Indians preferred living close to their places of work, and
he believed there was a need to economize on distances. City planning, however, was
done by the automobile-owning classes, both British and Indian. "Are not municipalities planning too much as if their city were like London, with numberless middle class
people able and willing to come up, by train, tram or motorbus to their shops and
offices?"

The overall impact of Geddes's work in India is difficult to measure. Although
his ideas were admired by some, he was also viewed as a crank by many officials. His
common sense approach, however, was difficult to fault. He approached his investigations with a receptivity to the local scene, seeking to understand the nature of the
Indian settlement, and making no attempt to impose a foreign conception of urban
environment.

Geddes's planning studies focused on the relatively small older towns of the
Madras Presidency, rather than on the city of Madras itself. He was, nevertheless, responsible for bringing to Madras a British architect, Henry Vaughan Lanchester, who

105. Mount Road, the principal commercial street in Madras.

106. North Beach Road. This street, facing the docks, was characterized by large mercantile houses, and its scale, as well as its relatively continuous building frontage, was exceptional in Madras.

did a detailed study of the city in 1916. Through Geddes's persuasion, Lord Pentland's government appointed Lanchester as the first official town planner in India. He had been editor of the *Builder* and had also served as an adviser in the creation of New Delhi. In addition to giving a series of lectures to municipal councillors and officials in Madras, Lanchester set up India's first city-planning class.

Like many visitors, Lanchester was struck by the unfocused pattern of settlement in Madras. The urban fabric had no cohesion and failed to convey the "impression of dignity that might be expected from its size." He acknowledged, however, that, "to many it is one of its charms that one can stand in the middle of Madras and see nothing suggesting that there is an important city around the wide Maidan" (fig. 105).[3]

In terms of urban design, he reported many weaknesses. Although the city contained a number of important buildings, few were well sited in relation either to one another or to the natural setting. The possibilities of axial planning had been ignored, and none of the important streets had focal points (fig. 106). As to large-scale composition, the effects of mass, skyline, and balance had been left completely to chance. He believed that the city also suffered from the "extraordinary variety of type in structures placed in juxtaposition to each other. There is not a single main thoroughfare but lapses at places into absolute squalor. . . . For nearly a century, there seems to have been no definite view as to the style of architecture best suited to the conditions, and the principal buildings exhibit so many experiments in treatment as to destroy the unity that should characterize a great city" (100). Under the circumstances, Lanchester saw no way in which Madras could achieve an architecturally defined streetscape. As buildings could not be depended on to enhance the line of the street, he believed that trees could be substituted, and he suggested a double row of planting along each side.

Lanchester's views were in harmony with those of Geddes with regard to the Indian quarters. He declared that "the Indian house at its best seems altogether admirable" (42), observing, however, that it was seldom at its best. In contrast to Calcutta and Bombay, where native districts were characterized by multistorey tenements, Madras had maintained its traditional pattern of low-rise houses. The problem lay not with the basic urban pattern, but with overcrowding and overbuilding. As he later described the situation, "the segregation of caste groups, and the tendency of families to remain together through several generations, are two important factors conducive to this state of affairs. A trade caste occupying a certain quarter is hemmed in by others, and has no other course open to it than to build more intensively. The expanding family is in much the same position, and in both cases this leads to encroachment. . . . A shop or house throws out a verandah in front, then closes it in; and later perhaps puts up another in front of that, besides filling up internal courtyards."[4] Like Geddes, he advocated conservative surgery in areas where clearance was deemed necessary.

Lanchester suggested that Madras expand by means of planned garden cities. He believed that if attractive new towns were provided, certain overcrowded castes or trades might be induced to move. Such new settlements would need to be true towns and not mere suburbs, however, for "many Indians have become inveterate town-dwellers, and to a large extent they will demand to be near busy bazaars and will submit to a great deal of overcrowding rather than remove to more suitable quarters." Commercial subcenters were also needed, as "the city has outgrown the single bazaar or the single centre."[5]

The garden city idea had evolved in response to a form of urban development very different from that of Madras. Ebenezer Howard had sought to counteract the problems of congestion and high land values seen in most modern cities, proposing a type of settlement designed to combine the advantages of both country and city. Although sprawling and disorganized, Madras might already have been considered a kind of garden city, with its relatively cheap land, abundant open space, and overall low densities (fig. 107). While the pattern of density in Madras was far from uniform, a comparison of building and street bylaws reported Madras standards to be comparable to those in Britain. It was noted that 40 percent of the city consisted of open space in roads and streets, the same as the British average. The amount of open space on each building plot was 33 percent, duplicating the British minimum, and building heights were generally low. The garden city idea, however, provided a concept by which future growth might be guided so as to counteract the tendency toward limitless sprawl.

At the time of Lanchester's study, the traffic problem was far from acute. He believed it would be useful, however, to segregate traffic going at different speeds, so that a lumbering bullock cart would not share the same street as a speeding motor car. He opposed widening bazaar streets to accommodate traffic flow, suggesting instead that heavy traffic should be routed around the bazaars. To facilitate circulation and open up additional areas of the city, Lanchester proposed a series of new streets, including a wide east-west artery through Georgetown (fig. 108).

Speculating about the differences between Indian and European cities, Lanchester considered European cities to have been more stable and long lived. He believed that European urbanization had arisen from an essentially economic base, while cities in India had often been founded at whim by reigning princes. He also described what he sensed to be a fundamental difference between the way Indians and Europeans considered cities. "The Indian," he stated, "regards the lapse of a great city with more equanimity than would be felt in Europe." Observing the lack of maintenance in Indian cities, he said it was "as if its inhabitants had doubts of its continuance."[6]

Although some planning survey work was pursued in Madras after Lanchester's departure, the development of the city remained piecemeal. The lack of a truly urban image was to persist, and it was noted in 1928 that "visitors are apt to leave with a positive dislike of Madras." For its British residents, however, the city afforded a relaxed style of living and a type of spacious housing no longer attainable in other colonial cities: "only those who have experienced the crowded, airless flats of Calcutta and Bombay can appreciate the open, breezy bungalows, with wide verandahs, overlooking fine compounds, which are found in their hundreds in Madras." As to Georgetown (formerly Black Town), "the farther one penetrates into its devious streets and byways the more does one realise that for certain parts time, figuratively speaking, has stood still. There are in evidence the same type of buildings, the same customs and the same dress as existed 200 years ago. Outwardly the place has not changed [fig. 109]. . . . [Madras resembles] an old English provincial town, with its aloofness from the main currents of national life."[7] For those who wanted to be at the center of things, there was always Calcutta.

Describing a visit he paid to Calcutta in 1888, Rudyard Kipling declared, "there is only one city in India. Bombay is too green, too pretty, and too stragglesome; and Madras died ever so long ago. Let us take off our hats to Calcutta, the many-sided, the smoky, the magnificent."[8] Coming to Calcutta from the provinces, the Briton would be reminded of "the lost heritage of London. . . . The dense smoke hangs low, in the chill of the morning, over an ocean of roofs, and, as the city wakes, there goes up to the smoke a deep, full-throated boom of life and motion and humanity." Viewing the waterfront, he might exclaim, "Why, this is London! This is the docks. This is Imperial. This is worth coming across India to see!" (13; fig. 110). In the business district, Kipling noted that "you must not, you cannot cross Old Court House Street without looking carefully to see that you stand no chance of being run over. This is beautiful. There is a steady roar of traffic, cut every two minutes by the deep roll of the trams. . . . It means business, it means money-making, it means crowded and hurrying life, and it gets into the blood and makes it move" (20; fig. 111).

However grand the initial impression of Calcutta, Kipling declared himself increasingly disillusioned with the Indian capital. It stank. "All India knows of the Calcutta Municipality; but has anyone thoroughly investigated the Big Calcutta Stink? . . . It resembles the essence of corruption that has rotted for the second time—the clammy odour of blue slime" (14). The inhabitants, moreover, had developed an astonishing indifference, assuring him, "Wait till the wind blows off the Salt Lakes where

107. *Madras street scene.*

108. *Lanchester plan for Madras, published in 1918. Proposed new streets are shown in black.*

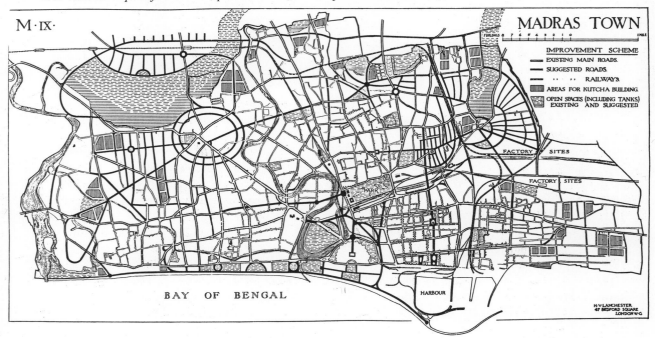

109. *Georgetown.*

110. *Calcutta waterfront in 1895.*   111. *Old Court House Street, 1895.*

112. A view of Chowringhee in 1859. By this time, the district was becoming congested, with mansions tending to crowd the edges of their plots.

all the sewage goes, and *then* you'll smell something" (15). The residential "palaces" of Chowringhee were not immune, and elegant drawing rooms received the penetrating stench of nearby stable and service quarters. To Kipling's astonishment, "they make no complaint. When they think the honour of the city is at stake they say defiantly: 'Yes, but you must remember we're a metropolis'" (24; fig. 112).

Kipling called his book *The City of Dreadful Night.* Although he had used the phrase previously to describe the city of Lahore, Calcutta apparently convinced him that for real all-out dreadfulness, particularly at night, nothing could match the city on the Hooghly. Should his readers have any doubts, he supplied an account of an evening ramble through the less salubrious quarters of Indian Calcutta. Escorted by a British policeman, he began by visiting a fire lookout in the police headquarters in Lal Bazaar. Northward, he noted, "the city stretches away three long miles, with three more miles of suburbs beyond, to Dum Dum and Barrackpore" (51). The spacious Maidan bordered by opulent quarters lay to the south, while to the east was the clamor of Sealdah Station. Westward were the business quarters and the lamps of river shipping. "'Does the noise of traffic go on all through the hot weather?'" Kipling asked. "'Of course,'" he was told "'The hot months are the busiest in the year . . . Calcutta *can't* stop, my dear sir.' 'What happens then?' 'Nothing happens; the death-rate goes up a little. That's all'" (51).

What Kipling wanted to see, of course, and his public to read about, were the sinister quarters of the native city. Braving the darkness (and who knew what dangers), he explored the congested reaches of what was termed the St. John's Wood of Calcutta, "a great wilderness of packed houses—just such mysterious, conspiring tenements as Dickens would have loved." Describing the house of a young woman he designated Dainty Iniquity, Kipling asked his reader to "stand at the bottom of a lift-shaft and look upwards. Then you will get both the size and the design of the tiny courtyard round which one of these big dark houses is built. The central square may be perhaps ten feet every way, but the balconies that run inside it overhang, and seem to cut away half the available space. . . . [Once inside, he found] English furniture of a gorgeous and gimcrack kind, unlimited chandeliers, and a collection of atrocious Continental prints" (59, 60).

Proceeding to "somewhere in the back of the Machua Bazaar, well in the heart of the city," Kipling noted that "there are no houses here—nothing but acres and acres, it seems, of foul wattle-and-daub huts. . . . The whole arrangement is a neatly contrived germ and fire trap, reflecting great credit upon the Calcutta Municipality. 'What happens when these pigsties catch fire?' 'They're built up again,' say the Police. . . 'Land is immensely valuable here.' All the more reason, then, to turn several Haussmanns loose into the city" (62).

In Kipling's view, the perpetuation of Calcutta's squalor was directly attributable to the participation of Indians in local government:

> It seems not only a wrong but a criminal thing to allow natives to have any voice in the control of such a city—adorned, docked, wharfed, fronted, and reclaimed by Englishmen, existing only because England lives, and dependent for its life on England. . . . The damp, drainage-soaked soil is sick with the teeming life of a hundred years, and the Municipal Board list is choked with the names of natives—men of the breed born in and raised off this surfeited muck-heap! They own property, these amiable Aryans on the Municipal and the Bengal Legislative Council. Launch a proposal to tax them on that property, and they naturally howl. . . . Why, asks a savage, let them vote at all? They can put up with this filthiness. They *cannot* have any feelings worth caring a rush for. [13, 15, 16]

Kipling acknowledged that "whether this genial diatribe be the outcome of an unbiased mind or the result of sickness caused by that ferocious stench, and secondly of headache due to day-long smoking to drown the stench, is an open question" (16–17). Even though Kipling's emotional response to Calcutta was ostentatiously bigoted, he was correct in realizing that a renovation of the city would have political implications and that Indian and British opinion might not necessarily be in accord.

The turn of the century was marked by an intensified concern for the sanitary condition of Calcutta and an awareness of the need for increased planning control. The *Indian Medical Record* of 1896 reported that "the vast area of Calcutta is a series of tortuous lanes, gullies and streets arranged according to no definite plan and devoid of those elements of modern city construction that make the work of effectual drainage . . . an easy matter. [Additionally, the problem is the] "enormous amount of *bustee* land covered with closely built tiled huts. . . . An inspection of these *bustees* is enough to sicken and disgust anyone. Their drains are elongated cess pools of filth and sludge made up of human excreta and kitchen refuse, that decompose and rot for days before any effort is made to get rid of such pestilential matter." Included in the recommendations of the report was the construction of new streets through the crowded central districts. These "would cut their way through localities whose population is constantly being decimated by zymotic diseases, parts in fact where dirt, overcrowd-

113. Burra Bazaar in 1895.

ing, squalor, poverty and disease offer a terrible menace to the well-being of the whole city." The inhabitants of Calcutta, it was maintained, were "practically living upon a dung heap with a festering cesspool underneath."[9]

A proposal for opening up congested districts was made in 1902, with the area of Burra Bazar given a high priority for renovation (fig.113). Many feared that taxes would be raised to pay for a plan that was devised primarily to gratify the British population, and opposition was expressed in the native press. It was declared that "any scheme which drove away the poor and middle-class people from Calcutta and forced them back to the ancestral village life they had given up, would lead to disaster."[10]

In 1911, the government created the Calcutta Improvement Trust and empowered it to undertake schemes for the extension and improvement of the city. Its chairman was an Indian Civil Service officer, C. H. Bompas. According to a present-day Indian historian, "there was no public body in Calcutta so intensely unpopular and so cordially disliked as the Calcutta Improvement Trust," and the press expressed dismay that Bompas should be the "supreme and undisputed master of the situation."[11] Realizing the control of the trust over the development of Calcutta property, the various communities of the city energetically sought representation on its board.

Bompas made a number of reports outlining the problems of Calcutta. He believed that the municipality and its surrounding suburbs needed to be considered as a unit for planning purposes. Deploring the lack of coordination between street planning in the city and in the suburbs, he observed that there was not a single road extending from the city center to the surrounding country. Within the city itself, especially in the congested districts of north Calcutta, the street system was totally inadequate for the volume of traffic, and large areas had virtually no streets at all.

Convinced that Calcutta required a comprehensive plan, Bompas invited a British engineer, E. P. Richards, to prepare a detailed study of the city's needs. The work was begun in 1913 and published in 1914. Included in Richards's report was a general summary of planning theory as it had been developing in Europe and North America, together with extensive comparative information about foreign cities. Throughout the report, Calcutta was contrasted to urban centers in the West, with recommendations for improvement based on standards developed in the Western context. The continual reliance in the document on Western prototypes may have reflected a dearth of information about Asian cities, as well as the cultural bias of the author.

Richards observed, as had others before him, that many of the British "possessed little or no knowledge of the dense back-blocks that compose three quarters of the city. . . . One can walk day after day for hours in the lanes of North Calcutta, without meeting a single European." Only a profound ignorance, he believed, could inspire such descriptions of Calcutta as "fairest city of the east." In Richards's view, "only prompt, big, and concerted action" would prevent Calcutta from becoming "the largest slum in the world."[12]

Richards's experience of cities had given him no preparation for the street system of Calcutta, and he was particularly struck by the extensive and densely built Indian districts served only by tortuous lanes and passages. Estimating the city to have a total of 2,500 acres of streetless property, he observed, "I know of no other city road-plan that closely resembles that of Calcutta" (77). The mesh of narrow streets divided the city into half-mile rectangles within which tangled footpaths separated property set at "every possible angle" (19). The suburbs, moreover, were "in a terrible mess, being without any street system whatever" (171).

To demonstrate Calcutta's deficiencies, he showed a comparison with London (fig. 114). Curiously, the London street pattern was illustrated by a district of bylaw streets of the sort often condemned by British urbanists. The noted planner Raymond Unwin, for example, had argued that such streets were wasteful of space as well as visually monotonous, and had urged an approach to urban design in which land parcels would be larger, and the number of streets reduced. A more innovative thinker than Richards might have seen in the Calcutta system the germ of a superblock concept.

In recommending alterations in the street system, Richards provided a series of plans ranging from those he considered ideal to more modest and presumably realistic schemes. Essentially, he proposed the development of additional north-south and east-west arteries together with new diagonal streets. An important focus for diagonal circulation was the terminus of a bridge leading from Howrah on the opposite side of the Hooghly. The river crossing, in the form of a floating bridge, had been constructed in 1873–74, and in 1893 a broad new street, Harrison Road, had been completed leading eastward from the bridge toward Sealdah Railway Station. It was proposed to create two new streets of similar width fanning outward from the bridge and leading through the city to the suburbs (figs. 115–18).

Richards's approach to Calcutta could be likened to that of Haussmann, whose

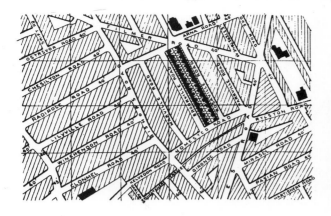

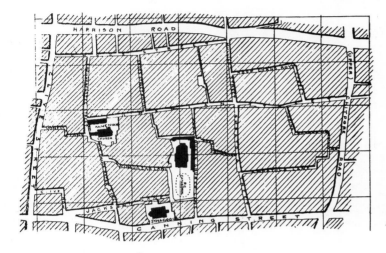

114. *Comparison of London and Calcutta streets from Richards's plan, 1914.*

influential work in Paris had involved extensive street construction by means of demolition. Like Haussmann's streets, those contemplated by Richards would be broad and straight and built without regard to what lay in the projected path. "The curved road," he noted, "is more picturesque than the straight road, but less noble, and less simple and safe for rapid traffic. . . . In the straight road alone can be used those large and beautiful artistic works that give grandeur and finish to a whole road or avenue, and indeed, to a whole city" (390).

Envisioning elements that might be employed in the beautification of Calcutta streets, Richards suggested that "fountains, rising from great basins of white marble like those of Paris would be very delightful and popular in the roads of Calcutta." He also recommended the use of great columns "soaring up at important main-road junctions." Unfortunately, he noted, "the time has long gone by when it was easy to create tree-planted boulevards in what is now built-up Calcutta," but such ornamental treatment might be attempted in the new radial roads traversing the suburbs. One of Richards's best suggestions was the arcading of streets. He pointed out that such arcades "will give valuable and grateful shelter from the painful enervating sun of the tropics, and protection from constant rain during the long monsoon months. . . . There is no valid reason why Calcutta should not come to be known as The City of Arcades" (390–93).

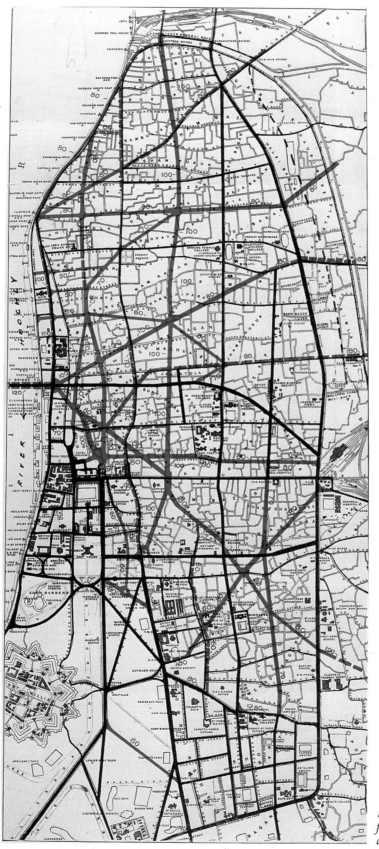

115. Richards's ideal plan
for Calcutta. Proposed new streets
are shown in red.

116. Harrison Road, constructed in 1893 to connect Howrah Bridge and Sealdah Station. The view is looking east near Howrah Bridge.

117. Cotton Street, a narrow artery running parallel to Harrison Road. Richards's proposed new Inner Strand Road would intersect at this point.

118. Radha Bazaar Street looking in the direction of Howrah Bridge. This street lay in the path of Richards's proposed southeast diagonal.

119. Trams on Chitpore Road. The tracks virtually filled the roadway.

Richards maintained that in addition to the aesthetic and functional aspects, "each great main road is, itself, a first-class sanitary measure. It is a great airway and a new lung" (39). Not only would the reconstruction necessitated by the street program result in improved building standards, but the extended circulation from the city to the outskirts would help to ameliorate housing conditions. In Richards's view, the Calcutta slums resulted in part from the inability of people to commute in and out of the city. Although a small tramway system existed, it was hampered in its expansion because of the lack of suitable streets (fig. 119). Richards hoped that with improved circulation, accessible and inexpensive housing could be developed in the suburbs, taking some of the population pressure off the center.

In the previous century, Calcutta slums had consisted largely of small huts. By the time of Richards's study, building densities had increased, and slums included tall, closely packed tenements. Richards noted that "collections of mud huts, tightly packed together and intersected only by paths and passages, have been replaced on the same sites by small brick dwellings, and these again by high dwellings" (236). Large buildings might have only a few feet of space between them. These narrow slits "make dark passages of great depth, and their walls are full of the windows of dark and airless dwelling-rooms; the ground floor often being occupied by the fronts of cave-like, dimly-lit bazaars, and the space from top to bottom between the opposite walls is frequently so hung across with the clothes, mats, rags, and bedding of the poor that the sky is scarcely visible" (236; fig. 120).

120. Richards used this view to illustrate the dense pattern of ground coverage in Calcutta. A new building was under construction in the center lot, and when it was completed there would be no separation from the adjoining buildings other than by narrow lanes at each side.

The report contained extensive analyses of slum conditions. Overbuilding was accompanied by overcrowding, with rooms subdivided by partitions, and families occupying tiny cubicles. Tuberculosis rates were high, especially among women. It was noted that "the women are indoors all day, and get the full effects of Calcutta's record overcrowding of buildings, of the wretched rooms, and the abnormal lack of light and air" (246).

Richards urged the creation of building regulations providing greater separation of structures. Similar studies had been underway in Bombay, but he felt the Bombay standards were too low to be adopted. "Considerable harm seems likely to occur from Calcutta following as good the example of Bombay, and vice versa, from Bombay taking Calcutta as an up-to-date example. . . . If it may be said without offense, it seems plain that both Calcutta and Bombay should not look to each other for guidance and example, but should rather draw experience from the far more highly advanced cities of other lands" (274, 277). Such a statement implies the absence of any local tradition of urban form that could supply an acceptable point of reference for planning standards. Richards may have had scant acquaintance with Indian cities, or he may have believed that only in the West could be found a scale of urban development comparable to that of the colonial metropolis. His failure to include examples of Indian townscape among his illustrative prototypes, however, was a major weakness of his report. The concept of the arcaded street was demonstrated through pictures of Paris and

Turin, and a map of Budapest was supplied to show "the road and street arrangement which would have suited Calcutta, and towards which we must especially work as regards creation of new intra-city main roads" (108–09, caption).

In any event, there appeared no simple solution to the problem of the Calcutta slums. They could not be dealt with through massive demolition, but would require a gradual program of repair. In addition, some new low-cost housing might be constructed to improved standards. Although Richards did not regard multistorey tenements as desirable, he admitted that "the block dwelling is an expedient, and seems to be an unavoidable necessity and stage in the gradual improvement of Calcutta" (82). High land costs in Calcutta lessened the feasibility of workers' housing within the city, and it was anticipated that increasing reclamation of the swampy lands surrounding Calcutta would provide opportunities for workers' colonies outside.

Like many city plans, the Richards report was not completely realized, but it did provide a general guide for future renovation. Elements of his proposed street plan were gradually achieved, and, through demolition, a number of broad arteries were cut through the dense urban fabric. The renovations continued to be controversial, and the Indian press often condemned the high-handed methods by which property was expropriated. In 1915, one journal reported that, "a vast number of non-political middle-class people in Calcutta were deeply moved, and shedding tears, because in the garb of improvement unlimited areas of land, dwelling houses, and everything standing within the zone of acquisition were being acquired." The authorities, it seemed, "could not sleep soundly until they saw Calcutta covered with a network of wide roads."[13]

In Europe renovation programs were sometimes opposed by preservationists desirous of maintaining old buildings for their architectural qualities. The Richards report, although it dealt extensively with the Indian districts of Calcutta, made no mention of architecture other than to deplore how much ground it covered. If Richards had ever heard of conservative surgery, he apparently believed it had no relevance to Calcutta.

Most Europeans presumed the native districts to offer little but noise and dirt, generally avoiding them altogether. Among the exceptions to the prevailing view was an account published in 1900. The writer declared that "one of the most wonderful sights in Calcutta is the Burra Bazaar, yet how few Europeans . . . ever visit it! . . . The houses are all very high, many rising to more than four storeys. They are built of stone or brick and, as a rule, are ornamented within and without, with rough but not unpleasing coloured frescoes. Some have balconies of wonderfully carved wood."[14]

Not surprisingly, one of the few British planners to respond favorably to Burra Bazaar was Patrick Geddes, who submitted a report on its improvement in 1919. The Improvement Trust, he noted, had proposed to open up the congested district by widening existing streets. Geddes pointed out that the best buildings lay along these streets, while the interiors of the blocks were often given over to bustees. It would be less destructive of valuable property, therefore, to direct new streets through the centers of large blocks, creating new frontages and leaving the existing streets intact. As to the network of narrow pedestrian lanes, he believed that this system of circulation was highly useful in getting foot traffic off the streets and providing short-cuts. "Lanes, it is true," he noted, "are much out of fashion; and with most large-scale plan-

121. Lane in Burra Bazaar.

ners especially." He pointed out, however, that "a lane, after all, is a pavement without a road beside it: and some people value its quietness; while its narrow width and shade give coolness." In Geddes's opinion, the system of lanes should be extended (fig. 121).[15]

He also appreciated the values of the courtyard house. Observing that this type of dwelling was traditional in many parts of the world, providing welcome shade in hot climates, he reported that "there are a substantial number of spacious courtyard houses in Barra Bazar . . . which, especially as the world now goes, no city can afford to destroy. . . . [and he suggested that] instead of regarding this clinging of householder and family to the old home as a mere old-fashioned conservatism, impeding modern progress, this sentiment might have been made a strong and effective argument for its repair and sanitation."[16] Geddes projected a new four-storey building type that he believed suitable to the mixed uses of the bazaar. It would consist of warehousing at ground level with offices above, together with two floors of dwelling space. The traditional courtyard would be preserved, but lifted up two storeys.

Geddes insisted that new housing be provided before demolitions were undertaken, and he opposed the view that displaced workers could always move farther out of the city. Only the middle and upper classes, he contended, possessed the time and money for commuting, and workers needed housing close to their employment. All in all, Geddes deplored the strong influence of Haussmann-type planning in India, contrasting it with what he termed more "modern ideas."

The Haussmann approach, however, continued to dominate the work of the Improvement Trust, and a number of broad thoroughfares were cut through the Indian quarters. Behind the new street facades, many districts remained relatively unchanged, with their dense building patterns, mixed activities, and dramatic juxtapositions of wealth and squalor. A network of twisting narrow pedestrian lanes still provided a large part of the circulation system, while in the wider arteries a pandemonium of assorted traffic prevailed.

The British generally praised the achievements of the Improvement Trust, citing the salutary aspects of the new streets. Great benefits had been effected by "cutting the spacious Central Avenue through the heart of the Chinese and Indian quarters. . . . The Central Avenue is 100 feet wide, and already shows what a great artery it will be in the future. Huge structures of four, five, and six storeys are already flanking it. . . . The southern end of this wonderful improvement has removed a congerie of small shops and dwelling-houses from the proximity of the mosque at the corner of Dharamtala and Bentinck" (figs. 122 and 123). Contemplating the extensive changes in Calcutta, a writer in 1928 declared that a visitor from 1900 "would today experience many visual shocks." He added, however, that "a few years after an improvement has been effected it is exceedingly difficult to recollect a locality as it appeared previously, and it is, of course, no one's business to make a photographic record of what is removed."[17] It had also been no one's business to record the fate of the people removed.

Even without the renovations of the Improvement Trust, economic forces would have fostered many changes. In 1930, it was reported that "the great mills, dwarfing the largest conception of Lancashire, extend for 40 miles along the banks of the Hooghly." Large office blocks characterized the commercial center, where "nearly all the banks and great business houses have rebuilt their premises in styles which have borrowed largely from the architecture of the great commercial cities of the West" (figs. 124 and 125). Along what was once the most fashionable residential street, "the 'palaces' of Chowringhee have mostly disappeared, their sites covered by commercial buildings, by clubs, or by the great blocks of flats which are springing up rapidly in days when the cost of living no longer permits the keeping of an army of servants" (figs. 126 and 127). It was noted that "the European no longer lives in a sort of proud isolation. Rich Indians increasingly invade the European quarter and outdo the merchant princes in the splendour of their dwellings."[18]

As older residential districts became commercialized, new neighborhoods were developed in the southern part of the city. Settlement of this area was facilitated in part by the works of the Improvement Trust and in part by private initiative. Such districts as Ballygunge began to attract Indian intellectuals, civil servants, and professional people, and building societies facilitated house construction.

The planning activity of Calcutta had a counterpart in Bombay, where an improvement trust had been in existence since 1898. The program of urban renovation in Bombay had come about not as a result of gradual pressures of growth, but in response to a disastrous outbreak of bubonic plague in 1896. To halt the spread of the disease, a Special Plague Committee was created by the government and given emergency powers to isolate victims and disinfect buildings. Meanwhile, as the death rate rose to over 2,000 per week, panic-stricken citizens fled the city in an exodus estimated at between one-quarter and one-half of the population. The mills stopped, business was brought to a standstill, and the ports of Europe were closed to Bombay

122. Demolition for the future Central Avenue and Chowringhee Square, shown in 1926.

123. Central Avenue and Chowringhee Square, 1935.

124. *Commercial buildings on Exchange Place.*

125. *Commercial buildings on Netaji Subas Road, formerly Clive Street.*

126. *Apartment house near Chowringhee Road built in 1926.*

127. *Apartment house in an Indian district of Calcutta, built in 1924.*

ships. Smoke from Hindu funeral pyres reportedly ascended day and night, and new burial grounds were sought among the Muslims. The plague continued for years, with weekly death rates as high as 2,820 in 1899–1900. As late as 1910, the plague was still considered epidemic, although the death rate had been reduced to 1,152 per week. A visitor in 1907 described houses that "had been visited by the plague again and again; on many a doorpost was the red circle, with date within, which is the sign that the pestilence had done its work and claimed its victim. On some of the lintels there were as many as five or six of these marks of doom."[19]

At the outbreak of the plague, the disease was not yet known to be spread by fleas that had bitten infected rats. It seemed clearly allied, however, to unsanitary living conditions, and it was heavily concentrated in densely built areas. The plague committee attempted to disinfect houses where plague had struck by washing the building with a solution of perchloride of lime, and when this was dry applying lime wash with quicklime laid on hot. The exterior might also be cleaned with steam (figs. 128 and 129). Certain dwellings were classified u.h.h., or unfit for human habitation. Attempts were also made at renovating houses to improve ventilation. Partitions might be removed or openings inserted, or portions of buildings closed off. The fact that the British community had been virtually untouched by the disease provided an effective advertisement for their way of life, and the plague is credited with accelerating the trend among well-to-do Indians to abandon the congested older districts in favor of suburban residences.

The Bombay City Improvement Trust, modeled on the Bombay Port Trust, was empowered to carry out such planning activities as creating new streets, opening up congested areas, reclaiming land, and constructing housing. At the time Richards was analyzing Calcutta, he observed that "the Bombay Improvement Trust has been and is still ridiculously hampered by lack of powers, by the timidity, the weakness, the incompetence, the amateurishness, and the lack of comprehension embodied in the Act and Acts under which it has to work; and . . . there is little enough to show for 15 years."[20]

Any planning organization is likely to be blamed for doing either too much or too little. Because its activities involved the compulsory acquisition of property for demolition, the trust was often unpopular with both landlords and tenants. Some believed it had usurped the role of the city government, while others considered its work handicapped by the continuing control of the municipality over building regulations and sanitation. In 1933, the Improvement Trust was absorbed by the municipality. Included in its work by this time was the demolition of 36,317 dwelling units and the construction of 61,868 units, including 3,500 housing units for city police. Additional achievements involved the creation of over 61 miles of roads, the planting of 12,000 trees, provision for parks and playgrounds, and various land-filling operations. The accomplishments of the trust, however, were considered minimal in relation to the overall needs of the city.

The housing crisis continued in intensity, and slum conditions of overbuilding and overcrowding persisted. Clearance efforts often exacerbated the congestion of adjacent areas, for many workers preferred to remain near their employment rather than to move to outlying Improvement Trust housing. One factor in lowering housing standards in both Bombay and Calcutta was the continuing predominance of single men

128. *Infected house in Bombay being washed with lime during the Bombay plague, 1896–97.*

129. *Buildings being steam cleaned using a "flushing engine."*

130. *Dense building in the Bombay fort area.*

in the working population. Most of these men lived as cheaply as possible in order to remit money to families elsewhere, and they would tolerate the most minimal housing provisions. Which city had the worst housing was open to question. It seemed apparent, however, that physical exploitation of the land was most intense in Bombay where densities in slum districts might be as high as 1,200 per acre (fig. 130). In 1911 it was reported that 80 percent of the population lived in single-room tenements.

Because of the shortage of space, Bombay housing was characterized by the *chawl* or multistorey dwelling (fig. 131). A British housing study done in the 1920s classified such buildings according to three main types. The worst was judged to be a dwelling house originally built for a single family, but converted to multiple occupancy and rented by the room. Often such houses had extensions built in the front and the rear, with additional storeys added as well. A single *chawl* five to seven storeys high might have from five hundred to one thousand inhabitants crowded into dark and unventilated rooms. Sanitation would be virtually nonexistent.[21]

Slightly better accommodation was reported for chawls built by private owners for profit. These were often two storeys high, and when they faced a road, they usually had commercial premises on the ground level. Access to dwelling rooms would be by means of external verandas or central corridors. Rooms would be about ten feet square with perhaps a small veranda attached. Buildings were often dilapidated, and the immediate surroundings unpaved and strewn with rubbish. Water might be available only from a single source and was often in short supply. Sanitary facilities were primitive and ill maintained (fig. 132).

In terms of physical standards, the best chawls were those constructed by the Improvement Trust and other public bodies. These were usually brick or concrete buildings ranging from three to five storeys in height. Although the basic dwelling type resembled others in the Bombay slums, the Trust chawls were solidly constructed and incorporated improvements in sanitation. A typical dwelling would be a single room ten-by-twelve feet with a four-by-six foot veranda. The veranda might be partially enclosed and contain a *chula* and a *nahini,* or bathing place. Like most public housing projects, however, the Trust chawls were mechanical in terms of site planning and often forbidding in appearance (fig. 133).

As frequently happens in such housing, the tenants were not gentle in their treatment of these buildings. One British observer noted that

> spitting of pan and betelnut juice and other nuisances are committed everywhere, especially on the staircases, in the passages and corridors. These places also serve as the chief repositories for the sweepings of the room. Goats, fowls and other animals belonging to the tenants are often to be found in the corridors. It is in these surroundings that one sees babies crawling, children playing and mothers nursing their infants. . . . The verandas are fitted with cooking places, but tenants prefer to cook in their living-room, especially on a windy day. It is not surprising, then, that the walls and ceiling are blackened, as there is little escape for the smoke. The "nahinis" and corners of rooms are often misused, especially by children. The floors are daily "cleaned" with cow-dung—a practice common throughout India; the occupants of the room eat their meals on the floor and sleep on it where space does not provide for "charpoys" (beds).

131. *Bombay chawl on Kalbedeve Road. Slender wooden props are used frequently in Bombay buildings to supplement an aging structural frame.*

132. *Bombay chawl courtyard.*

133. *Bombay Improvement Trust chawl, Mandvi district, built in 1908.*

Cooking and eating vessels are cleaned with earth, road scrapings and any kind of water which is procurable.[22]

People of rural habits do not adapt easily to high-rise housing. In addition to the permanent chawls, the trust provided some ground-floor dwellings of corrugated iron sheets, which were intended as temporary housing for construction workers and called semi-permanent sheds. They proved so successful that it was decided to replace them with permanent buildings designed on the same lines. By 1938, the trust had constructed 2,600 such dwellings. A government official reported that "they are very popular with the tenants, and if you visit one of these housing schemes, you will think that you are not in Bombay City but in some village laid out on scientific and hygienic lines."[23] In his Calcutta report, E. P. Richards had suggested that at the lowest level of housing a single room per family was adequate, provided that it was on the ground floor and had adjuncts for cooking, washing, and privacy. A dry-paved open

134. Mohammed Ali Road, created by the Bombay Improvement Trust.

yard and veranda would provide a sleeping area for most of the year as well as play space for children. Such housing had proved successful in Madras where the relatively low cost of land made single-storey housing feasible.

British housing studies, quite naturally, embodied an outsider's view of the chawl, focusing on its less-than-ideal physical standards and often emphasizing the worst examples. Deploring the chawls did not halt their proliferation, however, and in the densely built fabric of Bombay, they continued to provide the only affordable housing for much of the populace. Over the years the chawl was to become part of the image and legend of Bombay, even spawning writers who celebrated the intimate and supportive social life engendered by shared balconies and courtyards. Like many city neighborhoods despised by planners, the chawl districts could inspire deep affection and loyalty among their inhabitants.

Included in the Improvement Trust program was a series of north-south and east-west streets (fig. 134). The accompanying demolition made construction of these broad arterial roads both controversial and expensive, and the immediate impact was often to intensify overcrowding in the adjacent districts. To their proponents, though, the new thoroughfares were essential for traffic circulation and also desirable for the ventilation they were believed to provide in congested areas.

The Haussmann approach to city planning dominated in Bombay as it did in Calcutta, and although Patrick Geddes resided in Bombay between 1920 and 1924, his ideas seem to have had no impact on the development of the city. He condemned the Improvement Trust chawls as "Bolshevik barracks." His only contribution to local planning appears to have been a report submitted in 1915 on the redevelopment of six towns in the Bombay Presidency, of which two, Bandra and Thana, were in the vicinity of Bombay city. In the case of Thana, he suggested that the tank should be improved to create a water park which might become the focus of excursions from Bombay.

The activities of the Improvement Trust were to remain controversial. Although, in the long run, more housing units were constructed than were destroyed, the organization became associated in the public mind with wanton demolition. Sir Dinshaw Wacha, President of the Municipal Corporation of Bombay and a member of the Trust, once declared that the Improvement Trust itself needed to be, "improved off the face of Bombay."

Concurring, a versifier in Karachi assured his fellow citizens in 1905:

We may not have a Ballard Pier and passengers galore,
We may not have a Taj Mahal upon our sandy shore,
We may not have to live in an Apollo Bunder flat,
But we haven't got an Improvement Trust,
and thank the Lord for that.[24]

The Improvement Trust had been supplemented in 1920 by the Development Directorate, which was created to construct working-class housing, develop new industrial sites outside the central areas, augment communication between the city and suburban districts, and improve the supply and transport of building materials. The most ambitious work of the Development Directorate, however, was the reclamation of the Back Bay. This project had first been contemplated by a private company during the great boom of the 1860s, then abandoned when financing collapsed. In succeeding years, the government contemplated various proposals for resuming the project. It formed part of an inquiry sponsored in 1887 by the government of Lord Reay and was considered again by the Bombay Public Works Department in 1905–06. The idea was encouraged after the success of a shorefront reclamation project called Cuffe Parade on the west side of Colaba Point, where land was speedily and profitably occupied.

The government became further convinced of the feasibility of the Back Bay project when, in 1917, two private companies sought concessions to undertake the reclamation. It was decided that the profits of such a large-scale enterprise should be for public, rather than private benefit. Dredging operations began early in the 1920s and were to have been completed by 1926–27. Cost estimates proved inaccurate, however, and reclamation operations were badly organized. A trade depression, moreover, brought about a drop in land values. Fearing that reclamation costs might exceed profits on land disposal, the government decided to reduce temporarily the size of the landfill from 1,145 acres to 552 acres. The projected area of reclamation had been divided into eight blocks, and it was proposed to fill blocks one and two at the northern end and blocks seven and eight to the south. A shoreline boulevard called Marine Drive would connect the two districts, and it was anticipated that future reclamation would eventually complete the project.

A plan for the Back Bay had been commissioned in 1921 from a British architect and urbanist, W. R. Davidge. The land would provide an extension adjacent to the established government and commercial center. Just west of Bombay's major monumental buildings, Davidge projected a new government complex including headquarters for the legislative council. South of this enclave, about a hundred acres would be given over to offices "grouped round shady quadrangles on the lines of Gray's Inn or the colleges at Oxford."[25]

In its fusion of classical formality and ornamental landscaping, the Davidge plan reflected the currently fashionable tenets of Beaux-Arts planning (fig. 135). The street plan was laid out in a grid incorporating several broad, tree-lined avenues, including a landscaped boulevard along the seafront. Focal points such as the intersection of major streets were marked by ornamental squares or circuses. Extending north-south

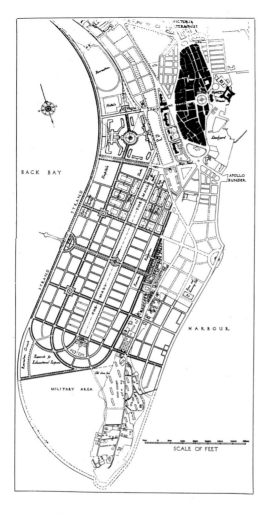

135. Davidge Plan for the Back Bay, 1921. The area of the old fort is shown in black. Just west of the fort can be seen the row of buildings added at the time the fortifications were demolished.

through the area was a landscaped mall designed to focus at its northern end on the tower of the university and at its southern end on a large public building.

As the reclamation area, which was given the name Marine Lines, was eventually built, the Davidge plan was set aside for a far more utilitarian scheme. The ornamental open spaces and the monumental aspects were eliminated, and the district was given over to private lots sold at auction. In 1937 a local British architect, Claude Batley, denounced "such callous meddling with so fine a scheme," observing that the changes in the plan "seem to have been made in order to sell the smallest parcel of land for the highest possible price, regardless of the inevitable result that the purchasers and their architects were then bound, in order to get any return at all, to overload the tiny plots to the maximum extent that the building regulations allow and, now, what someone has called 'a row of square boxes' overlooks Bombay's finest open space." He believed that "the grand Marine Drive should have been double its contemplated width, with fine public gardens and lawns stretching down to the seafront." Contemplating Marine Drive in 1944, Batley declared that the district had been "ruined forever." Instead of being partly set back to provide gardens and increased frontage views, the buildings along the seafront created an unbroken wall, and he predicted that when completely developed the new district would reveal "infamous monotony and congestion." The close placement of buildings would assure that "all privacy, indeed all decency of living, will be destroyed, and all that will be left as far as the rear blocks are concerned will be a huge higher-incomed-group slum" (fig. 136).[26]

The Back Bay was largely given over to apartment houses built close to the edge of the lot lines, with only narrow lanes and courts to illuminate and ventilate rooms without street frontage. Although the urban pattern was similar to that found in certain European cities, it did not reflect current thinking among urban designers. As developed, the Back Bay had neither the classical formality of the Davidge plan nor the innovative site planning of the contemporary modern movement. Like much urban development, it appeared to have been designed primarily by the forces of greed (fig. 137).

Another reclamation area was developed on the eastern side of Bombay on land excavated during the construction of Alexandra Dock between 1908 and 1914. The new district, adjacent to the docks, was called Ballard Estate and was planned by George Wittet, serving as a consultant to the Port Trust. Building construction took place during the 1920s, and the new district was described as being "like a miniature little European city with its handsome office buildings and wide well-kept streets, presenting a vast contrast to the narrow streets and noisy traffic of older Bombay" (fig. 138).[27]

Bombay, like Madras and Calcutta, was typical of modern commercial cities in the piecemeal nature of its planning activity and in the subordination of ideology to prevailing economic forces. It was only in New Delhi that an opportunity to plan comprehensively was afforded. The establishment of the new capital in 1912 had coincided with a period of intense interest in city planning among the British. Yet, in spite of the growth of the planning profession, the existence of a large body of planning theory, and the wide-spread awareness of the city as a highly complex organism, the plan of New Delhi embodied little beyond a formal diagram.

At the time New Delhi was created, the principal focus of attention among the designers was the monumental complex. The creation of the viceroy's palace and the accompanying secretariat buildings reflected an impressive clarity of concept. There was, however, no clearly defined vision of the city that would accompany the great government ensemble. It was not certain, in fact, that New Delhi was destined to be a city at all. New Delhi was intended to house the imperial government headquarters, nothing more. The only need that was anticipated was for office space, together with housing and institutional facilities for staff. The government was to be in residence, moreover, for only seven months of the year, migrating to Simla for the hot season. As the city neared dedication, *The Times* observed, "A question often asked is—will New Delhi ever become a city? Not in the sense in which the question is meant. It will be an annexe, an official suburb with a heterogeneous population drawn from all parts of India, but with a mere sprinkling of permanent residents. Only permanent residents can make a city, and New Delhi will not become one until it gets them."[28]

Whatever the future might bring, New Delhi was laid out on a grand scale and in the grand classical tradition. The design was produced by the New Delhi Planning

136. Marine Drive.

Committee headed by George Swinton, chairman of the London County Council, and it included John Brodie, City Engineer of Liverpool, and architect Sir Edwin Lutyens. Thomas Ward, an engineer, Geoffrey de Montmorency, a civil servant, and the architect Herbert Baker were attached to the committee, while H. V. Lanchester served as a consultant. Although the plan was a group effort, it has often been attributed to Lutyens, and there is no doubt that he was a powerful influence in its creation. In making its final report in 1913, the committee commented that

> a well-planned city should stand complete at its birth and yet have the power of receiving additions without losing its character. There must be beauty combined with comfort. There must be convenience—of arrangement as well as of communication. . . . [As to symbolism] Delhi is to be an Imperial capital and is to absorb the traditions of all the ancient capitals. . . . It has to convey the idea of a peaceful domination and dignified rule over the traditions and life of India by the British Raj.[29]

The expansive ordering of New Delhi was generally recognized as symbolizing the far-reaching powers of British rule. The system of axes and diagonals drawn from

137. Apartment houses behind Marine Drive.

138. Ballard Estate.

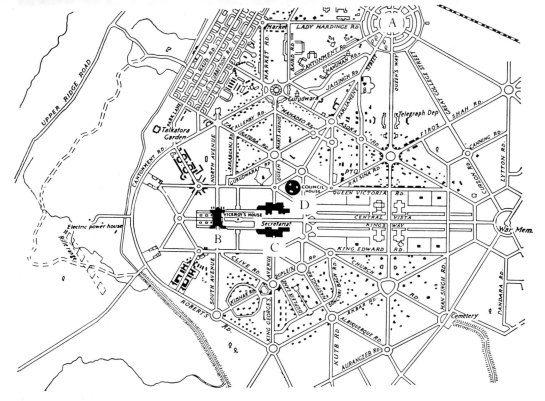

139. Plan of the official quarter of New Delhi. A. Connaught Place, the commercial center. B. Viceroy's Palace. C. Secretariat. D. Council House.

the tradition of baroque classicism provided a means of unifying a large-scale composition and of establishing visual hierarchy (fig. 139). As urban design, however, it had no specific political association and could effectively symbolize virtually any social system. The elements of the New Delhi plan had been used in papal Rome, in Versailles, in Paris, in Wren's unbuilt plan for London, and in Washington, D.C. Among these, the closest parallel was Versailles. Like the palace complex of Louis XIV, the city of the viceroy seemed intended to be primarily a ceremonial center, rather than a complete and balanced city.

New Delhi was to be built adjacent to and would be joined administratively to the old walled city of Delhi. Although the two would, in effect, function as a single urban entity, the possibility of creating the new city to harmonize visually with the old was never seriously considered. New Delhi was conceived as a purely British settlement juxtaposed to the Indian city in the manner of what some termed "glorified civil lines." Old Delhi, with its intricate web of narrow winding streets and densely packed buildings, and New Delhi, with its geometric plan and vast spaces, were to remain dramatically different in form, as well as physically discrete. As though to emphasize the separateness of the two urban entities, a large swath of land between them was cleared and landscaped (fig. 140). In the design of New Delhi, recognition of the Indian city was restricted to proposals for a linkage of axial vistas, and in the final plan, a wide street, Minto Road, was projected in the direction of the Jama Masjid.

140. The juncture of Old and New Delhi. The Jama Masjid appears at the top. The northern portion of New Delhi shown here contained housing for low-ranking government workers.

It was natural, however, that the development of New Delhi would direct the attention of British planners to conditions in the old city. Over the years, various proposals had been made by British administrators to facilitate expansion of the congested native settlement beyond its existing walls. In 1906, the Commissioner of Delhi declared that "the time has come to take up the question of extension comprehensively," stating that it was necessary to project roads, streets, and space allocation to provide growth for the next thirty years.[30] Little action had been taken, however.

The Town Planning Committee of New Delhi was convinced that the creation of the new capital should be accompanied by a renovation of the native city. They did acknowledge that such action would entail "months of patient investigation into the conflicting interests and the value of the various properties which will be encountered." And although they believed that "schemes for opening out are required combined with wide through traffic routes," they were aware that "compulsory improvements in crowded neighborhoods are not only costly but unpopular, and moreover actually produce a more unsanitary congestion—the tendency being for the dispossessed to huddle even closer into the side streets."[31] The committee suggested that if convenient access were given to areas beyond the walled city, people might move out of their own accord. The logical direction of expansion appeared to be west of the old city, and land for redevelopment was acquired in the district later called Karol Bagh. Little urban infrastructure was created however, and as late as 1931, a municipal subcommittee noted that the area still lacked unfiltered water and drainage.

In terms of planning, Old Delhi was essentially left to evolve spontaneously (fig.141).

The creation of the new capital promoted a dramatic rise in population. In 1921, the Delhi municipality had a population of 246,987; by 1931 it had risen to 347,592, an increase of 40 percent. At least 28 percent of this increase was directly attributable to the development of New Delhi, and while British planners concentrated their efforts to the south, the fabric of the old city had to respond to increasing pressures. The rapid influx of people into the already-dense district accelerated a tendency toward overbuilding, and new construction was often added to the roofs of existing structures.

The congestion of Old Delhi was subject to frequent discussion in the press and the municipal committee, and a deadlock developed between the central government and the municipality as to who was responsible for the development of the old city. In 1936, a British report summarized conditions within Old Delhi. Using British standards of reference based on a required minimum of fifty square feet of living space per person, the walled city was judged to have an excess population of 100,000. It was declared that the settlement needed to be planned to accommodate not only these people but also an additional 133,000 over the next fifteen years. Most houses were built in disregard of a bylaw that required two-thirds of every plot to be left open, and it was noted that "crooked, narrow alleys, flanked by two and three storeyed houses overcrowded with ill-ventilated single-room tenements are a commonplace in many wards of the city."[32] Internal courtyards, the traditional source of light and air, had often come to be roofed with iron gratings that were then covered with mats, which blocked out the sky.

To facilitate expansion of the city, it was suggested that the southern portion of the city wall between Ajmeri Gate and Delhi Gate be demolished to provide housing sites. The wall was declared to be both "non-historic and non-aesthetic," and its removal, together with the filling-in of the adjacent ditch, would provide 64,830 square yards of new land. As the new plots would face the landscaped area separating Old and New Delhi, they would presumably create a desirable residential district. It was also proposed that Minto Road in New Delhi, aligned with the Jama Masjid, be extended into the old city, creating a wide thoroughfare all the way to the mosque. No action was taken on these suggestions, however, and Old Delhi remained essentially intact.

Just as the planning of New Delhi emphasized the separateness of the British city from the Indian settlement, it also emphasized class distinctions among the British. The civil service embodied an elite class sometimes likened to the Brahmins, or "heaven-born." Although the colonial conquest of India had been instigated by the desire for trade, the merchant, or "box-wallah," was looked down upon. Imperial rhetoric emphasized a divine mission to lead and enlighten, and many preferred to forget that the empire had been founded on profit. New Delhi placed the imperial administration in a purified setting, removed both from the squalid associations of trade and from the social promiscuity of the commercial metropolis. There was to be no encouragement of commerce and industry in the new capital. "We do not," stated the viceroy, "want factory chimneys on every side."[33]

New Delhi seemed designed to counteract the trends toward racial and social mixture that were found in the other major colonial cities. The residential pattern of the city reflected the civil service hierarchy, with upper-level employees segregated from lower-level employees, and the British separated from the Indians. In some ways,

141. *Street in Old Delhi.*

142. New Delhi bungalow.

the distribution of population was like the caste distribution of a traditional Indian town. The highest ranking officials, the gazetted officers, were placed nearest the government center, with Indian princes at the eastern end of the monumental axis. European clerks were housed beyond the officers' district, and Indian clerks still farther away. At the greatest distance were the lowest ranking Indian employees. Land elevation was also used to emphasize status, with European clerks on higher land than the Indian clerks, and gazetted officers higher than the clerks. Within the various housing districts, a pattern of fine distinctions was developed in which rank was defined by size of plot, cost of house, and street location.

With a projected population of 30,000 to 57,000, and abundant land, plot sizes were ample. In the original plan of 1912, the allotments ranged from 6 acres down to 1.75 acres. This was later revised, with ruling princes given sites of 4 to 8 acres, gazetted officers 2 to 3.5 acres, and 0.25 acre for members of the legislature. Private residential sites ranged from 1 to 3 acres. A free-standing bungalow was provided for all upper-level employees, with various types of terraced housing for those at lower levels (fig. 142).

Although the placement of the lowest-income employees at the greatest distance from the government center would clearly create hardships in the absence of a good system of public transportation, the planning committee had no practical proposals for this problem. Tramway systems existed in other cities in India, but it was considered that in Delhi they would not prove satisfactory given the local conditions. The committee report indicated that "should a necessity for public means of conveyance arise, it will probably best be met by the provision of a motor omnibus service. . . . in any case many of the residents will utilize their own means of conveyance."[34]

New Delhi, with its vast dimensions, has been described as the first city specifically designed to the scale of the motorcar. The placement of the commercial center, for example, midway between the government complex and the old city, and at a distance of two to three miles from the upper-class residential districts, reflected the assumption that its patrons would be arriving by automobile. With its low-rise building and spacious layout, it had some of the characteristics of a modern suburban shopping mall. Yet although the scale of New Delhi could be linked to advances in modern transport, the British in India had shown a taste for far-flung settlement long before the invention of the internal combustion engine. New Delhi reflected in a systematic way the type of low-density city that had existed in Madras and Calcutta as early as the eighteenth century. For those without automobiles, transportation would continue to be a problem. Cecil Beaton, who visited the city during the Second World War, complained that "even to-day there is no adequate tram or bus service to Old Delhi; those unable to find accommodation in the New Town must cover the distance of seven miles by bicycle, for a tonga moves almost as slowly as the proverbial bullock cart, while the cost of a taxi is out of the question."[35]

Walter George, an architect involved in the initial construction of New Delhi, described the design as a "Road plan, rather than a Town Plan."[36] The Beaux-Arts classicism of the street layout defined the city in advance of any conception of urban architecture. The largest street was a 440-foot-wide ceremonial avenue called Kingsway, leading eastward from the viceroy's palace (fig. 143). The remaining street widths were designed to range from 60 to 300 feet. Second in intended importance was a processional route called Queensway, projected southward from the commercial center to intersect Kingsway. The abundance of great ceremonial routes led some critics to complain that the city seemed designed for a perpetual Durbar, rather than for practical needs. The planners had sought to provide streets wide enough for all eventualities, however, and it was suggested that building frontages be kept back to facilitate future street widening. A detailed program for landscaping accompanied the development of the street system (figs. 144 and 145).

In contemplating the New Delhi plan, some observers were disturbed that the streets would have little flanking architecture. The aesthetic of an urban street usually derives from the scale and character of the adjacent buildings, and the viceroy believed that Delhi's broad arteries should be lined with five-storey buildings as "in the Champs Elysées and Bombay." There was no budget for such construction, however; nor was there any anticipated need for so many buildings. "European street effects" were not deemed feasible.[37] New Delhi consisted primarily of a monumental government complex surrounded by open space and scattered, low-rise housing.

143. Kingsway, the great ceremonial way leading eastward from Raisina Hill.

144. New Delhi Street.

145. *Landscaping on the government axis.*

Summarizing the plan in 1913, a *Town Planning Review* editorial called attention to the lack of social planning:

> taken as a whole the scheme is boldly conceived, and the principal features are relatively in the right place, but the enthusiasm of the authors for the attainment of fine architectural effects precluded them from giving much study to the problems of the individual and to the growth of the city as an organisation of social units. Town planning as a study has recently made great strides in its recognition and analysis of the social structure from which the city springs, and to those who have surveyed cities and analysed their organisation, noted the tendencies of their growth, and . . . studied their human nature, the report is disappointing.[38]

In addition to certain weaknesses in the plan, there were inevitable problems as construction got underway. Housing lagged behind the demand, and in 1930, *The Times* reported that "the accommodation for the thousands of clerks who have flocked to Delhi with the Government has been utterly inadequate. Houseless clerks and their families crowd into the old city and add to the congestion within the walls." The planners were often criticized for failing to provide for schools, markets, clinics, and the like. Walter George noted that such facilities had, in fact, been projected but, because of disorganization and lack of funds, were not built. He reported that "since 'houses' for Government Servants was the cry, the sites allocated for amenities became swallowed up in housing."[39]

While lacking in visual urbanity, New Delhi provided for the comfortable classes a comfortable way of life. An English couple recalled that "New Delhi of the 30's was one of the quietest, most spacious and traffic-free cities in India." To those who preferred the excitement of a great metropolis, though, New Delhi would long seem both pompous and provincial. According to Cecil Beaton, the general effect of New Delhi in the 1940s was of "a complacent yet callous centre without gaiety or the strength for cruelty; a heartless, bloodless Display-City, without a past or the necessary roots to develop a future."[40]

In making its final report, the planning committee had stressed "the need for foresight. There must be a readiness to meet every requirement of the future."[41] Yet they clearly had little notion of Delhi's future. No one in 1913 could have foreseen the speed with which independence would arrive, nor could anyone have anticipated the advent of partition and the vast flood of refugees that would subsequently inundate the capital. A well-conceived city plan, however, should have incorporated provisions for population growth, and for the augmentation of building densities over the years. The planning of New Delhi might, in this respect, be contrasted to that of Washington, D.C., at the end of the eighteenth century. In spite of the meagerness of their resources, the government of the struggling American republic envisioned the capital as a future metropolis. From the beginning, land plots and street frontages were designed to produce a relatively dense fabric of terraced buildings. As a result, the urban pattern of Washington remains essentially intact and functioning to the present day. The planners of New Delhi ignored the possibility that the city would ever attract a large population or require a truly urban architectural fabric. The rapid and chaotic evolution of Madras, Calcutta, and Bombay apparently embodied no lessons, conveyed no warnings. The city the New Delhi planners bequeathed to the future was grand in its general outlines but, except for the monumental complex, deficient in architectural conception. It was a city in many ways destined for obsolescence.

In spite of its defects, the metropolis had become increasingly accepted as a focus of modern life by the mid-twentieth century. Although the 1931 Indian census report had declared that "city dwelling is not generally congenial to the Indian," this view was contradicted a decade later. The 1941 report stated that "city life has begun really to appeal to the ordinary middle class or lower class Indian, because for the first time accommodation within his means and his taste has become available. The huge blocks of flats which in less than a decade have completely altered the face of Bombay and parts of Calcutta, with their amenities of running water, electric light and the city features of the tram, the bus, the cinema, etc., have meant that every year sees an increase in the number of persons who seek to pass their retirement or their leisure in a city instead of their farm houses."[42] In India, as elsewhere, the power of ancestral roots was yielding to a new way of life.

5.

The Modern Movement

In the 1920s, Aldous Huxley visited Bombay. "Architecturally," he declared, "Bombay is one of the most appalling cities of either hemisphere. It had the misfortune to develop during what was, perhaps, the darkest period of all architectural history. Most of its public buildings were designed and executed between 1860 and 1900." Apparently at a loss for words to describe the astonishing stylistic mélange before him, he made recourse to the terminology of a Bombay guidebook:

> "The Presidential Secretariat, we are told, is in 'the Venetian Gothic style.' The University Hall (completed 1874), which is 'in the French Decorated style of the fifteenth century,' rubs shoulders with the 'Early English' Law Courts (opened in 1879). The University Library, harking back to an earlier century than the Hall, is 'in the style of fourteenth century Gothic.' The Old General Post Office 'was designed in the mediaeval style by Mr. Trubshawe.' The Telegraph Office . . . is 'Romanesque.' The Victoria Station, of which the style is 'Italian Gothic with certain oriental modifications in the domes,' confronts the Municipal Buildings, in which 'the oriental feeling introduced into the Gothic architecture has a pleasing effect.' More frankly oriental are the Gateway of India ('based on the work of the sixteenth century in Gujarat') and the Prince of Wales Museum ('based on the Indian work of the fifteenth centuries in the Presidency.') The architecture of the Hotel Majestic and the Taj Mahal Hotel is not described in the guide-book. It is a remissness; they deserve description. The Majestic is more wildly Mohammedan than anything that the most orthodox of the Great Moguls ever dreamed of, and the gigantic Taj combines the style of the South Kensington Natural History Museum with that of an Indian pavilion at an International Exhibition."

Seeking respite from these architectural horrors, Huxley, "in self defense," contemplated the classical town hall. "Long and low, with its flight of steps, its central pediment, its Doric colonnade, it has an air of calm and quiet decency. Among so many architectural cads and pretentious bounders, it is almost the only gentleman. In Bombay, it seems as good as the Parthenon."[1]

The eyes with which Huxley viewed Bombay were those of the European avant-garde. In the years following World War I, a new artistic vision emerged, and to those who accepted the precepts of the modern movement in architecture, much of nineteenth-century building was anathema. Confronting the styles of the past, one confined one's admiration to the relatively disciplined forms of classicism. But, in any event, the past was not to be copied. To the modernists, debates over style, such as that surrounding the creation of New Delhi, were obsolete. The very concept of style was deemed irrelevant in the modern world.

The modern movement, as it is usually defined, is linked to a variety of architectural innovations appearing in the latter part of the nineteenth century. Industrialization and the growth of the modern commercial city provided a new array of building types, as well as an increased range of technical possibilities. In the realm of style, alternatives to revivalism arose from many directions. The unadorned grandeur of certain industrial structures inspired concepts of a new monumentality, while commercial blocks provided an aesthetic based on the expression of structural framing elements. The British Arts and Crafts movement, although backward-looking in some respects, promoted directness and simplicity in domestic furnishings. Stylistic innovation also characterized the Art Nouveau, with its sinuous plasticity and sumptuous ornamentation. Although the turn of the century lacked a unified vocabulary of design, there was a growing conviction that the styles of the past would no longer suffice to express the needs and spirit of a changing society.

Following the World War I, the rhetoric of modernism became increasingly forceful. Nostalgia for the past, together with its architectural forms, was emphatically renounced by the avant-garde, who sought to attune their work to the contemporary world, to its technical possibilities, its intensive urbanization and progressive social concepts. Architectural visionaries projected schemes for new commercial metropolises, dazzling their admirers with images of vast motor expressways and towering glass-walled skyscrapers interspersed with landscaped parks and sport grounds. Traditional building crafts were to be supplanted by industrialized methods using mass-produced standardized components. Those architects who adhered to the new modern concepts often felt themselves embattled revolutionaries within an unenlightened profession. However enthusiastic and dedicated, the modernists remained a minority, and while they dreamed optimistically of a dawning new age, major commissions often remained in conservative hands.

The most striking aspect of the modern movement was the stylistic unity that emerged during the 1920s. Modern designers repudiated not only traditional modes, but also the ornateness of the Art Nouveau and the plasticity of Expressionism. By the close of the decade, the mainstream of the modern movement reflected what came to be called the International Style. It was characterized by simple geometric forms, smooth, finely finished surfaces, generous use of glass, and an absence of ornament. The term "machine aesthetic" came into use to denote the precise "machined" finishes inherent in the style, and to suggest a relationship between the new architecture and the products of industrialism.

The artistic ferment of the European modern movement initially had little impact in India. India's link to the West lay primarily through Britain, and Britain remained relatively conservative in artistic matters. Britain had no skyscrapers; nor had it ever adopted the more extravagant manifestations of Art Nouveau or Expressionism. As the

International Style evolved during the 1920s, British building reflected little of the stylistic extremism seen on the Continent.

Not surprisingly, British architects in India mirrored the conservatism of their colleagues at home. Classical detailing persisted in Calcutta, where it was adapted to multistorey office buildings and apartment blocks. The only structure in that city that might have been inspired by the Art Nouveau was Esplanade Mansions, built by Martin and Company in 1910. Designed to contain both apartments and offices, it dramatized its corner site with an opulent, undulating facade that would not have been out of place in Barcelona (fig. 146). During the same period, Bombay remained a focus of the Indo-Saracenic mode. In the impassioned controversy arising over the design of New Delhi, the debate concerned European tradition as opposed to Indian tradition. That the associational symbolism of traditional styles might be abandoned altogether had occurred to none of the city's founders. A. G. Shoosmith, a British architect working in New Delhi, observed in 1938 that the "quickening change in direction of architectural aim in Europe . . . undermined New Delhi as a future influence. Bereft now of the support of imported architectural thought for the classical spirit which informed it, . . . it is in danger of appearing as a splendid culmination to the old epoch instead of inaugurating a new."[2]

Although the major buildings of New Delhi reflected an artistic consensus on the legitimacy of historicism, some of the minor structures of the city embodied innovative departures from stylistic orthodoxy. The construction of the new capital attracted a number of British architects to India, including Walter George, H. A. N. Medd, A. G. Shoosmith, and Robert Russell. Shoosmith was responsible for St. Martin's Garrison Church, a brick structure designed in 1928. Lutyens had advised the architect to "get rid of all mimicky Mary-Ann notions of brickwork and go for the Roman wall." The result was a fortresslike geometric mass, its sharp profile and unadorned surfaces creating a powerful imagery almost beyond time. One British critic noted that "had this church been the work of a French or German architect, Europe would have been flabbergasted by the magnificently simple and direct design. But since it is the work of an Englishman, it will probably never be heard of abroad" (fig. 147).[3]

Another architect whose work in Delhi embodied a departure from traditional style was Walter George. St. Thomas's Church, designed in 1929, and intended for Indian sweepers, was modest in scale, but similar to Shoosmith's Garrison church in its use of unadorned brick and simple geometric forms. The careful economy of the structure was such that, in the architect's words, "every brick is doing its duty" (fig. 148). Walter George was to remain in India for the rest of his career. Regarding the predominant classicism of New Delhi's major buildings, he commented, "the Renaissance began in Florence with Brunelleschi's small Pazzi Chapel in the 1420's. It died in Delhi with Lutyens' Viceroy's House in the 1920's, a run of 500 years."[4] In designing for the demanding Indian climate, George believed that it was "folly to turn our backs entirely on the past: we should build on it, and gradually add to it the newer materials and methods."

One of George's most distinguished works in Delhi was St. Stephen's College, designed in 1938. Employing a combination of brick and gray stone, the school displayed a simple horizontal massing, incorporating a series of arcaded walkways and

146. Esplanade Mansions, Calcutta, designed by Martin and Company, and built in 1910.

147. St. Martin's Garrison Church, New Delhi, by A. G. Shoosmith, 1928.

courtyards. In the words of the architect, "nothing has been designed for effect except that the accommodation . . . has been built so as to keep out the rain, the wind and the sun . . . and so as to last indefinitely" (fig. 149). Walter George's work was attuned to the local climate and existing technology, and the exposed brick surfaces of his buildings weathered well. In his view, "the aim of flush surfaces, throughout, both external and internal, should be abandoned. In this climate, every material moves and produces cracks, and provision made for movement usually means some disturbance of surface. . . . Why do all 'modern' buildings begin to look shabby within a year or two, and why do cracks begin to show? It is not all bad workmanship or cheating by the contractor." George's common-sense philosophy and sensitive design thus might have provided an admirable precedent for the creation of a modern Indian architecture.

Twentieth-century India was in many ways far removed from the society which the modernists idealized. The country as a whole remained unindustrialized, with the bulk of the populace inhabiting rural villages. In the major cities, however, there was a counterpart to the Western industrial metropolis and ample opportunity to create the urban building types favored by modern designers. As early as 1906, a visitor to Bombay had observed, "great blocks of flats, and flourishing shops, some of which might have been transported from Bond Street and others brought from the Edgware Road." Increasingly, pressures on land and the high cost of servants induced both the British and Indians to abandon their spacious bungalows and traditional houses for more constricted quarters. Those contemplating residence in India in 1923 were informed that

148. St. Thomas's Church, New Delhi, by Walter George.

cities situated on the coast, such as Calcutta, Bombay, Madras, Karachi and Delhi, the seat of the Government of India, are naturally very cosmopolitan in character, and in them Europeans of different nationalities and Westernized Indians live in common residential districts. . . . The old, roomy, almost palatial bungalows set in a large compound, with spacious, well-proportioned rooms and wide verandas, are rarely to be obtained nowadays. They are being rapidly replaced by flats or small modern houses with very limited garden space. Rents are very high, ranking with those of London and Paris . . . [In compensation, one could count on] European sanitation, with the water-carriage system of conservancy and fixed baths with hot and cold water supply.[5]

Some, reportedly, welcomed the new way of life. An Indian architectural journal noted that "young people, fed on the international outlook day by day, by the newspaper, the cinemas and the radio, with the speed lines of the motor car and the aeroplane as familiar as were once the family bullock cart and the richly caparisoned elephant, bearing aloft its purdahed howdah, are not satisfied with the old traditional family home that took generations to come to its fruition. They require a little home of their own and one that does not require an army of servants to keep tidy; the modern flat-let is the only possible solution, at any rate in the large cities."[6]

To many, however, apartment living remained, at best, a compromise. An Indian woman in Bombay reported in 1936 that, "during the last eleven years of my stay in this city, I have changed a number of flats. I am not very happy about these constant changes but I have done so because I could not find a single flat that would come up

149. *St. Stephen's College, Delhi, by Walter George, 1938.*

to my expectations of comfort or convenience. During my flat hunting I have seen flats and flats. Those which are styled Hindu flats have certain peculiarities. The front room generally extends to the whole length or breadth of the flat. It is more like a durbar hall. The rest of the rooms, bedrooms, etc., are too small in proportion. One can hardly move in them." (This type of apartment plan appears to be an attempt to retain certain elements of the traditional Hindu house containing a central hall, or *mazaghar,* around which subsidiary rooms were grouped.) She also observed that

> very often the bedrooms have small water enclosures called chokadies, which not only mar the beauty of the room but are bad from even the sanitary point of view. Those, therefore, who have some conception of beauty and proportion and also comfort are unable to live in such flats in spite of their being Hindus. The house agent takes them round to see flats built in what he would call the European style. These flats have generally low ceilings where one feels like being in a box and a feeling of suffocation comes over. The drawing-room and the dining room are generally combined, which can suit only those who are actually living in the western style. The sanitary arrangements are good, and yet bath tubs are not particularly desirable. From the point of view of health and cleanliness, the Indian system of bathing in running water is much more commendable. The real drawback to such flats, however, is that hardly any provision is made for the servants' quarters. Those of us, therefore, who are neither Europeans nor are orthodox enough to live anyhow find it extremely difficult to get suitable places to live in or else have to pay very much beyond their means.[7]

Apartment living was also disliked by many of the British. One writer observed

150. Watson's Hotel.

that "the spaciousness of Anglo-Indian life had always been a much-vaunted compensation for the discomforts of the climate . . . [In spite of] the amenities of frigidaires, English baths, built-in radios and electric cooking ranges [one might] wonder whether Anglo-Indian life had not lost much of its distinctive character, and whether these bright little flats with tiled floors and imitation-Heal furniture were not more appropriate to New York or Berlin than to Bombay."[8] To the doctrinaire modernist, of course, a common mode of dwelling was a fact of modern life. Many modern designers made a standardized, presumably universal housing type a major focus of their efforts. The ideal living unit was to have been freed of waste space and outmoded symbolism in favor of compactness and functional efficiency.

The technical device that made the multistorey building feasible in India for both offices and apartments was the electric ceiling fan. The bulky, hand-operated punkah required a lofty space. With the introduction of electric fans in the late 1890s, rooms could be scaled down to European dimensions. As a result, it was noted, ceiling heights in luxury apartments became comparable to those of workers' chawls.

Just as European architectural styles had been imported into India over the years, certain advances in European building technology had also been reflected there. During the nineteenth century, the development of metal framing, together with techniques of prefabrication, had a notable impact on building forms. In the colonies, as in Europe, iron construction was used openly in such utilitarian structures as bridges and train sheds, and in conjunction with traditionally styled masonry in more ornamental buildings. Many of the Gothic Revival and Indo-Saracenic buildings of Bombay, for example, had imported metal framing elements and staircases. One of the most innovative buildings of the 1860s in Bombay was Watson's Hotel (fig. 150). Framed in metal, with a plain surface of brick infilling, it eschewed traditional style for a direct expression of the structure. An 1875 guidebook described the building as "pretentious, but somewhat unsightly," noting that it had been "built, at an enormous cost, of iron and brick, on perhaps the best site in Bombay." It inspired no imitators, and it was noted during the 1920s that "Watson's Hotel was at the time of its erection the most up-to-date building in Bombay, and with its airiness and cleanliness was to have served as a prototype, whereas it now merely marks a new departure which did not lead to anything."[9]

In addition to metal framing, European modernists energetically promoted the use of reinforced concrete for a wide range of building types. Addressing a group of his colleagues, Robert Cable, a British architect working in India in the 1920s, declared concrete to be "a material that defies all the accepted canons of Architecture and which is going to upset all the traditional forms which have grown out of the expression of construction, a material, moreover, the universal use of which . . . will tend to produce throughout the world one more or less universal and international style of Architecture." While the use of concrete in Britain had been mostly limited to utilitarian works, on the Continent it was evident that "a courageous architectural spirit has seized upon the possibilities, artistic as well as practical, of this novel substance and construction, and that results which can only be described as revolutionary have already appeared. Here in India we have as yet scarcely begun to be conscious of this revolution at all."[10]

The audience to which Robert Cable directed his remarks was the Bombay Architectural Association, formed in 1922. Its creation was one of a series of landmarks in the development of the architectural profession in India. By the 1920s, professional training had become available in India, although it was restricted to a single institution, the J. J. School of Art in Bombay. A two-year draughtsman's course had been offered beginning in 1896. This was expanded to four years in 1908, under the direction of George Wittet, then consulting architect to the government of Bombay. The modest intention was "to afford instruction to those students intending to enter architects' and engineers' offices as assistants."[11] In 1913, Cable, then of the Architectural Association School in London, was appointed to develop a full-fledged architecture course, with a teaching staff that included the consulting and assistant architects to the Bombay government, as well as local practicing architects.

Gradually, the curriculum was brought into line with British professional standards, and in 1922 the course was extended to five years. By 1923, passing the qualifying examination for the government diploma in architecture provided exemption from the intermediate examination of the Royal Institute of British Architects (RIBA) in London. By 1929, the curriculum, based on the syllabus laid down by the Board of Architectural Education in London, was raised to the level of the final RIBA examination, and in 1930, for the first time, the RIBA Special and Final Examination was held in Bombay.

The necessity for duplicating British methods and standards remained unquestioned by most architects in India. When a school of Indian architecture was proposed in Calcutta in 1935, Claude Batley of the J. J. School of Art insisted that "there is no doubt whatever that a proper Architectural School is required in Calcutta, but any scheme is doomed to failure which does not ensure that its students, after receiving their training, shall win the confidence of the public and possess that status among the other learned professions, which members of the architectural profession enjoy in other countries. To do this the School must gain the recognition of the Royal Institute of British Architects, as regards its degree, since that body stands for the soundest architectural education and the highest ideals of architectural practice throughout the Empire."[12]

Accompanying the growth of architectural education was the development of a professional organization modeled along British lines. The Royal Institute of British Architects had been founded in Britain in 1834 as a professional society, and, beginning in 1863, it became responsible for examining and qualifying prospective architects. Although it was not a teaching organization, the RIBA controlled the standards of professional training, as well as establishing rules for professional practice. Its Indian counterpart was begun in 1917 as the Architectural Students Association, with a membership composed of former students of the J. J. School. This evolved into the Bombay Architectural Association, which achieved affiliation with the Royal Institute of British Architects in 1925. The RIBA itself was an empire-wide organization that included many Indian architects among its members. The Indian Institute of Architects was formed as an allied society in 1929, with an initial membership of 158. Twenty-five years later, membership had risen to 262.

Although the organization was intended to represent all of India, the architectural profession was largely centered in Bombay. As late as 1942, it was not considered feasible for the governing council to have "representatives from various parts of India assisting in its deliberations, as is the case with the council of the RIBA. Such members, though many, are as yet comparatively few for the needs of the country and are still too scattered throughout the vast expanse of a sub-Continent and further afield, to enable such representation to be a practical reality."[13]

The institute was engaged in promoting the architectural profession in India and with establishing standards of professional practice in such matters as ethics and fee schedules. It sponsored exhibitions, competitions, and lectures, and the pages of its *Journal* provided both a sounding board for opinion and a means of publicizing the work of local designers.

Although the architectural profession in Bombay included a number of British firms, by the 1930s it was no longer dominated by them. Indian architects controlled some of the largest and most successful offices, and some firms had both British and Indian partners. During the period between 1917 and 1942, the Indian Institute of Architects had eleven presidents, of whom five were Indian and six were British.

In spite of their professional progress, architects in India continued to struggle for recognition. Engineers remained dominant in government public works departments, as well as being active in private construction. The general public seemed often unaware of the unique role of the architect. Thus at a time when certain modern architects in Europe idealized the work of the engineer, and exhorted their colleagues to emulate the engineer's rational method, architects in India energetically sought to establish a separate identity. They greeted with dismay certain attempts in engineering schools to supplement courses with architectural classes. The *IIA Journal* insisted that "any attempts to mix up engineering and architectural training require to be firmly discouraged."[14]

The role of Indian tradition in contemporary architecture continued to inspire discussion among designers, and many remained convinced that the styles of the past could be well adapted to modern uses. When Patrick Geddes prepared his studies of towns in the Bombay Presidency, he urged the continuance of traditional architecture. He objected to innovative styles, pointing out that "even if good, they bring a new standard before the town, and this tends to depreciate, in the eye of the public, existing buildings in the older traditional styles." In terms of economics as well as aesthetics, old buildings needed to be protected from, "depreciation by new fashions."[15]

When inaugurated as vice president of the association in 1925, Claude Batley urged architects to make use of traditional craftsmen. He believed that "a sincere attempt at an Indian revival is fully justified now and here; in due course the world-style may carry us along with it, but by studying our old work and by trying to apply what we study to our modern problems we shall, unconsciously, be offering our country's contribution towards that same coming world-style which will be based on the world's needs and signify the growing unity of mankind."[16]

A policy of fostering traditional styles had led the association to direct a memorandum to "various Public Bodies, asking for their cooperation in encouraging the adoption of traditional Indian Architectural treatment as a basis for the design of modern buildings erected under their aegis."[17] In response, the Bombay Improvement Trust had organized a competition for facade designs suitable for its redevelopment projects. The prizewinners were all characterized by the use of pointed arches, overhanging balconies, and tiled pitched roofs.

Among the enthusiastic supporters of the local building tradition was a Calcutta architect, Chandra Chatterjee. Convinced that in art "India is at last coming into its own," he predicted a veritable "Renaissance of Indian architecture." In his view, Indian architecture would not only hold its own against foreign influences, it would itself influence foreign cultures. "People who have been deeply pondering over the problems of life and society, whether in Europe or in America, look forward to India for the solution of the knottiest problems of life which are baffling the best endeavors and the best understanding of the modern world." The Western world had already developed an appreciation of Chinese and Japanese art, and "the turn of India seems at last to be coming." Chatterjee seems to have been received with particular favor in the United States, where he lectured and where an exhibition of his work at the Architectural League was organized by Raymond Hood. A publication of his work in 1935 included testimonials from Henry Saylor, editor of *Architecture,* and architects Claude Bragdon and Harvey Wiley Corbett. Declaring that "India is today threatened by the march of Western civilization," Corbett praised Chatterjee's work for its fusion of rational plans with motifs recalling "the best of Indian art."[18]

By the 1930s, the modern movement that had begun on the Continent was making noticeable inroads in Britain, and it was inevitable that its persuasive ideology would have an impact in India. In some respects, the new architecture might be viewed as yet another foreign fashion imposed on the local scene. To the true believer, however, modernism was not a superficial style, but an embodiment of fundamental and universal principles. It was thus advocated as a rational, functional, culturally neutral mode of design. The visual qualities of the International Style were such, in fact, that when it was introduced in the West, many complained that it was not sufficiently

European. To the eyes of many Westerners, plain white walls and flat roofs had North African associations. Le Corbusier's International Style housing project at Pessac had been derisively dubbed "the Moroccan district," and the 1927 Werkbund exposition at Stuttgart inspired a photomontage in which the houses were juxtaposed with camels and caftan-clad Bedouins. A German critic once denounced the new architecture as "inappropriate to the German climate and customs. . . . It is immediately recognizable as the child of other skies and other blood."[19] Through its elimination of traditional ornament, the new design could be viewed as equally alien, and to some eyes equally appropriate to almost any culture.

Claude Batley, addressing the Indian Institute of Architects in 1934, insisted that "this New Architecture is really but a return to primary essentials." Although he was to remain an admirer of Indian tradition, he was not immune to the new ideology. Indicating some of the errors of the past, he noted that

> it is hard to realise how much that we were taught was architecture in our younger days, and how much that most of our clients think is architecture, even today, is mere dress, purposeless and unfunctional. . . . Look at almost any facade on the West side of Hornby Road, in our own Bombay, and any reasonable man will agree that it would be transformed for the better if one of us took an axe and chopped off every bit of ornament, including the mouldings and pilasters, for none is essential and practically none even significant. [Repeating the modernist dictum that the architect must adapt to a changing world, he invoked] the gramaphone, the cinema, broadcasting and the popular picture paper, cheap transportation resulting in tubes, trams and motor buses, . . . the telephone, the "streamlined" motor and the aeroplane, all these, spreading themselves through every sphere of life, mechanical ploughs, reapers and threshers in agriculture, submarines, tanks and motor tractors in the military sphere, great luxury liners, pullman and sleeping cars, all have familiarised us with new forms and new materials, some of which have a very definite relation to this new architecture. . . . the functionalism of the great grain silos, of the bolder of the reinforced concrete bridges, the economy of space suggested by the luxury cabins, the saloon motor and, even the tube carriage, have necessarily given us architects inspiration. Together with such inspiration the manufacturers have given us new materials, cement and its bye-products like "big-six", synthetic marbles and stones, with plywood and "celotex", aluminum and "staybrite", asphalt and wired glass. It would be far stranger if we had not been relentlessly swept along the stream of progress but had allowed ourselves to comfortably stagnate in the still backwaters of the day-before-yesterday.

To Batley, the new design was no mere style, but possessed "an inward and spiritual grace."[20]

Not all of Batley's audience responded favorably. An Indian architect declared that modern architecture was "only another type set for us over here to copy from abroad . . . full of corrupt mannerisms and entirely unnatural from an Indian point of view." Another condemned its "crudity and ugliness," deploring the loss of "mouldings and ornaments which gave such charm to much of the traditional work." It was also pointed out that in India "the dispensing of weather-shades and fanlights was altogether indefensible." Batley himself conceded that "this new architecture could not be universally applied." The key to modern architecture, he believed, "rested entirely on functionalism, and it would have to be studied in India from that point of view alone, in which case it must, subconsciously at least, take upon itself an Indian character."[21]

Among the supporters of the modern movement in India was an engineer, R. S. Despande, author of a popular series of books on house design published in Poona in the Bombay Presidency beginning in 1931. These books presented a common-sense layman's guide to residential planning and construction, including numerous model house designs. In the early editions of his work, the houses presented for emulation were relatively traditional bungalows with pitched roofs. In 1936–37, Despande took a trip around the world, during which he was completely won over by avant-garde European architecture and the theoretical writings of its architects. From this time onward, the model house designs in his books all reflected the International Style (figs. 151 and 152).

His travels convinced him that "it was not a revolution which was sweeping over the Western countries, but a natural, inevitable evolution." Employing the familiar rhetoric of the modern movement, Despande informed his readers, "the *Esprit Moderne* consists of functionalism and simplicity and devising new methods of construction to suit new materials. . . . To copy productions of historical periods is not to maintain traditions of those periods at all. They were suitable for those times only."[22]

Repeating the argument that architecture must be brought into harmony with modern life, Despande saw no essential difference between India and the industrialized West. "It is only when we enter the garage that we are in contact with reality for a short time. So many changes have taken place, in our food, dress, habits and social customs, so many new discoveries and inventions have been made, such as railways, telegraphs, telephones, television, gramophone, radio, electric appliances, aeroplanes, air conditioning etc. that our entire out-look of life is metamorphosed" (80).

Like other modernists, Despande insisted that the new architecture was "more in keeping with the fundamental principles of true architecture than the conventional architecture which we have long been accustomed to" (81). In Despande's view, "the Modern Architecture seems to transcend not only the limitations of time and space, but even national traditions and bias. It is not the property or patent of any particular body of any one nation, but a universal art offering boundless scope for development" (81).

As to the aesthetic of the International Style, Despande judged it "most suited to our country. In the first place, it is in keeping with our philosophical ideal viz. 'plain living and high thinking'. . . . in a land of sunshine with a contrasting effect of light and shadow, bold, clear-cut features with smooth, sweeping lines present a more effective appearance" (81). Plain surfaces, moreover, would help prevent the deposit of dust.

Despande was an advocate of Western furnishings, insisting that "dining on tables is infinitely better than dining on floors in a squatting position" (92). Like European modernists, he favored built-in cupboards and storage, and he welcomed the introduction of new materials. "The use of bakelite and glass in the furniture is a very great advance, particularly as a covering on tops of tables, teapoys, shelves or window-

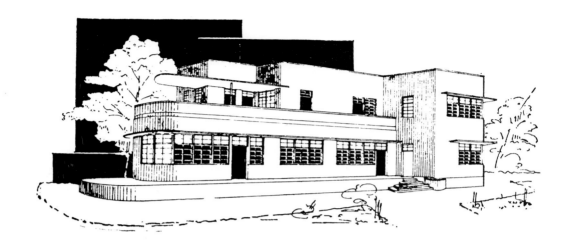

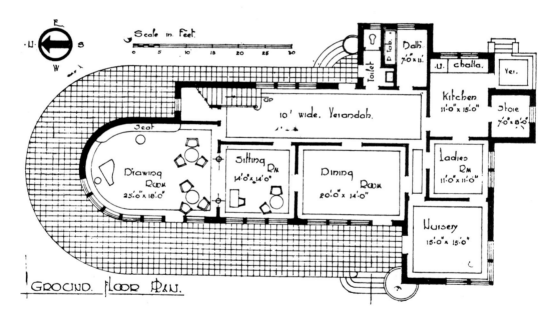

151. Model house design from Modern Ideal Homes for India, *1939. The house plan appears essentially Western, with European furniture, including a grand piano indicated.*

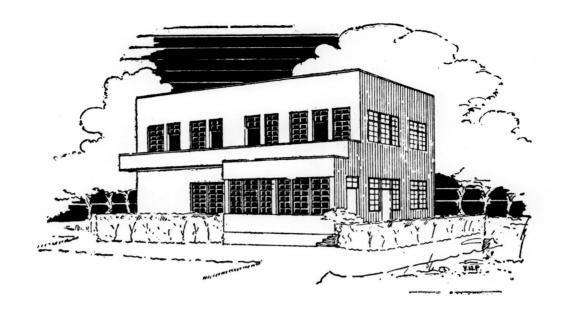

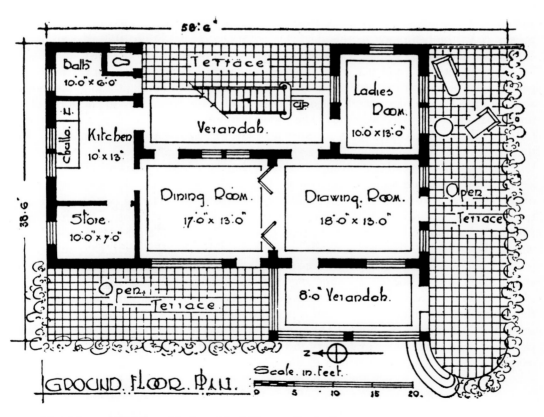

152. *Model house design from* Modern Ideal Homes for India, *1939.*

sills, etc. Similarly furniture with a frame work of pipes of stainless steel, or chromium plated ordinary steel, is also very good. They look elegant, do not rust and are very easy for cleaning and handling because of their light weight" (92–93).

He also promoted redesigning the Indian kitchen, which he deemed

> the very embodiment of drudgery. Firstly, our cooking range rests on the floor, in which position it does not get any draught of air from the bottom. The result is that a lot of smoke is caused. . . . Then, again, cooking is done in a squatting posture in which, if one sits long for hours, pain is caused in the back. For reaching every little thing the lady has to get up every now and then as there is very little storage space as compared with the modern western kitchen, she has to make unnecessary trips to and fro. . . . Cooking in a standing position, on the other hand, simplifies everything. It necessarily requires the chulla range to be installed at a higher level, which allows easy draught of air from below. This arrangement affords a considerable cabinet space below the range, makes the sink very easily accessible and increases the storage space enormously. [55]

Arranging cabinets up to a height of six feet would, he believed, minimize the common risk of a woman's sari catching fire.

Despande informed his readers, "I introduced this system of doing cooking work in a standing position in my own home, and also persuaded several friends to adopt it, and thus am in a position to speak from experience that though ladies offer some resistance in the beginning to this deviation from age-old tradition, still after some experience they come round to find great ease and comfort in it" (55–56).

The modernist emphasis on health and sanitation had particular appeal to Despande. Like many European designers, he was obsessed with sunlight and ventilation, and his model house designs included large areas of glass, frequently in the form of unshaded horizontal window bands. The modern movement had developed in northern Europe, where cool, cloudy skies inspired a desire to increase natural illumination. In the tropics one normally sought protection from the sun. Sunlight was courted in Europe not only on aesthetic grounds, however, but as a health measure. The tuberculosis bacillus had been found to flourish in dark, badly ventilated buildings, and much of the effort at revising standards of building placement and altering patterns of fenestration had been directed at thwarting this major disease. Tuberculosis was also rampant in India, especially in crowded urban districts. Because the *purdah* tradition kept women housebound, they had a much higher mortality rate than men. Despande pointed out that "the high death rate, particularly amongst infants and women, has its origin in the overcrowding of rooms and deficiency of fresh air and light in ill-built, congested houses. Men go out into the open air at least for some part of the day, but the females of the middle classes and especially those in *purdah,* have to confine themselves for 24 hours in the house. The young and innocent infants whose strength and power of resistance are naturally very low, are further devitalized by want of sufficient oxygen, and consequently succumb to diseases" (94). If the women could not go outside, it was essential to get abundant sun and air inside.

Not everyone welcomed expansive fenestration, however, and H. J. Billimoria complained that "the restraint that was so successfully practised in traditional work in creating a restful coolness in a room now generally goes by the board in the following

*153. Tubular metal furniture exhibited at the Ideal Home
Exhibition in Bombay, 1937.*

of the Western craze for glass and still more glass on the external faces of our buildings."[23] On many buildings, a small amount of sunshading was provided by thin projecting cornices reminiscent of the traditional *chujja*.

One aspect of modern design that might have been considered appropriate to
the Indian tradition was the simplification of interior furnishings. Modernist rhetoric
was filled with exhortations against domestic clutter. Traditionally, Indians had employed almost no furniture. It was from Europeans that they had learned to fill their
houses with heavy, carved sideboards, chintz-covered sofas and assorted bric-a-brac.
Now they were instructed to admire the clean lines and pure forms of tubular steel.
The opportunity for a concentrated display of modern furnishings came with the Ideal
Home Exhibition organized by the Indian Institute of Architects in 1937. Model interiors consistently displayed the simplified geometry, lightness, and streamlining of European modernism. In the West, much of the new design had been inspired by hopes of
creating objects suitable for inexpensive mass production. In the Indian context, however, the new simple forms were luxury items with no implications for large-scale
consumption (fig. 153). The occasion of the exhibition, quite naturally, inspired reminders that most of the city's inhabitants had no urgent need to have their taste
improved. In 1931, approximately 80 percent of the population lived in one-room
tenements, with furnishings that were doubtless already simple and functional.

A. G. Shoosmith predicted that, because of its rigorous geometry, modern design
would never really catch on in India. He maintained that, to the Indian, "architecture
means vivid light and shade, with abundance of enrichment, and a style whose appeal
lies in fine line and an alien science, will have scant virtue in his eyes."[24] Modern
design, however, offered more than the austerity of the International Style. From the
mid-1920s, an alternative to the rigor of the Bauhaus had been evident in what came

154. Liberty Cinema, Bombay.

to be called Art Deco or the Moderne. This variant of the modern mode employed a variety of zig-zag and curving streamline forms, together with sumptuous materials and colorful decoration. Although a few relatively pure examples of the International Style were created in India, most modern buildings reflected the exuberant Art Deco. It was employed in office buildings, shops and restaurants, and, perhaps most conspicuously, in motion picture theaters. As film going became increasingly popular, ornately styled cinema houses became notable landmarks (figs. 154 and 155).

Just as the architectural profession was centered in Bombay, the city was also the site for most modern building. In addition to its application to industrial and commercial structures, the new style was enthusiastically adopted by the affluent classes for residential building. On Malabar Hill and along the fashionable seacoast, traditional bungalows began to give way to streamlined mansions and apartment houses (figs. 156 and 157). One of the most extensive concentrations of the new architecture was found in the Back Bay Reclamation project. The construction of this new district coincided with the flowering of the Art Deco, resulting in an architectural ensemble of remarkable stylistic consistency. By 1940, Marine Drive with its adjacent buildings was almost complete, ornamenting the seafront with a row of apartment houses and hotels not unlike similarly colorful confections in Miami beach (figs. 158–61).

The construction of large modern buildings in India generally employed poured-in-place concrete framing with brick infilling panels and surface finishes of painted stucco. The modern movement in the West had presupposed rapid advancements in

155. *Eros Cinema, Bombay.*

156. *Mayfair apartments built in 1937 in the Cumballa Hill district of Bombay. The architects were Merwanji Bana and Company.*

157. Carmichael House apartments built in the Cumballa Hill district of Bombay in 1937, and designed by K. P. Burjo-Behram and H. J. Billimoria.

159. Building on Marine Drive, Bombay.

160. Apartment house in Marine Lines.

161. Apartment houses in Marine Lines.

158. *Hotel on Marine Drive, Bombay.*

162. Surface damage on building on Marine Drive.

163. Surface damage on a building in Calcutta.

building technology. An age of prefabrication and factory production was foreseen, and the new style was perceived as singularly appropriate to, and symbolic of, the industrialization of building. Even in the West, however, technology lagged behind the expectations of many modernists, and in India there was little hope of rapid change in methods or materials. The image of mechanization was often achieved without standardized components, through abundant hand labor. A study of building construction during the 1920s noted, "it is surprising what is accomplished with the crude methods and implements that are used—the bamboo scaffolding, the pulleys worked by manual labour instead of cranes, and the absence of any kind of machinery."[25]

Limitations in local materials were remedied to some extent by the importation of British building products. Included in the pages of the *Indian Institute of Architects Journal* during the 1930s were advertisements for steel scaffolding, standardized metal windows, asbestos cement sheets, cement tiles, masonite, glass tiles, and aluminum sheeting. Among the domestic appliances shown were gas refrigerators, cooking ranges, and hot water heaters, together with electric fans and portable air conditioners. The style of living portrayed in the *Journal* was exclusively Western. Advertisements reflected the latest Art Deco fashions, and the interiors that were illustrated were all furnished in a European style. Bathrooms were shown equipped with British bathtubs and water closets, never with the showers favored by Indians or with Asian toilets. The concerns of the architectural profession seemed entirely keyed to the needs of the industrial metropolis, and to the tastes and preferences of the well-to-do anglicized classes.

In India, although the smooth stucco surfaces preferred by modernists were achievable, building maintenance remained a problem. The monsoon was brutally damaging to building surfaces, and without an annual refinishing, modern facades became conspicuously cracked, chipped, and discolored (figs. 162, 163). Aesthetically, Art Deco was never everyone's cup of tea, and cubical buildings with colored surface decoration were sometimes derisively characterized as the "box and band style." An Indian architect in 1935 deplored the "cleverly forced mannerisms of the decadent *style moderne*," pointing out that "the ubiquitous terrace balustrades with streamed bars, the unprotected, mid-air projections, the garish colour and decoration are more than indicative of the indiscriminate ransacking of catalogue modes. This naval architecture, if it could be so called, for stationary structures, the projections uncovered to the blazing sun and the monsoon downpour, are illustrative of the grotesque and imitated decadence."[26]

The introduction of the modern movement in India coincided with the intensification of the independence movement. Many anticipated a future when India would become free of Western domination and able to assert her own cultural identity. One Indian scholar mused in 1934, "have we ever imagined to ourselves an India, politically and economically free, but artistically and culturally dominated by Europe, slave to the ideals of modern commercialism, dragged at the chariot wheels of the modern machine age?"[27]

A conviction that Indian tradition was antithetical to the tenets of modernism was retained by many architects. A. G. Shoosmith perceived the modern movement not as a universal mode of design but as a local phenomenon arising from purely European circumstances. The revolutionary changes in European architecture had arisen from the social upheavals of the nineteenth century and the trauma of the First World War. India, he believed, had no social basis for modern architecture. "India is a deeply conservative country, and has experienced as yet no social revolution. . . . [The nationalist ideal, moreover,] aims at self-sufficiency and freedom from alien interference, and is therefore in direct opposition to the foreign commercial interests which share with novelty-seeking potentates responsibility for the importation of modern European architecture into India." The modernist contention that a single architectural imagery could provide a means of universal expression he found both unrealistic and aesthetically objectionable. "This internationalism has brought about a lack of change in the architectural scene in which the traveller . . . misses much that gave interest to his wanderings."[28]

The Second World War slowed the pace of construction in India, and as architects anticipated the resumption of peacetime activity, the debate over modernism persisted. Discussing the work of the J. J. School of Architecture in 1940, Claude Batley concluded that while some of the faculty had hoped for "a real Indian Architectural Renaissance, . . . it seems this is not to be for the present since the young Indian architect is bitten by what we know as Modern Architecture, and sees no reason why his country, alone, should revert back to mediaevalism." The following year, an editorial in the *Indian Institute of Architects Journal* pointed out that "in India today Western influences have and are playing an important part in the life of the country," arguing that "an archaeological exhumation of Indian forms and details will lead us nowhere along the path of rational progress."[29]

Surveying Calcutta in 1942, a British architect, Bernard Matthews, predicted that "any development on the lines of Indian architecture is not to be expected. [The city has] no Indian traditional building background, and the modern functional motif has been found to be more suitable to the customs of the inhabitants." While voicing concern for the survival of traditional design, an Indian architect, L. M. Chitale, predicted that there was "every danger" of its "now being merged and absorbed into the present craze for modernism." Old buildings, meanwhile, were fast disappearing, and with them, the memories of the past. In 1939, a Bombay architect, Janardan Shastri,

164. A vision of the Indian future. An advertisement for concrete from the Journal of the Indian Institute of Architects, April 1946, the year before independence.

had produced a study of the remaining vernacular houses in the city. Presenting his work, he expressed regret that nothing could be done "to preserve at least a few specimens of this architectural heritage." His drawings, he hoped, would at least "serve as a record of the glory which is bound to vanish before the onrush of modernisation."[30]

Indian independence in 1947 provided a stimulus to redefine and clarify cultural identity. Within the architectural profession, however, a Western orientation persisted. The Indian Institute of Architects maintained its affiliation with the RIBA, and through its English language journal members kept abreast of the international scene. Educational institutions continued to employ the English language and follow Western models. British architects with established practices in India often chose to stay on, retaining positions of professional leadership. Among these was Walter George, who was elected president of the Indian Institute of Architects in 1950, an appointment deemed noteworthy because, for the first time, an Institute president came from outside Bombay.

Summing up the British achievement in India at the time of independence, one British writer regretfully concluded that, "in one respect, indeed, we have grievously failed. . . . We shall leave behind us no monuments in stone comparable to those which perpetuate the memory of the Moghul dynasty."[31] The judgment was arguable, and, in any event, to most modernists, might have seemed irrelevant. Both the forms and the symbolism of traditional monumentality were judged outmoded and inconsistent with the needs of contemporary society. The British historian, John Summerson, declared in 1941 that "all those things which suggested and supported monumentality are in dissolution. . . . Monumentality in architecture is a form of affirmation; and affirmations are usually made by the few to impress the many."[32] From this viewpoint, the splendor of New Delhi was as dead as Ozymandias, the last great affirmation of the ruling few. Modern architecture, on the other hand, was often seen as the architecture of democracy. In any event, the British architectural legacy represented far more than monuments in stone; it included a continuing receptivity to Western ideas. The metropolis that had been open to the modern movement would continue to be a window toward the outside world. For many Indian architects, national independence would imply, not a turning inward, but expanding opportunities to participate in a world design community characterized by shared ideas and a common aesthetic sensibility (fig. 164).

6.

The Post-Independence City

It is recounted that when some Indian villagers were asked if they thought conditions had become better or worse since the departure of the British, they responded, "who were the British?" The story, of course, reinforces the myth of an eternal India fundamentally unchanged by centuries of British domination. The foreigners had presumably planted their flags, paraded their troops, made their money, and disappeared without causing so much as a ripple of disturbance in the profound depths of the Indian soul. Such a belief might be supported or contradicted depending on one's viewpoint. Certainly much of India's rural culture survived unaltered, and in 1981, 75 percent of India's 700 million people still lived in agricultural villages. Prime Minister Nehru once stated that "the fundamental problem of India is not Delhi or Calcutta or Bombay but the villages of India."[1] National planning policies of the newly independent Indian government strongly emphasized the improvement of the dominant rural sector. Yet the westernized metropolises bequeathed by colonialism could hardly be ignored. By 1979 India had attained an urban population inferior in numbers only to the United States and the Soviet Union.

The place of the city in modern India became subject to extensive discussion as officials sought to define their goals for national development. In the view of one urbanist, "It is high time we realized that the (so-called) western path of industrialization-urbanization-modernization is not the best path for us. . . . The British, when they built New Delhi, for example, were clear about what they wanted—they wanted an Imperial City. They were also clear in their mind when they developed Calcutta, Bombay and Madras—they wanted colonial cities. But what sort of cities do we want in free, democratic, socialist, secular India?"[2]

Independence had been accompanied by partition with Pakistan, and the new municipal administrations were often forced to cope not only with normal problems of urban maintenance and expansion, but also with a sudden inundation of refugees. The euphoria of creating a new nation could not deaden the awareness of monumental problems, and in meeting these problems, India continued to turn toward the West. To most Indian leaders, independence did not imply a return to the past, but an opportunity for India to take her place as a modern progressive nation. Indians did not seek to break ties with the outside world, but to broaden and redirect those ties. Relations with the West had long been governed by India's subordination to Britain. Now India was free to pursue her own goals and serve her own interests.

The end of the Second World War was marked by dramatic political realignments. Yet while colonial empires collapsed, relations between industrialized nations and former colonies retained certain elements of the past. Colonial administrators and technicians departed, only to be replaced by administrators and technicians supported by a variety of foreign aid programs. It is possible, of course, to see in Western foreign aid a new species of imperialism. However generous and well-intended, such programs could be instruments of political and social coercion. Those engaged in assistance activities have often been accused of misguided zeal in the promotion of Western ideas and methods, and of an insensitivity to local conditions. In the case of India, though, many of the new government officials had been part of the colonial administration and had long been oriented toward Western ideas. Indian technicians continued to seek training abroad, usually in Britain or the United States, and there was a resulting harmony in thinking between Indian administrators and their foreign advisers. Far from rejecting westernization, many Indians persisted in equating it with progress, optimistically anticipating an era of technical advancement and industrial prosperity.

One of the areas in which foreign consultants frequently were used was city planning. The post-war era was characterized by unprecedented urbanization throughout the world, and as cities became subject to redevelopment and expansion, the planning profession achieved growing prestige. Planners of the 1950s experienced some of the hubris that affected modern architects of the 1920s. There was a sublime confidence that with sufficient planning power in force, the unruly urban environment could be ordered and perfected.

In India, the socialist orientation of the government made it strongly receptive to the concept of large-scale planning, and its first five-year plan called for a national town and country planning act. Individual states were empowered to enact planning legislation as well as machinery for its implementation. Administrative progress was slow, however, and because of a lack of technical staff, few municipalities were in a position to carry out comprehensive planning programs. In an effort to remedy the shortage of Indian town planners, the government encouraged the establishment of academic programs in this field. As in the training of architects, British models were followed, with the noted planning school of the University of Liverpool providing a strong influence. A Department of Architecture and Town and Country Planning was created by the Bengal Engineering College in 1949, with a similar program, the Department of Architecture and Regional Planning begun in 1955 by the Indian Institute of Technology at Kharagpur. In the same year, the School of Town and Country Planning was established by the government in New Delhi. It was subsequently attached to the University of Delhi as the School of Planning and Architecture. India's first city planning journal, *Urban and Rural Planning Thought,* was published by the school. These programs were modest in scope, and by 1958, only thirty planners had graduated. In succeeding years, courses in city planning were developed at Madras University, the College of Engineering in Poona, and the J. J. School of Architecture in Bombay.

Professional training was accompanied by the creation of professional organizations. The Indian Board of Town Planners, formed in 1949, became the Institute of Town Planners, India, in 1951. Modeled on, and allied with, the Town Planning Institute, London, this organization sought to publicize city planning concepts and foster exchange of ideas through conferences and publications. It also conducted a professional examination recognized as an equivalent to a university degree.

In the years following independence, India's major cities were subjected to numerous studies, surveys, projections, recommendations, and long-range plans. Planning documents, frequently prepared with the help of foreign consultants, reflected attempts to summarize information, analyze problems, and suggest directions for future urban development. The plans served primarily to document what could be readily observed—that India's cities were in an appalling state of crisis. Both the alleviation of immediate problems and the accomplishment of long-range plans seemed to require financial and technical resources as well as administrative efficiency far beyond Indian capabilities. While the paper plans accumulated, the cities of India became legendary as urban disaster areas (fig. 165).

Among the major metropolises, New Delhi was the subject of the most comprehensive planning efforts. As the national capital, it was the visual symbol of a new republic. As a planned city, moreover, it conveyed an implied obligation to continue its ordered development. New Delhi, however, had originally been conceived to house a small, migratory colonial administration. The post-independence city needed to accommodate the pressures of a rapidly expanding bureaucracy, a diplomatic colony, a variety of new institutions, growing commerce, and a population vastly exceeding that envisioned by the British.

Although New Delhi had been systematically designed, the metropolitan area as a whole had received no comprehensive planning. An improvement trust had been created in 1937, but an inquiry committee reported in 1951 that it had failed to produce either a civic survey or a master plan, "with the result that the growth of Delhi has been proceeding in a haphazard way with little foresight and imagination and without any co-ordination."[3] The war years had accelerated the pattern of unplanned growth. A population of 348 thousand in 1931 had risen to 522 thousand by 1941. Industrial and commercial enterprises mushroomed as Delhi became a major center for the distribution of goods to the north and northwest. Government activities also increased rapidly, and new residential areas for government personnel sprang up.

Hasty and disorderly growth also characterized the period immediately following independence in 1947. As the result of partition, a sudden influx of about 500 thousand refugees from West Punjab, Baluchistan, Sind, and the North West Frontier Province arrived in Delhi. Desperately seeking to shelter this unforseen addition to the city's population, the Rehabilitation Ministry began a series of new settlements on agricultural land outside the city. Hordes of new government workers also needed immediate accommodation, and the Ministry of Works, Housing, and Supply undertook the construction of a series of housing estates. In addition, the government created tracts to be sold to private developers. There were, needless to say, many immigrants who were forced to become squatters. Shack colonies sprang up wherever open land was available, often along roads, railway lines, or canals. In spite of various attempts at relocation, by 1971, 350 thousand people were still officially homeless.

For more than a decade after independence, Delhi continued to sprawl in all

165. Calcutta slum-dweller.

directions, producing a series of disjointed settlements with marginal utilities, inadequate roads, and almost no public transportation. The rapid and disorderly spread of the city was in some ways comparable to the suburban expansion of many North American cities during the same period. The American pattern of decentralization was made feasible by extensive road construction, almost universal automobile ownership, and sufficient wealth to provide and maintain extended utility systems. With virtually no resources to sustain it, Delhi adopted the world's most costly form of urban settlement (fig. 166).

A series of tentative planning efforts culminated in the establishment of the Delhi Development Authority (DDA), created by an act of parliament in 1957 and charged with the preparation of a master plan. Collaborating in the creation of the plan was an eight-member team of American city planners supported by the Ford Foundation.[4]

Dominant in Western planning at this time was the concept of decentralization through regional development. It was hoped that through systems such as planned satellites, excessive congestion could be avoided and balanced patterns of residence and employment established. A particular focus of attention among planners in the 1950s was the New Towns program in Britain, where the growth of London was guided by means of a greenbelt surrounded by a series of new urban centers.

The Delhi plan, published in 1962, reflected contemporary planning ideology in its attempt to develop guidelines for growth until the year 1981. The Delhi metropolitan area was defined to include the Union Territory of Delhi, an area of about 800 square miles, together with a group of satellites. The plan explained that "what is visualized is a compact orderly growth of urban Delhi, with six Ring Towns, self-contained in matters of work and residential places, but with strong economic, social and cultural ties with the central city. This is the only way to prevent the increasing urban sprawl which is threatening to grow into one giant urban mass with its long and senseless commuting to work, substandard services and lack of social cohesion."[5] The population of the planned region was anticipated as 6 million by 1981.

While acknowledging that Delhi would continue as the major government center, the plan stressed the desirability of having a balanced economic base, anticipating that Delhi would continue as a major financial, commercial, and distribution center. Large and heavy industries were to be excluded, however. In projecting future development, the city was divided into eight planning districts, each of which would have a distinct character. Each of these districts was projected to have its own principal shopping and employment center, as well as a series of subcenters. The land-use pattern was based on planning areas with populations from 25 thousand to 100 thousand people.

The plan did not seek to halt existing trends of decentralized expansion, but to provide instead an orderly framework for this expansion. Transportation was to be based on an augmented street system employing ring roads and new north-south, east-west arteries. It was hoped, of course, that decentralizing work centers within the city would help reduce commuting distances.

The master plan, like many similar documents, was never realized in detail, but served to provide general guidelines for the activities of the Delhi Development Authority. Its projections had extended only to 1981, and in 1985 the authority presented a scheme to modify and update the plan to the year 2001. Increasing population remained a cause for concern, and by 1985 had reached 5.7 million, assisted by an annual growth rate of 4.69 percent during the decade 1971–81. Not surprisingly, the new plan emphasized policies that would slow the rate of immigration, which was averaging more than 160 thousand per year. It was declared that only such new central government offices as directly served the ministries of the government of India be located in Delhi. Existing public-sector offices within Delhi should be encouraged to move, while new offices should, if feasible, be set up elsewhere.

To encourage balanced regional development, the National Capital Region Plan-

166. *Delhi. A. The Ridge, site of the original British military settlement. B. Civil Lines, the initial British civilian settlement. C. Old Delhi. D. Red Fort. E. Connaught Place. F. Rashtrapati Bhavan, formerly the Viceroy's Palace. G. Diplomatic Enclave. H. Yamuna River.*

167. Construction activity in the southern part of Delhi. The area is characterized by a disjointed proliferation of housing colonies, government offices, institutions, and commercial centers separated by large tracts of undeveloped land.

168. Office building and shops in Nehru Place, a commercial center in south Delhi.

ning Board was created in 1985 to coordinate planning in the Union Territory of Delhi and adjoining states. The Delhi Metropolitan Area, it was estimated, would be able to accommodate about 8 million people in 2001, "by judicious infill and selected modifications of densities."[6] An additional 4 million would need to be absorbed in urban extensions.

Like the 1962 master plan, the 1985 scheme attempted to formulate a land-use pattern by dividing the city into zones, each of which would be given a development scheme planned according to its specific character. Fifteen such zones were delineated within the Union Territory of Delhi. What appeared on paper as a guide for controlled development proved, however, to have little practical effectiveness. There was no real control at the regional level, and within Delhi development was disjointed and chaotic. As with many other government functions, achievement was hampered by an ossified bureaucracy, and the DDA was frequently accused of inefficiency and corruption.

One of the by-products of the 1962 master plan was the proliferation of unauthorized housing colonies. In order to facilitate the implementation of the plan, the government had instituted a freeze on new land development in 1959. Nevertheless, developers would often acquire tracts of agricultural land on the outskirts of the city and, without seeking municipal authorization, sell it as small house lots. Pressure for the legalization of such housing colonies resulted in part from the sluggish develop-

169. Outdoor café in Yashwant Place, a commercial center in south Delhi.

ment of planned housing areas by the DDA. Land sales by the authority, moreover, were held by auction, producing prices far beyond the means of many citizens. So intense was the competition for land, that costs often exceeded those of comparable property in major cities in Europe and North America. However much planners might deplore the unauthorized colonies, they provided housing for many—clerks, teachers and small traders—who otherwise could never have afforded it. By 1985, over 600 unauthorized colonies had been considered for regularization.

Colonial New Delhi was planned by, and essentially for, the automobile-owning class. Post-independence planning continued this pattern, promoting an extended urban fabric of relatively low density based on a system of road transportation. In what one critic called "the world's most energy inefficient city,"[7] most citizens would remain condemned to tedious hours of commuting on a notoriously inadequate bus system. Another inheritance from colonial times was the class division of the city between north and south. In New Delhi, the British rulers had established themselves south of the old Indian city. Within New Delhi itself, there was an overall class separation, with the most prestigious lots south of the great monumental axis and the low- and middle-income groups mostly housed on the north, or "wrong side of Rajpath." After independence, the south continued as a magnet for middle- and upper-class residence, as well as providing sites for prestigious governmental and educational institutions. District commercial centers containing offices, shops, theaters, and luxury hotels also came to characterize the southern edge of the city (figs. 167–69).

The prevailing pattern of post-independence growth gave Delhi a doughnutlike configuration, with the verdant expanses of Lutyens's colonial capital encased by a ring of far more intensely urbanized settlement. In view of the shortage of land in the area, it was natural that consideration be given to increasing the density of New Delhi. Urging a complete reconstruction, Inder Malhotra insisted that "there can be no two opinions that sprawling bungalows, surrounded by acres of lushgreen lawns,

170. The vicinity of Connaught Place.

have long been ripe for the hammer of the demolition squad."[8] The renovation of New Delhi was to remain controversial, however. To some, the city embodied an obsolete imagery and a waste of urban land. To others, it seemed a precious artifact to be preserved (fig. 170).

One district that became the focus of changing attitudes among planners was Old Delhi. In colonial days, British planning reports had emphasized its congested building pattern and high population densities, leading many administrators to consider it essentially a slum. Similar views were retained by many Indian planners after independence. The removal of the wall along the southern edge of Old Delhi and a slum clearance project near Ajmeri Gate, recommended by the British in the 1930s, were accomplished by the Indian government during the 1950s, with the city wall giving way to a new commercial street, Asaf Ali Road (fig. 171). The British had proposed to replace the wall with housing, justifying the demolition as an effort to remedy congestion in the old city. As built, Asaf Ali Road seemed less an attempt to ameliorate conditions in Old Delhi than to hide it behind a drab new wall of modern money-grubbing.

The Draft Master Plan for Delhi published in 1960 referred to Old Delhi as "a planners' nightmare with its multiplicity of conflicting uses and its million problems created by acute congestion, unsanitary conditions, and dilapidated structures."[9] Surveying the 1,135 acres comprising the old city, the plan recommended that 469 acres be conserved, 476 acres be rehabilitated, and that an area of 190 acres, containing a population of 37,108, be entirely demolished. The district proposed to be razed lay just north of Asaf Ali Road between Delhi and Turkman Gates. Like previous planning studies, the Draft Plan acknowledged that the complexities of Old Delhi presented particular difficulties for urban renewal, and that citizen support was essential. The

171. Asaf Ali Road.

potential conflict between officialdom and the inhabitants of Old Delhi was dramatized in 1976, when the government precipitously bulldozed about 6.7 acres of building in a populous district adjacent to Turkman Gate, and forcibly relocated its
inhabitants across the river. The razing of the city wall had inspired criticism; the
demolition of the Turkman Gate area provoked outrage, and the resulting protest
ranged from bloody rioting within the city to high-level political lobbying within the
government. It seemed apparent that no matter how difficult conditions within the old
city might appear to outsiders, many of its inhabitants were deeply attached to their
homes and their way of life. In any event, what were their alternatives?

Increasingly, Old Delhi came to be recognized as a vital embodiment of traditional Indian townscape (figs.172, 173). The 1985 plan designated Old Delhi as requiring special treatment, and while the upgrading of sanitation and utilities was deemed
desirable, no extensive rebuilding was recommended. It was urged, moreover, that "re-
vitalization should be taken up keeping in view the traditional character and style of
the buildings."[10] Meanwhile, having been spared systematic alteration at the hands of
government planners, Old Delhi had been evolving spontaneously. Previously a focus of
varied urban functions, between 1961 and 1981 the old city was subject to rapidly
increasing wholesale and commercial activity. It was proposed, therefore, to shift certain industrial and commercial enterprises outside the city in order to preserve a balanced residential component within its boundaries.

Although the plan was primarily concerned with practical matters, the question
of Delhi's overall visual image was considered. The city's growth had been manifested
in a series of unrelated, widely separated districts, and it was observed that, except for
Old Delhi and the planned area of New Delhi, the Indian capital was an 'amorphous
aggregate of masses and voids.' In recent planning, "neither urban form nor visual
characteristics were given due consideration."[11]

Within Delhi, the DDA was often criticized for its minimal achievements, yet
outsiders often protested the favored position of the capital. A resident of Bombay
judged Delhi to have "more money than town planning and architectural sense; therefore, an example not to be imitated in any form. In point of fact, Delhi is an economic drag on other cities, when one knows how much central revenues are poured

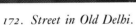
172. Street in Old Delhi.   *173. Street in Old Delhi.*

into its maintenance." In the view of some, post-independence planning supported the colonial image of Delhi as a sheltered enclave for the administrative elite. The city has been condemned as "an anachronism in present-day India, and like all anachronisms it continues to inflict social and moral damage. Anyone who lives in this city for any length of time is bound to lose touch with the reality that is India."[12]

Not everyone begrudged Delhi its privileged status, though, and a former government official, Ashok Mitra, pointed out that "persons with experience of unplanned chaotic and sorry growth in numerous cities ... have during their periodic visits marvelled at the way Delhi has succeeded in holding on to a semblance of order and supervised growth where so many others have failed."[13] His reaction was understandable as his point of comparison was his native city of Calcutta (fig.174).

Assuming that Delhi embodied the best of city planning in a land where—as Kipling informed us—the best is like the worst, with what can the worst be compared? Mitra observed in 1968 that "in the last thirty years, particularly between 1945 and 1965, Calcutta seemed poised on the road to slip, slide, decay and perish, kept going by some strange animal vitality.... A Calcuttan is thus used to squalor and ugliness, reconciled to rapidly disappearing civic amenities, inured to hope ... of any worthwhile urban renewal and reconstruction" (figs.175–77).[14]

Even at the height of its wealth and power, Calcutta had been known for its dramatic juxtaposition of grandeur and squalor. In the years following independence, the grandeur was fast fading, and the whole city appeared to be degenerating into a massive slum. A group of foreign urbanists, invited to Calcutta in 1967, declared, "we

*174. Calcutta. A. Hooghly River. B. Howrah. C. Howrah
Bridge. D. Burra Bazaar. E. B.B.D. Bag (formerly Dal-
housie Square). F. Fort William. G. Chowringhee Road.
H. Maidan. I. Circular Road.*

175. Calcutta. Billboard on the Maidan.

have not seen human degradation on a comparable scale in any other city in the
world. This is a matter of one of the greatest urban concentrations in existence rapidly approaching the point of breakdown in terms of its economy, housing, sanitation,
transport, and the essential humanities of life. If the final breakdown were to take
place it would be a disaster for mankind of a more sinister sort than any disaster of
flood or famine. It would be a confession of failure, at the first major confrontation, of
mankind's ability to organize the vast, rapidly growing urban concentrations into
which humanity seems inevitably destined to move."[15]
   Of all the major Indian cities, Calcutta was the most adversely affected by partition. An estimated 3 million people fled from East Pakistan to West Bengal, with 700
thousand inundating Calcutta. One of the most characteristic features of the city became the sight of homeless people camping out in the streets, and by 1960 their
numbers were estimated at over 300 thousand (figs.178, 179). The division of Bengal
separated Calcutta from its source of jute, destroying an industry that had been one
of its economic mainstays. The reduction of territory, moreover, eliminated a large hinterland that had previously been served by Calcutta commerce.
   Economic activity was increasingly affected by a deterioration in conditions of
navigation on the Hooghly. Silting had been a problem for some time, requiring expensive dredging to maintain the channel. There also was an increase in dangerous

176. *The once elegant intersection of Esplanade Row and Chowringhee.*

177. *Chowringhee signscape.*

178. *Street dwellers in Calcutta.*

179. *Street dwellers.*

180. The Hooghly. Major shipping activity has almost disappeared from Calcutta.

bore tides. By the mid-1960s, the port commissioners calculated that the port would soon be unable to function economically. The increasing size of oceangoing vessels provided an additional reason for abandoning Calcutta as a major port, and alternate docking facilities were begun at Haldia, about forty miles downstream (fig. 180).

Although the river had been a major source of drinking water, by 1959, the salinity had risen well beyond the tolerance limit for human consumption, or even for the needs of local agriculture. At a time when urban services in many parts of the world were improving, the most basic utilities were growing scarce in Calcutta. The per capita supply of filtered water dropped from 59.6 gallons in 1931 to 28 gallons in 1964–65; that of unfiltered water from 44.1 to 30 gallons over the same period. The lack of potable water promoted high disease rates, making Calcutta the "cholera capital" of the world (fig. 181).

The low-lying, swampy site had always had drainage problems, and in the monsoon season streets were repeatedly flooded. With the city's combined drainage and sewerage systems chronically overloaded, pedestrians were often compelled to wade through what was virtually liquid sewage. Surveys taken in the 1960s revealed that only 54 percent of Calcutta city had sewers, and that there were none at all in Howrah across the river, or in any other municipality in the greater Calcutta area.

At the same time, transportation facilities were totally inadequate to serve a modern metropolis. The street pattern still lacked adequate main arteries, and from dawn to dark the poorly maintained roadways were clogged with a seething mixture of automobiles, trucks, handcarts, rickshaws, bicycles, bullock carts, and various beasts of burden, including human draft animals. Lacking adequate sidewalks, pedestrians were forced to share the vehicular roadway. Traffic jams were particularly bad in north Calcutta and in the vicinity of Howrah Bridge, the only river crossing (figs. 182–84).

181. Men bathing at a street pump.

183. Beasts of burden.

182. *Mahatma Gandhi Road, formerly Harrison Road. Calcutta streets carry a bewildering assortment of traffic.*

184. *Chitpore Road. The street continues to carry a double line of trams in addition to a heavy volume of mixed traffic.*

185. Calcutta bus.

186. Calcutta bustee.

Major public transportation was provided by a system of buses and tramways, carrying 802 million passengers annually. Trams designed for a maximum capacity of 80 frequently carried 200 passengers, while buses packed to suffocation were festooned with passengers desperately clinging to bumpers and door frames (fig. 185). An equally overloaded system of commuter railways brought over 200 thousand people into the two main railway stations of Howrah and Sealdah. Like the local transport vehicles, the suburban trains habitually operated over capacity, with trains designed to seat 580 carrying peak loads of over 2,000. In rush hours, the area surrounding the rail terminals was a solid mass of stalled traffic.

Housing conditions in Calcutta seemed beyond remedy. In addition to those with no dwellings at all, there were vast numbers living in conditions of chronic congestion and squalor (fig. 186). According to official estimates in the 1960s, more than three-quarters of the population lived in slums, with two-thirds in *kutcha*, or semi-permanent buildings. More than 57 percent of multimember families lived in single rooms. The housing crisis was not restricted to the poor, and a planning study of the mid-1960s pointed out that "the situation, hopeless as it seems for the low-income groups, may be yet more frustrating for families in the middle-income ranges. They have a consistent income stream, some savings and rising expectations, but often are as unable to secure decent new housing as those at the very bottom of the ladder."[16]

By the beginning of the 1960s, the Calcutta crisis became a matter of more than local concern. Prime Minister Nehru declared that "its problems are national problems . . . and it is necessary that something special should be done. If the whole city went to pieces, it would be a tremendous tragedy."[17] In the same year, the West Bengal government created the Calcutta Metropolitan Planning Organisation and charged it with the preparation of a development plan for Calcutta.

Active in the creation of the new plan were specialists from the World Health Organization and the Ford Foundation, as well as more than fifty Indian officials recruited from all over the country. Calcutta's problems appeared virtually unsolvable, however, and although the development scheme reflected a reasoned effort, Nehru observed that "with all the experts coming from different parts of the world, nobody can really figure out how Calcutta can be saved."[18]

For planning purposes, the Calcutta Metropolitan District was defined to include the municipality of Calcutta together with its adjacent urbanized area along both banks of the Hooghly River. Altogether it comprised an area of 490 square miles and a population estimated in 1966 as 7.5 million. Stressing the symbolic importance of the city, the plan considered Calcutta to be the "true capital not only of its State of West Bengal but of all eastern India."[19]

The development plan was described as a "perspective plan," which attempted to outline possibilities for the succeeding twenty years. The emphasis was to be "less on a hard-and-fast, once-and-for-all 'master plan' " than on "creating the developmental machinery and planning institutions whereby a full control, and positive encouragement of the development process can be exercised." It was hoped to create an environment which would be "socially satisfactory" and capable of serving a population of 12.3 million in the metropolitan district by 1986.[20]

Serious administrative problems were foreseen, however, and it was noted that "a major obstacle to the planned development of essential facilities and utilities in Metropolitan Calcutta is the chronic inadequacy—in technical staff and financial resources—of the numerous municipal governments and governmental agencies in the Metropolitan District." Calcutta could not expect to receive aid "from international agencies such as the World Bank or the World Health Organisation—if it does not give a clear demonstration of its capacity to use its own resources effectively, of its willingness to put its own house in order to achieve the most efficient governmental and administrative arrangements." Administrative reform was urged to counter the confusion of the existing welter of separate, uncoordinated governmental agencies at central, state and local level.[21]

In terms of economic activity, the Calcutta metropolitan district was placed within the framework of a regional development plan promoting a series of major urban centers. It was anticipated that although Calcutta would decline in relative importance in manufacturing and shipping, it would still remain an important center for

187. Sidewalk on College Avenue, Calcutta. In terms of civic maintenance, the motorist is always favored over the pedestrian. Street paving is regularly renewed, while sidewalks deteriorate into rubble-strewn dirt.

engineering, for textiles and chemicals, for trade and commerce, for specialized business services, and for governmental and cultural activities. In any event, the city would not cease to grow. In an effort to take some of the pressure off Calcutta, it was proposed to develop an alternate urban center twenty-five miles to the north at Kalyani-Bansberia.

The most urgent need was simply to arrest the appalling deterioration of the existing urban fabric, to provide "safe and potable water, proper sewerage and drainage, and proper refuse disposal. . . . Massive improvements in housing were needed, "in particular, to provide shelter for the thousands with no shelter at all who now sleep on the streets or in improvised hovels on vacant land, and to improve conditions in the bustees." The plan also called for "clearing metropolitan traffic arteries . . . renewal of the central business areas . . . a reawakening of citizen interest in civic affairs and a revival of hope in the possibility of improving the urban condition."[22]

The twenty years following the publication of the development plan did little to revive hope in the possibility of improving the urban condition. Although various public works were put into effect by the Development Authority, assisted by World Bank financing, the overall decline of the physical environment continued unabated (fig. 187). Political changes, moreover, had no discernible impact on Calcutta's chronic problems. Although in 1977 a Left Front government dominated by the Communists came to control both the local council and state assembly, it was noted that "these shifts did not bring about any change in the inefficient, stagnant functioning of the Corporation. Service facilities for the city, garbage collection, water supply, and street cleaning and lighting, continued to deteriorate."[23]

Accompanying the steady decline in the urban fabric were some ambitious public works. New peripheral roads were built to alleviate pressure in the central street sys-

188. *Subway construction along the Maidan.*

189. *Subway construction workers.*

tem. In addition, a second bridge across the Hooghly was begun. A nineteenth-century pontoon bridge linking central Calcutta with Howrah was replaced in 1943 by a metal suspension bridge that had continued as the only river crossing in the city. The new bridge was projected to link the industrial area at Garden Reach-Kidderpore in the southern part of the city with expanding districts to the west. Although the initial completion date was estimated as 1983, construction has been subject to lengthy delays.

Another project promising a distant completion date is the underground rail system. In 1949, a French consulting team recommended a rapid transit system for Calcutta, and subsequent studies by the Metropolitan Planning Organisation established a projected routing to run about ten miles from Dum Dum in the north to Tollygunge in the southern suburbs. An additional east-west route was also contemplated. Russian consultants were employed in the initial stages of design, and construction began in 1972, with cut-and-cover excavations following the eastern edge of the Maidan and leading southward along major streets. Invoking images of the building of the pyramids, an army of workmen carried the excavated mud in baskets on their heads as they ascended bamboo ladders from the deepening muddy trench (figs. 188, 189). Late

190. Salt Lake City apartments.

191. Salt Lake City office buildings.

in 1984, after twelve years of laborious activity, the inaugural run took place on a two-and-one-half-mile stretch leading southward from the Esplanade to Bhowanipore. A shorter section starting at Dum Dum was also opened. At that time the estimated completion date for the system was 1989–90. Needless to say, many questioned the wisdom of attempting a staggeringly expensive underground system in a city with so many other desperate needs. It might be said to have the same relation to the transportation problem as a five-star hotel to the housing problem. Still, when the necessities are scarce, occasional luxuries assume great importance, and like the hotels, the new rail system may be prized as a symbol of modernity and progress.

The presence of swamps, together with a salt lake directly to the east of Calcutta, promoted expansion north and south, rather than east. Land shortages, however, have led to increased reclamation of this area and the creation of new settlements. Beginning in 1960, silt from the Hooghly was employed as landfill to create a new

192. *Burra Bazaar, Calcutta.*   193. *Burra Bazaar, Calcutta.*

township in the Salt Lake area (figs. 190, 191). Although the Richards plan had suggested this location for workers' colonies, the new Salt Lake City, planned for 250 thousand, was initially designed to provide housing and white-collar employment for the middle classes. Future phases are intended to include industrial establishments and working-class dwellings.

In spite of its social problems and a physical environment that deteriorates steadily, Calcutta retains much of its old fascination. The narrow streets of the bazaar districts are still the scene of frenzied commercial activity in an ambience that seems to have remained basically unchanged for over a century. Although much of the old architecture has crumbled, there are still remnants of once-elegant mansions, all the more poignant for their altered surroundings. And there is, above all, the human pageant. In no other city in the world is the pressure of the crowd so vivid and intense. It seems at times like a living juggernaut, an astonishing manifestation of vitality in a decayed and brutal environment (figs. 192, 193).

It has been suggested that today, just as in colonial times, many of Calcutta's inhabitants are simply indifferent to the physical condition of their city. As always, many of the working-class are single men laboring to support their families in rural villages. Willing to accept the most minimal subsistence during what they consider a temporary stay, they are unlikely to feel great personal concern for civic improvement. Even at the upper economic levels, there is a reputed lack of civic responsibility. Ashok Mitra has indicated that

> the city's big businessmen came from elsewhere with no thought of a stake in the city to start with. Very many of them remained, and still remain, aloof from the affairs of the city, some out of a sense of diffidence, and of not belonging, others from an unwillingness to get more involved than is good for their work. The bulk of them have been content to get the most of what the city has had to offer, but have hardly ever thought of placing themselves as a group at its service.

He contrasted Calcutta in this respect with Bombay (fig. 194), a city which had benefited from a "band of dedicated industrialists, businessmen and entrepreneurs who were large in vision, big in money and unsparing of effort. Bombay was their passion, their destiny, and apart from straining all their surplus energy for the good and prosperity of the city, they gave away their own money in trusts and charities to make Bombay strong, cultured, beautiful. Their skill in managing big industries was reflected in the municipal tax structure; their planning acumen bore fruit in the municipal building laws. Their ideas of growth compelled them periodically to appoint expert committees to plan on a larger and still larger scale."[24]

Expert committees, however, had not prevented Bombay from evolving into a chaotic agglomeration with many of the same problems as Calcutta (fig. 195). As elsewhere, paper plans for directing urban development were often ineffectual in the face of administrative lethargy and overwhelming economic and social forces. Post-independence Bombay did, however, have the advantage of relative prosperity. The city even profited from partition, for when the port of Karachi became part of Pakistan, Bombay acquired a virtual monopoly on west-coast shipping. Although the city continued to expand as a varied industrial and commercial center, the cotton textile industry maintained its primacy, employing 46.93 percent of the workers of Greater Bombay in 1961.

Suggestions that the municipal territory of Bombay be expanded had been made as far back as 1907, and were taken up for consideration several times before independence. The first detailed effort to create a master plan for a new "greater Bombay" was made by the Bombay City and Suburbs Post-War Development Committee created in 1945, under the direction of I. H. Taunton. Comprehensive planning was deemed essential to counteract a process of growth and redevelopment that had "been going on practically unplanned and uncontrolled for the past 60 years."[25] Inspiration was taken from recent planning proposals in Britain, specifically the Barlow, Scott and Uthwatt reports which outlined programs of national planning, decentralization, and public land control. The need for planned expansion was underlined by the rapid increase in Bombay population during the war years. Although the 1941 census had reported 1,660,800 for the city and suburbs, the total had grown to 2,765,634 by 1945.

The development committee envisioned the extension of greater Bombay to incorporate the northern suburbs, creating a balanced dispersal of industry, commerce,

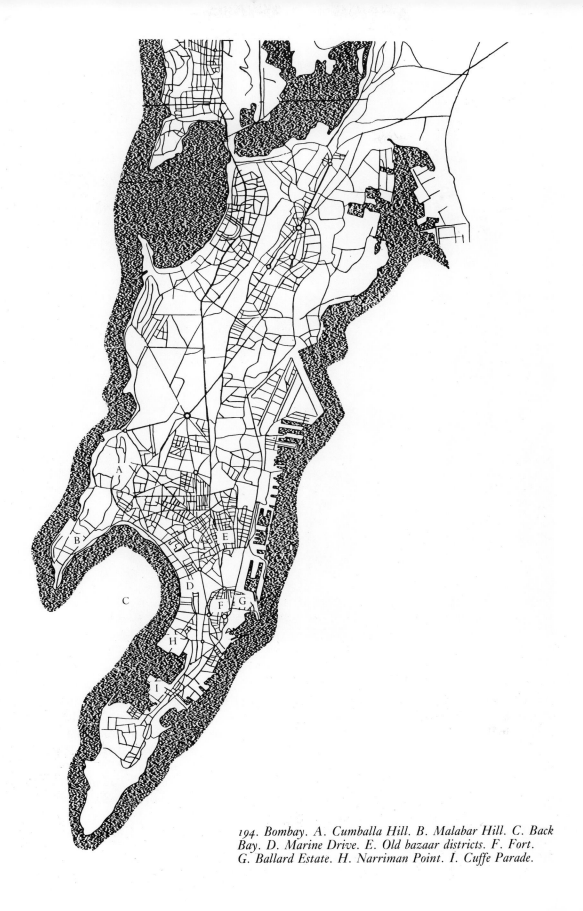

194. Bombay. A. Cumballa Hill. B. Malabar Hill. C. Back Bay. D. Marine Drive. E. Old bazaar districts. F. Fort. G. Ballard Estate. H. Narriman Point. I. Cuffe Parade.

195. Bombay street scene.

and residence. It was also proposed that the territory to the east on the opposite side of the bay be urbanized. This had been urged by Foster King in his presidential address to the Indian Institute of Architects in 1945. As an alternative to continual northward expansion, he speculated, "would it not be wiser to boldly strike out laterally in an eastward direction across the harbor to the inviting mainland?"[26]

The development committee noted, "we are, for the first time in the history of our comparatively young City, trying to look seventy-five to a hundred years ahead.

Our vision will have to be keen and penetrating to visualise that distance."[27] The extent to which the keen and penetrating vision of the panel foresaw the approach of Indian independence is unclear. In any event, the departure of the colonial administration had little effect on planning policies. Although the Greater Bombay Scheme had been directed by Englishmen, it had involved the collaboration of a large number of Indian officials and technicians, many of whom remained in government service following independence.

In 1948, an *Outline of the Master Plan for Greater Bombay* was prepared by N. V. Modak, Special Engineer of the Bombay Municipality who had also been involved in pre-independence schemes, together with the American planner, Albert Mayer. They described their plan as one "which has the benefit of the last 30 years of mistakes and successes in European and American planning. . . . One of the big questions is whether Bombay's citizens will be able to leap over these 30 years, save the time and waste, the trial and error which America and other countries have gone through or whether every country must make its mistakes and learn from them." In any event, immediate action was considered essential. "Bombay is desperately overcrowded, and the overcrowding appears to be constantly worsening . . . Numerous instances can be cited where adequate planning and execution are now impossible except at enormous expense and dislocation of people, where even a few years ago it would have been simple and inexpensive."[28]

Retaining a number of ideas from previous studies, the Modak-Mayer plan suggested that the municipality be expanded to incorporate the northern suburbs. Greater Bombay, as they conceived it, would extend as far north as Bassein [Vasai] Creek, a waterway providing a natural boundary. New north-south express highways were projected through the suburbs as far as Thana and Borivli. The idea of urbanizing the territory across the bay was also included. Two satellite towns were suggested for this area, along with a third town beyond the new northern city boundaries.

The Modak-Mayer plan had been merely advisory and was superseded by the *Development Plan for Greater Bombay,* published in 1964. Territorial boundaries had been periodically expanded northward so that, by 1957, Greater Bombay extended as far north as Dahisar on the Western Railway side and up to Mulund on the Central Railway side, providing a total area of 169 square miles. The population had reached 4,152,056 by 1961, with an increase to 7,062,073 anticipated by 1981. The *Development Plan* also incorporated many of the suggestions from previous plans, providing an overall summary of current conditions, together with a generalized series of recommendations for future development. It was hoped that by 1985 "Greater Bombay [would be] a better place to live in than it is today."[29]

As might be expected the plan deplored the heavy concentration of activity at the southern tip of Bombay, favoring a balanced distribution of commerce, industry and housing throughout Greater Bombay. Large-scale industry was to be discouraged in order to assist development in other parts of the state. Noting the uneven population densities, often rising to 1,400 per acre, the plan suggested a goal of 250 to 600 per acre in the central city, and from 150 to 250 in the suburbs. Although increases in parks and open spaces were considered desirable, it was stressed that "obviously the Western standards of open spaces cannot be adopted."[30]

Tramways and bus transportation had been taken over by the municipality in

1947, with the tramways phased out beginning in 1954. The system provided excellent coverage of the entire area of Greater Bombay, carrying an average of 1,809,000 passengers per day during 1962–63. Loading was heavy, however, owing to a chronic shortage of buses and the constant need for extensions into newly developed areas. The most popular and effective means of mass transportation were the suburban railways. Greater Bombay was served by the Central and Western railways, which led respectively to Victoria Terminus and Churchgate Station. Counts made at gates of Victoria Terminus between seven and eleven A. M. recorded 330,000 incoming passengers, with similar tallies at Churchgate amounting to 165,000. As in Calcutta, service was far below the need, with carriages jammed to overflowing and some commuters hanging from doors and windows. Increasing decentralization of employment, as well as technical improvements and additional track would, it was hoped, alleviate conditions somewhat. Recommendations for improved street circulation included the creation of expressways together with the widening of existing streets.

Housing conditions were found to have deteriorated sharply since the beginning of the Second World War. Construction during the 1920s and 1930s had been such that, "by the beginning of World War II in 1939, more dwelling units for the middle class at least were available in the City than were tenants." During the war, however, building activity slowed, while population grew, and an influx of post-independence refugees exacerbated the acute overcrowding. The Rent Restriction Act froze rents at pre-war levels, and landlords found it difficult, in a climate of rising costs, to maintain buildings in satisfactory condition. Housing construction became a relatively unattractive investment except for luxury units, which could be sold. The housing shortage affecting the middle classes was naturally far more acute among the poor. A pre-war survey had reported Bombay to have 85 slums spread over 330 acres. By 1956–57, the number of slums had risen to 144, with a total acreage of 877 and a population of 415,875. Although the elimination of such areas was deemed desirable, it was admitted that the "clearance of slums is frought with difficulties" (figs. 196, 197).[31]

In projecting the northward expansion of Bombay, the development plan reflected prevailing demographic trends. Southern Bombay, though retaining its old prestige, was simply becoming saturated. A northward movement of commerce and industry along the rail lines was happening spontaneously, with strip development along motor roads, and rapid expansion of the suburbs. By and large, the hopes that Bombay would be a "better place to live" in 1985 than in 1964 were far from realized. The basic problems of the city remained essentially unchanged and even exacerbated by the increasing population. Utilities and transportation systems continued to be strained to the limit. The housing crisis persisted, with delapidated chawls remaining the basic housing form for many, and squatters and pavement dwellers still much in evidence. The 1976 census had reported 2.85 million people, one-third of the population of Greater Bombay, to be living in slums, and it was estimated that by 1981 this would have risen to 45 percent, or 3.75 million. As elsewhere, urban improvement continued to be a matter of isolated, piecemeal efforts, hampered by political and economic circumstances, and accompanied by corruption and inefficiency.

An inheritance from the pre-independence epoch was the great reclamation project of the Back Bay. Filling operations had begun during the 1920s, with the tidal flats divided into eight segments. At the time work was halted in 1930, blocks one

196. Bombay slum district.

197. Shanties built along railroad tracks.

and two to the north had been reclaimed, together with blocks seven and eight at the southernmost tip of Bombay. The southern landfill had been given over to military use, while the northern blocks became a district of apartment houses called Marine Lines.

In 1958, a government study group recommended that reclamation of the remaining 550 acres of the Back Bay project be resumed in order to create additional

198. Cuffe Parade landfill seen from Narriman Point.

land close to the commercial and administrative center. By 1975, about 200 additional acres of the Back Bay had been reclaimed, comprising block three to the north, which was named Narriman Point, and part of block five adjacent to Cuffe Parade to the south. Narriman Point was largely given over to prestigious office blocks, while the Cuffe Parade segment was dominated by luxury apartment towers set in dense formation (fig. 198).

As the new Back Bay area began to take form, it was subject to increasing criticism both inside and outside the government. At a time when planned decentralization was gaining favor, it seemed contradictory to encourage additional commercial activity in an already constricted area. The office complex at Narriman Point notably increased the burden of commuters on an overloaded suburban rail system and put an additional strain on scarce urban utilities. The conspicuous complex of high-priced apartments at Cuffe Parade did little to alleviate Bombay's housing problems. It was disclosed, moreover, that plots had been leased to developers on singularly advantageous terms, providing windfall profits at the expense of the taxpayers. Between Narriman Point and Cuffe Parade the shoreline had for many years been occupied by a colony of fishermen. What was to become of them when the land was reclaimed? The image of the laboring poor being threatened by the encroaching bastions of wealth and privilege reinforced the conviction that the Back Bay reclamation was an extravagance drawing

199. Looking from Colaba toward Narriman Point with fishermen in the foreground.

heavily on public funds, but contributing little of public benefit. Following proposals to revise and truncate the plan, it was decided, in the mid-1980s, to stabilize the shoreline without further extension (fig. 199).

By this time, Bombay's planners were convinced that extensive new construction should take place not adjacent to the historic core of Bombay, but across the bay in what had come to be called New Bombay. This project, first proposed in the 1940s, seemed increasingly feasible as metropolitan Bombay continued to expand. In 1967, in accordance with state directives, a metropolitan regional planning board was set up in Bombay, its proposals subsequently published as a *Plan for the Bombay Metropolitan Region 1970–1991*. Regional boundaries were expanded as far north as the Tansa River, and included extensive territory on the eastern mainland. The regional population in 1981 was 11,091,792, with 9,860,163 in urban areas and 1,231,629 in rural districts. Bordering the western side of the bay was a fifty-five-thousand-acre tract projected as the site of a "new metro center."

The development of New Bombay was placed under the direction of the City and Industrial Development Corporation (CIDCO), and a draft development plan for the settlement was given state approval in 1979. The plan envisioned a series of urban centers linked by a railway and motor routes. Each population center was projected at between 100,000 and 150,000, with twenty such nodes ultimately envisioned. The site

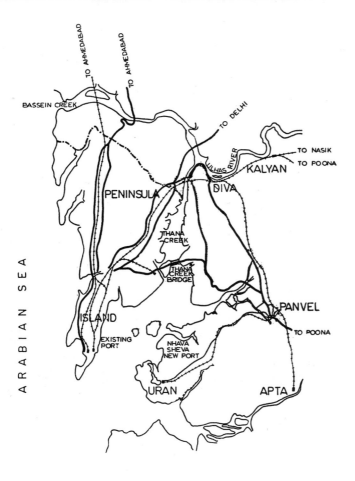

200. The Bombay region. In the years following independence, city boundaries had been repeatedly extended northward, reaching Bassein Creek in 1965. New Bombay embodies an attempt to deflect the pattern of urbanization eastward across the bay.

of New Bombay incorporated some districts to the north that were already beginning to industrialize, as well as the site of a new port projected by the Bombay Port Trust at Nhava Sheva to the south. Access to New Bombay was to be facilitated by rail and motor bridges constructed over Thana Creek, a northern inlet of the bay. An additional bridge connection leading across the bay from the southern districts of the city was also considered a possibility (figs. 200–202).

As in many Indian projects, realization was slow and uncoordinated. Although a motor bridge was created across Thana Creek, there was no railroad link, and industrial establishments that might have located in New Bombay continued to adhere to the existing rail lines leading northward instead. It was suggested that the state government might take the lead by moving its headquarters there, but few high-level administrators were tempted to leave the comforts and distractions of Bombay to pioneer a new city.

201. *Looking westward toward Bombay from Vashi in New Bombay.*

202. *Belapur in New Bombay.*

By 1985, economic activity in New Bombay was primarily supported by the shifting of wholesale storage and marketing from the city of Bombay. The center of Vashi became the site of the produce market, together with cold storage and food processing facilities. With a population of 85,000 in 1985, Vashi had begun to acquire some of the attributes of a normal town. Meanwhile, a projected central business district, together with a government office complex, was begun at Belapur. Other centers of development included Kalamboli, intended as the site of the wholesale iron and steel market. In 1985, it was estimated that by 1989–90 New Bombay might have a population of 500,000.

Of the four major Indian metropolises, the city that has appeared most resistant to the forces of rapid transformation has been Madras. On the occasion of the Madras Tercentenary Celebration in 1939, one official recorded that "the scenes around the city's temples, tanks and squares are still the same as those witnessed in distant days, the crowds which chatter in the Kotwal and Triplicane Bazaars are little different from their predecessors in earlier years, and the Madras fisherman still goes out in his frail craft . . . exactly as his forefathers did many centuries ago." Quoting the statement in 1981, S. Muthiah happily observed that "it is still true today, nearly four decades later. May the charms of airiness, courtesy and tradition never fade in this gracious city" (figs. 203, 204).[32]

By that time, the Madras metropolitan area, as the fourth largest city in India, had attained a population of 3,660,000 in the city itself, 4,510,000 in the Madras

203. *Madras street.*   204. *Mount Road, the major commercial street of Madras.*

urban agglomeration, and 4,960,000 in the metropolitan area (fig. 205).[33] But while population continued to grow following independence, economic activity failed to keep pace. A survey of the port in 1960, for example, showed no increase in cargo activity over the preceding two decades, as well as indicating a decrease in the number of vessels using the harbor. Madras had few large industries, except for textile mills, and although it was an important administrative and educational center, the commercial base was relatively static. Migration to the city might be attributed less to the lure of employment than to the prevailing poverty of the surrounding areas. A comparison of income levels in India's major cities in the early 1960s showed per capita annual income in Greater Bombay to be 1,180 rupees, that of Delhi to be 872, and that of the Calcutta metropolitan district to be 811. In the Madras metropolitan area, per capita income was only 437 rupees, with many employed in domestic service and casual labor.

205. *Madras. A. Georgetown. B. Harbor. C. Poonamallee Road. D. Fort St. George. E. Cooum River. F. Mount Road. G. Marina. H. Adyar River.*

The image of Madras as an overgrown village persisted. The buildings in the city remained essentially low-rise, and a survey taken in 1960 indicated that 56.2 percent of Madras dwellings still consisted of traditional houses with courtyards. At this time, 30 percent of the land of the city was lying vacant and undeveloped. Although the general sense of openness, the relatively clean air, and abundance of trees gave Madras an agreeable ambience, there was ample evidence of poverty. Sixty-nine percent of households shared their dwellings with co-tenants, and nearly 65 percent of all dwellings consisted of only one room plus a kitchen. Overcrowding was frequent, and nearly one-third of all houses were judged to need replacement or renovation. At least one-quarter of the population lived in slums, most of which were huts on low-lying ground subject to flooding (fig. 206).

Population densities varied widely throughout the city, ranging from as little as 10 per gross acre to over 600 in parts of Georgetown. The old native quarter retained its lively mixture of residence and commerce (fig. 207), comprising a population of 300,000 in 1960. Physically, it was in a state of deterioration, and judged to need both redevelopment and a reduction in population.[34]

Like other major cities, Madras became the subject of various planning studies. As in other Indian cities, planning proposals drew heavily on foreign ideas, employed foreign consultants, and were often developed in the hope of attracting foreign financial support. An interim development plan had been created in 1967 by the state directorate of town planning. In 1969, "it was decided to explore avenues for securing financial assistance for the development of the city from institutions both national and inter-national and it was then found that the plans prepared earlier were inadequate, in that the problems of the metropolis had not been viewed from a long range perspective."[35] To remedy this, the *Madras Metropolitan Plan, 1971–1991* was created by the Tamil Nadu government under the coordination of Thiru S. Parthasarathy. Included was a projected physical framework for the development of the metropolitan region. In presenting possible patterns of expansion, Western examples were employed. London, it was shown, had attempted to control expansion through the creation of new towns beyond a greenbelt. Paris had developed a new town pattern comprising two strips of east-west development north and south of the old city. Washington, D.C., and Copenhagen had been planned in configurations of radial corridors.

For Madras, the radial corridor scheme was proposed, projecting a series of urban nodes and satellite towns. It was anticipated that "the nodes would be connected with rapid transit rail systems and expressways to the city on the one hand and to the Satellite towns on the other. The nodes amongst themselves would similarly be connected by both rail and road systems to facilitate intra-urban-movement."[36] According to estimates, the city's population would be 3 million and that of the new urban centers 2.1 million by 1991.

The plan seems in many ways a fantasy totally unrelated to existing conditions. It implied that money would be available for extended road construction, expanded utility lines, new railway development, and for the maintenance of a system of public transportation sufficient to serve a far-flung metropolis. In general, Madras was not densely settled, and a more feasible provision for expanding population would have included a more efficient use of land within the city. While projecting large-scale development for the end of the century, the plan acknowledged the city's current inabil-

206. Madras slum.

207. Georgetown.

ity to cope with the most urgent problems of housing, water supply, drainage, and sewerage. As in Calcutta, water supplies were falling, and the per capita supply of filtered water in 1961 was half that of 1931.

As the city deteriorated, planning activity continued. In 1972, the Madras Metropolitan Development Authority was created and empowered to create a master plan. In addition, the organization became, in 1977, the coordinating agency for a World Bank urban project that was to include slum improvement, water supply and sewerage, and roads and traffic. Deciding that the existing master plan needed to be reviewed, the Metropolitan Development Authority engaged a consulting team, Alan Turner and Associates, appointed by the British Overseas Development Administration. It was hoped that the result would be a development program for five years and a general program for the next ten years. The consultants, however, found themselves unable to create "a conventional master plan related to a specific point in the future and containing a finite and quantifiable number of projects." They described their work as, "a framework for growth within which many separate but coordinated activities will take place."[37]

The general urban situation of Madras was disclosed to be much the same as indicated in other studies. It was noted, however, that previous estimates of population growth had been too modest. Population appeared likely to reach 7.31 million by 1991, 2 million more than suggested in previous forecasts. New growth, moreover, was concentrated in the city and its periphery rather than in the radial corridors anticipated by the 1971 plan. Although it was believed that the development of the corridors was a laudable objective, it was judged to depend on a high and unlikely degree of coordination among government bodies in the provision of utilities, employment, housing, and transportation. For the moment, the location of new development was more likely to depend on the existing road network than the ambitious system of rapid transportation previously outlined.

Slums were judged to be increasing at the rate of about 5,500 households a year, with nearly 200,000 households already existing in unimproved slums, and 360,000 families in unsatisfactory conditions in older areas of the city. As part of an effort to provide housing at the lower end of the economic scale, Madras became the focus of a series of site-and-service housing projects sponsored by the World Bank. Begun in 1977, this program attempted to create affordable housing for the poor by making improved land plots available and permitting occupants to build their own houses. Although generally successful, the program could assist only a small proportion of those in need of dwelling. A housing deficit of 200,000 units was predicted by the close of the century (figs. 208, 209). Like similar documents, the *Structure Plan* attempted to suggest plausible directions of urban development, yet it also underlined the ineffectualness of conventional planning recommendations in the Indian situation.

Conditions in the post-independence metropolis have become such that the colonial period is occasionally viewed with a certain nostalgia. It is not uncommon for residents of Calcutta to recall the British Raj as the time when the streets were washed every night. One critic, Patwant Singh, demanded in 1969, "why is it that when others have achieved dazzling successes in science and technology, we are unable to keep even our telephone, power and water supplies running at minimal levels of

208. *Site and services housing. The sites provided plumbing units, together with one-storey party walls and roofs.*

209. *Site and services housing with additions by occupants.*

efficiency? . . . These were areas which were functioning adequately and satisfactorily before we became independent." As to the visual qualities of Indian cities, he commented, "Let's face it. As a people, we are insensitive to our physical environment. People who did not belong here and ruled over us during the last few centuries were far more sensitive. Look at their vision. They built and planned more lovingly, more rationally than we are doing today." The Englishman, he maintained, "had a feeling for environment, whether in India or elsewhere. We don't. We abuse it instead."[38]

Many of the flaws of Indian cities, though, are attributed to a misguided emulation of Western models. Charles Correa once pointed out that "our cities are based on the private automobile, because they still copy the cities of the West. It's sheer lunacy. Obviously an Asian city built in this century should . . . base itself on mass transportation."[39] Mass transportation, however, might also be considered an expensive Western import, and no Indian city seems able at present to maintain such a system adequately. It might be better to envision a city without mass commuting.

Among Westerners as well there have been repeated doubts, not only as to the applicability of Western models, but as to the usefulness of Western expertise. A conference at Oxford Polytechnic in 1979 reported a "new humility" among city planners. The experts of the 1950s and 1960s "now see that they have been meddling dangerously in the affairs of developing countries, often in complete ignorance of deeprooted culture considerations."[40]

Inevitably, many Indians have begun to question the large city as a feasible form of settlement in India. One writer observed that, "in the absence of any structural change in the urban situation, the only futuristic projections one encounters are the doomsday projections of exploding population or worsening environment, rising unemployment, increasing housing shortages, growing bankruptcy and collapse of urban infrastructure, in short, increasing *per capita misery*."[41]

It has sometimes been suggested that most Indians are not natural urbanites, that they have been thrust into urban living by necessity rather than inclination. There is an Indian saying: "after ruin go to the city." While it implies that the city offers opportunity for survival, it also indicates that without compulsion one would never go there to live. The modern metropolis is a demanding environment at best, and the technology that can make it manageable, together with the comforts that can make it palatable, do not exist in India except for the well-to-do. The Indian metropolis does not treat its inhabitants well. They, in turn, do not treat the city well.

A city does not exist, of course, on a purely physical level, and the defects of Indian cities do not preclude social, intellectual, and cultural life. The relation between the built environment and fundamental human well-being can never really be measured. Yet, unless one is a total mystic, the material world is hard to disregard. While the teeming crowds of the Indian metropolis display an astonishing vitality and resilience, there is also a sense of human resources strained to the limit.

The period of rapid urban expansion following the Second World War produced abundant study and theory directed at understanding and managing urban form. Even in societies with ample resources, the big city presents an amalgam of social and physical problems for which no clear remedy has appeared. While alternative patterns of settlement have been envisioned, and efforts to control urban expansion attempted, the sprawling accretion of metropolitan centers has been universal, and universally de-

210. Calcutta street scene.

plored. Even in the West, decentralization has continued to attract a diverse band of supporters. In India, the customary arguments against massive agglomerations can be bolstered by the circumstance that such centers have, from inception, been foreign outposts planted on Indian soil, without roots in Indian culture. No one can say just what pattern of development would have prevailed without colonialism, but given the present situation, what alternatives are possible? Discussing trends of urbanization, an Indian writer insisted that "we cannot fully erase the past settlement pattern but the hangover of colonial urban development cannot last forever."[42]

Nothing, of course, lasts forever, and one can presume that all cities come to dust in the end. Yet, in the meantime, the troubling metropolis remains. It has been estimated that by the year 2000 half the world will live in cities, with Indian centers projected among the largest. Delhi's population at that time is anticipated at 13.3 million, with Bombay at 16 million and Calcutta 16.6 million (fig. 210). In India, as elsewhere, there seems no way back to Arcadia.

7.

The Architecture of Independence

In celebration of its one-hundred-fiftieth anniversary in 1984, the Royal Institute of British Architects awarded its prestigious gold medal to an Indian, Charles Correa. Praising Correa's work, the *RIBA Journal* noted that he had "avoided the insensitive imposition of inappropriate western forms of building in a country where radically different cultural, economic and climatic circumstances and conditions prevail, preferring to seek inspiration from local traditions."[1] In its reflection of the fashionable pieties of post-modernism, the statement was not likely to astound. Among architects, in 1984, local culture was decidedly IN, at least in terms of lip service. Yet rather than reflecting a new appreciation of tradition, the award was primarily indicative of the emergence of Indian designers into the international architectural scene. While some of Correa's designs might be seen as local in inspiration and uniquely appropriate to India, much of his work is well within the modernist mainstream. Like many of his Indian colleagues, Correa studied abroad, and after training at the University of Michigan and the Massachusetts Institute of Technology, he worked for Minoru Yamasaki in Detroit. Having established his practice in India, he continued to travel extensively, securing himself a place in the community of world-class architects suffering from chronic jet-lag.

At the time of independence, many architects in India continued to support the concept of an essentially universal modern architecture. The rhetoric of modernism stressed not style but a presumably rational approach to design unhampered by historical or cultural restraints. Some, however, saw modern architecture as symbolic of the colonial past. Architecture could play an important role in providing the new republic with unifying symbols, and it was inevitable that some would demand a specifically Indian imagery. In 1947, the architect V. R. Talvalkar proclaimed, "now that we are free, it will be the duty of our National Indian Government and our patriotic public workers, as well as our clients, to see that our national and other public buildings be designed hereafter only in indigenous style." Foreign architectural styles could be viewed as both symbolically inappropriate and functionally unsuited to Indian conditions. The editor of an Indian architectural journal complained that Indian architects "are invariably and obsessively influenced by the architectural trends of the west. . . . In

India, no acceptable or logical justification is possible for imitation of western building forms, since neither the technology nor affluence exist to justify them, nor obviously can there be an acceptable philosophical base for such techniques and forms here."[2]

Presumably a mode of design could be created that would be recognizably Indian as well as appropriate to the needs of contemporary life. The same quest, in colonial days, had produced the Indo-Saracenic style, in which contemporary buildings were clothed in traditional decorative motifs. Indo-Saracenic architecture had often been derided for its superficiality, and to those familiar with twentieth-century modernist doctrine, its perpetuation seemed absurd in the context of the contemporary city. A critic in Delhi reported that "we saw modern office blocks capped with domes because that was supposed to make them look Indian." Pointing out that the dome had no symbolic association with office buildings, he complained that "it focuses our minds on the old and the quaint, and inhibits us from identifying ourselves with the science and technology of today." In contrast, he cited the Japanese, who "have met the challenge of the 20th century most realistically, by not allowing themselves to be deflected from their avowed national purpose through a sentimental attachment to the past. . . . Their urban architecture is modern to the hilt—what else can it be?"[3]

Those opposed to traditional motifs tended to be architects and critics; those who liked them were often high-ranking government officials. In Delhi, in 1955, a large government-sponsored hotel, the Ashoka, reportedly in response to bureaucratic pressure, was redesigned to provide a surface of Indianized decoration (fig. 211). While some deplored the "political decision to clothe it with its present bizarre trappings," visiting tourists may have responded to the decor in the same spirit that they enjoyed the elephant rides provided through the grounds. In Delhi, the plain cubical mass of a government conference hall, the Vigyan Bhawan, was entered through a green marble Buddhist arch (fig. 212), described as symbolizing "the Indian heritage of peace and culture."[4] The arch motif became an easily recognized and frequently employed symbol of Indian identity, applicable to a wide variety of structures (fig. 213). This historical tokenism, though derided by critics, might, from the present-day viewpoint, be judged a manifestation of premature post-modernism.

Just as many modern buildings in India have been embellished with historicizing decoration, some structures maintain the elements of traditional composition, while displaying a modernized pattern of ornament. In Delhi, the Lakshmi-Narayana temple recalls the forms of ancient Gupta temples, but the garish decoration conspicuously fails to emulate the quality of the past. Although the temple is highly popular, S. K. Saraswati described it as "an instance of over-enthusiastic revival without reason and understanding" (fig. 214).[5]

Some architects concluded that the search for a national design should focus not on the revival of traditional styles but on the employment of traditional patterns of building placement. The courtyard house, with its sheltered interior, was advocated as far more suitable for India than the free-standing bungalow. Vernacular townscape, with its pedestrian scale, spatial enclosure, and short vistas came to be studied and admired. The architect Ranjit Sabikhi reported that "for many of us who started work in and around Delhi in the early sixties the traditional architecture of the Indo-Gangetic Valley has held considerable fascination. . . . The traditional cities of North India have a closely built organic structure with a clearly defined hierarchy of open spaces.

211. *Ashoka Hotel in Delhi, by J. K. Choudhury and Gulzar Singh, 1955.*

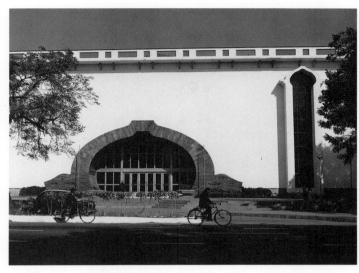

212. Vigyan Bhavan conference center designed by R. L. Ghalot, 1955.

213. Taj Mahal Hotel in Bombay, and new addition.

214. Lakshmi-Naryan temple, Delhi. It was built by the industrialist Raja Baldeo Birla, and it is sometimes popularly known as the Birla temple.

They are dense and compact constructions designed to effectively counteract the intense heat to which they are exposed for the major part of the year."[6] The Mogul capital of Fatehpur Sikri and the city of Jaiselmer in Rajasthan were frequently cited as sources of inspiration.

For those Indians still oriented toward the West, there was now a bewildering variety of form from which to choose. Pre-war modernism had been dominated by a clearly defined body of theory and a general consistency of style. Although the period following the Second World War coincided with a victory for the modern movement, the old ideological unity had dissolved, and the stylistic range was characterized by a remarkable freedom of expression. Noting that "there is greater diversity in design today than there has been for many years, perhaps than ever before," an American architectural journal in 1961 termed the prevailing movement, " 'Chaoticism'—the acceptance and practice of the principles of chaos." The architect Minoru Yamasaki spoke of "the explosion of architectural ideas, which indiscriminately gush forth to fill the streets of our cities. . . . producing almost every conceivable shape and form." Declaring that "the only principle that I can conceive of believing in is the Principle of Uncertainty," Philip Johnson observed that "the very best known of my own generation do one building one day and the very opposite the next. We seem, even more so than in that much-maligned 19th Century, to be making a new architecture every day."[7] The formal aspects of contemporary Western building ranged from a stringent geometry derived from the International Style, through a variety of sculpturally expressive shapes, reflecting not only the machine aesthetic of smooth, finely finished surfaces, but also the massiveness of rough concrete and exposed brick.

An attention-getting addition to post-independence Delhi was the American Embassy of 1958 (fig. 215). Official handouts described the building as both "ultra-modern" and attuned to Indian tradition: "Edward Durrell Stone . . . has used the pierced walls of South Indian temples, the elevated platform of Mughal tombs and mosques and the rectangular interior courtyard found throughout India to produce a blending of American and Indian styles." Reflecting a form of modernized classicism, the exterior was marked by slender gold leaf columns and ornamental cast concrete screens. The building was favorably received in the Indian press, and the *Statesman*'s account of the dedication declared that "before the morning was old, it was obvious that America's contribution to Delhi's architecture was a big success." The architectural critic Patwant Singh noted, however, that, "not infrequently, a 'big success' is confused with a successful something." The templelike imagery provoked a sense of "visiting a shrine," and Singh believed that something "less of an eclectic, unapproachable monument . . . would have been more appropriate to the time and place." The landscaped interior courtyard, covered with aluminum mesh, failed to provide a cool shelter for the interior, acting rather as "a pocket for hot air which has nowhere to go."[8]

Many Indian architects favored the geometric form of the International Style combined with the decorative flair of the Art Deco. Screens and sunbreakers were widely used, becoming a fashion as much ornamental as functional (fig. 216). Characterizing Indian design in 1961, an architectural journal noted

> we find flatness, continuous window-glazing, either horizontal or vertical, a few cantilevered balconies pushed here and there with horizontal grills, sand-pebble stones and random-rubble stones, brick work plastered. . . . Those who cannot afford to use imported materials imitate by using materials such as brick-plaster surfaces painted to represent marble. For factory and office buildings, out of proportion glazed windows are provided, creating the problem of glare. In some cases, glass is used from the plinth level to the roof. Often, facades are treated with a series of sun-breakers, vertically or horizontally. Doubts arise as to their efficiency.[9]

The post-independence architectural achievement had proved disappointing to many, and in the same year the editors of the *Journal of the Indian Institute of Architects* complained that the magazine consisted largely of a potpourri of inadequate articles and filler material. This was "not the fault of the *Journal,*" they insisted, but the result of there being "so little new work that is good enough to document."[10]

The most celebrated architectural project to follow Indian independence was the creation of Chandigarh, the new capital of Punjab begun in 1950. Although the pro-

215. *U.S. Embassy by Edward Durell Stone, 1958.*

ject, which was strongly supported by Prime Minister Nehru, was intended to symbolize the newly independent nation, it had been designed by foreigners. The monumental government buildings were created by the French architect Le Corbusier, a leader of the European modern movement since the 1920s. Although he had been one of the formulators of the International Style, his post-war work was characterized by massive sculptural forms in exposed concrete. This mode of design, sometimes called brutalism, created a dramatic alternative to the smooth geometry of the machine aesthetic and was highly influential, especially in Britain and Japan. The major monuments of Chandigarh were concrete, but most of the buildings throughout the city were constructed in exposed brick, the most abundant local building material. In addition to his work in Chandigarh, Le Corbusier received commissions in Ahmedebad, a city which also became the site of a major project by the American architect Louis Kahn.

Although the designs of Le Corbusier and Kahn were sometimes controversial, their work embodied a vocabulary of powerful architectural images that seemed in many ways timeless and universal. Their use of materials, moreover, gave their work a certain suitability to India. In a land where building maintenance was often lacking, and where surfaces were subject to strong weathering, brick and concrete seemed feasible alternatives to the smooth, plastered surfaces of the International Style and Art Deco. Attempting to develop buildings appropriate to tropical conditions, both Kahn and Le Corbusier had experimented with sun shading devices such as inset balconies and fixed sunbreakers.

The impact of Le Corbusier and Kahn was particularly felt in Delhi among a group of young architects who were beginning their careers in the 1960s. In some instances, the inspiration was rather specific, as in the Akbar Hotel by Shivnath Prasad. This building, which formed part of a new commercial center built in south Delhi in the 1970s, echoed many of the qualities of the Chandigarh secretariat in its use of concrete and in its sculptural surface pattern (fig. 217).

The expanded formal range of modernism suggested a new compatibility with Indian tradition. Modern buildings could now incorporate thick walls, rough surfaces, and restricted fenestration. In the creation of planned housing complexes, moreover, designers often found opportunities to infuse modern architecture with evocations of

216. Delhi building with screen.

217. Akbar Hotel by Shivnath Prasad, in the Yashwant commercial center in south Delhi.

218. Shared space in the Yamuna housing complex by Ranjit Sabikhi, 1973–81. A strong sculptural element is provided by the projecting stairways.

traditional townscape. In 1963, for example, an ensemble of YMCA staff housing in Delhi by the Design Group partnership attracted favorable attention through its use of exposed brick, internal courtyards, and narrow pedestrian lanes. A more sizable grouping by the same firm was the Yamuna apartment complex built in Delhi between 1973 and 1981 (fig. 218). This project, created for a housing cooperative of south Indians, consisted of a series of four-storey blocks surrounding a central square from which pedestrian streets radiated. According to Ranjit Sabiki, a Design Group partner, "the winding traditional street with its community activity along it was recalled."[11] In contrast to the YMCA housing of exposed brick, the Yamuna housing employed a surface facing of gray stone aggregate. It had become apparent that, although concrete and brick were relatively resistant surfaces, both suffered continual deterioration in the Indian climate. The use of stone surface aggregates became popular with a number of architects who were seeking a durable finish. Similar in concept was the Tara housing complex designed by Charles Correa. This ensemble, built in Delhi between 1975 and 1978 for a housing cooperative for members of parliament, consisted of maisonette units focusing on a central court. Constructed of concrete and exposed brick, it depended for its aesthetic impact on the sculptural massing of simple cubical forms (fig. 219).

A variation on the theme of vernacular building occurred in the Asian Games

219. *Tara housing by Charles Correa, 1975–78.*

Village, which was constructed on a thirty-five-acre site in Delhi in 1981–82. This complex, consisting of two hundred houses and five hundred apartments, was intended to be sold to private buyers once it had served the purpose of housing visiting athletes. The designer, Raj Rewal, attempted to create spatial variety by planning terrace houses and apartment units around a series of squares connected by pedestrian lanes. He likened the individual groupings to the traditional *mohallas* or wards, in Indian towns. Another attempt to enclose shared spaces within a courtyard formation appeared in multistorey housing designed by Rewal for the National Institute of Immunology in Delhi. Both ensembles employed surface finishes of stone aggregate (figs. 220, 221).

In the ideological climate of Western post-modernism, the high-density Delhi housing complexes drew high praise, and foreign critics eagerly accepted at face value the architects' claims that such building appropriately accorded with both tradition and contemporary living patterns. The author of a British history of modern architecture considered the pink and brown bands of the Institute of Immunology housing to recall the "polychrome marble stripes of Mogul architecture," and the tan surface of the Asian Games housing to evoke "the honey-coloured stone of old desert towns."[12] The beauty of traditional building, however, is heavily dependent on its decoration, and surface detailing may be as important as patterns of building placement in creating an effective evocation of the past.

220. *Asian Games housing by Raj Rewal, 1981–82.*

221. *Housing for the National Institute of Immunology by Raj Rewal, 1985.*

The shared spaces and the implied social intimacy of the tradition-inspired housing complexes do not necessarily reflect the lives of the inhabitants. The Yamuna housing was commissioned by a group of people from Tamil Nadu who already formed a cohesive community, sharing a local language and set of customs. The backers of the Tara complex came from diverse backgrounds, having in common only their connection with parliament. The occupants of the Institute of Immunology housing have no link other than their common employer. The Asian Games housing was built by the government with no particular group of occupants in mind, but with the assumption that it would be sufficiently attractive to be readily salable. In spite of Delhi's chronic housing shortage, the Asian Games units proved difficult to market, although it remains unclear whether the problem lay with the nature of the architecture or with the high prices.

Interestingly, the compact housing complexes dramatize a contradictory vision of planners and certain architects in Delhi. Both before and after independence, planners promoted the development of a sprawling, automobile-based, low-density metropolis. Within this unfocused ambient, the new housing enclaves create a counter-image, as though small bits of Old Delhi had been broken off and scattered about in the southern reaches of the city. Unlike Old Delhi, however, the new complexes are purely residential and their inhabitants, like their neighbors in more conventional housing, are dependent on motor transport for access to employment, shopping, recreation, and other urban facilities. Published pictures of the housing generally emphasize the interior pedestrian spaces, but not the surrounding parking lots and access roads.

It is difficult to create effective townscape except at the scale of a town. A project large enough to have afforded scope for a truly urban concept was Jawaharlal Nehru University, planned for the southern edge of the city. This sizable complex might have been advantageously conceived on the lines of a traditional town, incorporating continuous frontages, spatial enclosures and sheltered pedestrian circulation. The university might be considered a social entity with sufficient unity to be appropriately expressed in a visually coherent environment. It was, however, developed on the model of an American campus, with an amorphous spread-out assortment of unrelated buildings.

The praise given to the achievements of high-art designers is balanced by the scorn with which conventional housing colonies are regarded by critics. In such areas, usually based on a grid plan, free-standing dwellings face the street on separate, but crowded plots. The house types might be regarded as a legacy of British taste, with the "Indian" aspect apparent primarily in the decoration. According to the varied whims of their owners, exteriors are embellished with colored plaster and stone veneers, ornamental arches and metal filigree.

There is clearly more than one way to evoke tradition. Modern Indian architects have been taught to emulate the "fundamental" attributes of traditional form and avoid the "superficial" trappings of style. Middle-class householders, however, often seem quite content with a modern bungalow ornamented in local style (fig. 222). With ceiling fans and airconditioning, the rooftop terrace (such as that provided in the Asian Games housing) is no longer essential as a sleeping area, and with the decline of the purdah tradition, the courtyard has lost much of its old function. Observing that "an American brought up in completely different conditions does not find it difficult to

222. Dewdrops. An Indianized bungalow in the Salt Lake district of Calcutta.

live in a house designed for an orthodox Indian family in any of the suburbs of new Delhi," an Indian architectural journal concluded in 1962 that, "a uniform pattern of living is unconsciously forging itself out the world over."[13]

One of the notable aspects of post-independence India was a shift in the creative center of modern architecture from Bombay to Delhi. The capital became an important center for architectural training and the headquarters for many innovative practitioners. While the commercial builders of Bombay seemed primarily interested in the greatest profit per square foot, both government and private clients in Delhi appeared willing to support unconventional designs. Among some of the more novel experiments in Delhi was the National Co-operative Development Corporation headquarters by Kuldip Singh, an office building employing a vertical core connected by footbridges to sloping office blocks (fig. 223). In the diplomatic enclave, an area once described as "whimsey on a grand scale," one of the most imaginative ensembles was created for the Belgians as their embassy by a sculptor, Satish Gujeral. Using exposed brick, he created a chancery that evoked an expressionist image and an ambassador's residence that conveyed the romance of a habitable ruin (figs. 224, 225).

A conspicuous feature of the post-independence era was the introduction of the skyscraper into India. Largely restricted to the United States before the Second World War, the high-rise building began to proliferate throughout the world in post-war years. Although the skyscraper can be thought of as a necessary evil resulting from intense urbanization and high land values, it had long held a glamorous attraction for modern architects. For its early proponents, the skyscraper seemed the inevitable frui-

223. The National Cooperative Development Corporation by Kuldip Singh.

tion of modern technology, and destined to characterize the modern city. The seductive symbolism of the high-rise building was to have particular appeal in the Third World, where, in spite of their costliness, technical problems, and cultural inappropriateness, such structures would often be prized as visible evidence of progress.

Although accepted by some as inevitable, tall buildings became a matter of continuing controversy in Delhi, where many felt that the low-rise character of the city should be preserved. At the same time, increasing shortage of land inspired a variety of proposals to augment densities. In 1951, the Delhi Improvement Trust Enquiry Committee suggested the introduction of multistorey buildings on certain major streets and along the central government axis. Gordon Cullen, a British architect who served as a consultant while the 1962 plan was in preparation, had also suggested the introduction of high-rise buildings in some areas, including the government complex.

Responding to those who feared a transformation of New Delhi's government center, a letter published in the *Statesman* in 1962 noted that "influential opinion is wedded to maintaining its monumental character. Good luck to those of this opinion, but they are opposed by the forces of democracy, the concept of architectural monumentality having changed with time. The Central Vista as a showpiece can now be considered to have performed its function; monumental pomp is not a feature of democracy, even in architecture."[14] Presumably, there was no reason why vast soaring blocks should not be constructed along the central axis to accommodate government offices.

224. Belgian Embassy chancery by Satish Gujeral, 1980–83.

225. Ambassador's residence, Belgian Embassy.

Gradually, high-rise buildings began to appear in the old bungalow districts, often in the form of luxury hotels, and also near Connaught Place, primarily in the form of office blocks. In response to concern about the changing face of New Delhi, the Urban Arts Commission was set up by parliament in 1973 and given powers of approval over structures of "public importance." Its members proved either unwilling or unable, however, to halt the spread of high-rise building.

The 1962 plan had included a system for controlling the height of buildings by creating a floor-area ratio in which height was related to plot size, with ratios varying according to the zone of the city. Among the sites considered logical for tall buildings were the new commercial centers in the urban periphery. Not surprisingly, the most generous height allowances were projected for the business district adjacent to Connaught Place. In fact, many thought that this entire complex, with its modestly scaled classical buildings, was ripe for demolition. One writer declared, "if we do not dismantle Connaught Circus, it will represent that we have not progressed."[15]

Planning policies, however, advocated retaining Connaught Place intact, even though adjacent areas might be subject to high-rise renovation. Included in various proposals for the district was a scheme produced by Raj Rewal and Kuldip Singh in 1968 for the controlled redevelopment of Barakhamba and Curzon roads. They suggested that tower blocks be set back from the street alignment, to be partially screened by a raised pedestrian plaza and an irregular line of relatively low buildings. A similar proposal was made in 1969 for Janpath, another broad artery leading into Connaught Place. This street was to continue as a shopping area, with low-rise buildings bordering the street and tall buildings set within the blocks. In practice, however, the district had no unified plan, becoming instead the focus of spontaneous high-rise development. In 1971, Patwant Singh predicted that "once the fifty or so projected skyscrapers which are abuilding around Connaught Place and along Parliament Street are completed, this area will be a living nightmare" (fig. 226).[16]

Within a few years, the skyline viewed from Connaught Place was broken by towers. The old unity of style, moreover, was supplanted by flamboyantly competing forms. Contributing to the dramatic new profile of the commercial center was the Life Insurance Corporation of India building by Charles Correa, together with the State Trading Corporation building and the new town hall by Raj Rewal and Kuldip Singh. The town hall became particularly controversial because its tapering concrete bulk loomed conspicuously over the historic structures of an eighteenth-century observatory, Jantar Mantar (figs. 227–29).

In India, the most logical site for skyscrapers was Bombay with its constricted site and expanding economy. Under pre-independence building bylaws, heights were restricted to seventy feet in the city and three storeys in the suburbs. Following independence, building height had no specific limits, but was based on a floor space index, which related height to ground coverage and permitted buildings of twenty to thirty storeys. As population and land values rose, fashionable areas such as Malabar Hill and Cumballa came to be dominated by high-rise apartments. The prevailing gap between rich and poor in Bombay became noticeably dramatized through the image of shack colonies huddling in the shadow of towering luxury blocks (figs. 230–31).

A conspicuously augmented scale of building appeared in the new Back Bay reclamation area. This district, previously criticized for the close placement of its Art

226. *High-rise buildings near Connaught Place.*

227. *State Trading Corporation building by Raj Rewal and Kuldip Singh, shown under construction in 1986.*

228. Life Insurance Corporation of India building by Charles Correa, shown under construction in 1986. This building faces directly toward Connaught Place.

Deco apartment houses, became the focus of a far greater concentration of buildings in the high-rise office complex at Narriman Point (figs. 232–33). The architectural idiom of this burgeoning commercial center—rectilinear slabs of concrete framing and glass infill—had become commonplace throughout the world. Although the quality of design varied somewhat from building to building, all were similar in their disregard for climate, with large areas of unprotected windows necessitating a costly burden of air-conditioning.

To many, the glass-walled skyscraper would always remain an extravagant symbol of rampant commercialism. An Indian architectural journal once queried

> Do our social priorities and economic resources permit us to allow a handful of developers, in a nation of 700 million, to make fortunes and use up colossal energy resources for these skyscrapers (airconditioning, elevators, waterpumps and generators) when millions of urban dwellers live in dark and dingy hovels, and ten times their number in our rural areas do not have electricity with which to run their tubewells? Are we prepared for the sake of these few developers and the new corporate sector elites to allow India's oil import bills to keep mounting, or its other energy resources channelised towards these inappropriate, expensive, and impractical status symbols? If at present we are unable to supply even our single and double storied buildings with water and electricity, how will we supply 30 storied buildings and more with these facilities? . . . [Moreover,

229. Delhi Town Hall, viewed from Jantar Mantar.

230. *The Cumballa Hill district of Bombay.*

231. *High-rise and low-rise housing in Bombay.*

232. Narriman Point.

building services are often out of order. How would the occupants of such struc-
tures] survive in summer temperatures of 110° and more during periods of
power failures? How will they reach the top floors during power blackouts when
the elevators do not work? [Could such buildings provide] all that is required for
eventualities like firefighting and emergency evacuation?[17]

The validity of the last question became clear in 1986, when a high-rise, luxury
hotel in Delhi, the Siddarth Continental, caught fire. Alarm systems failed, and many
occupants were trapped. Attempting to fight the blaze, the city brought in over sixty
pieces of firefighting equipment, only to discover that most of it was inoperable. Following the fire, it was disclosed that the government had permitted a number of hotels to disregard safety regulations to enable them to open in time for the Asian

233. Commercial building on Narriman Point. The building with the glass facade is the Indian Express Building, designed in 1967–70 by Joseph Stein, an American architect with a practice based in Delhi.

Games of 1982. Although it had been understood that the breach of code would be remedied eventually, it was doubted that any of the hotels had complied.

In addition to attracting opposition to its architecture, Narriman Point was also criticized for its lack of comprehensive site planning. The street system was rudimentary, and there was no effort to develop greenery or open space within the complex. Provision for pedestrian circulation was minimal, and the highly functional arcade characterizing the old business quarter was not even considered. No attempt was made to orient buildings with regard to sun or view, or to group them for either functional or aesthetic effect. Design standards were even lower at the nearby Cuffe Parade site, where apartment towers were jammed side by side on minimal plots. Although the apartments were among the most costly in Bombay, their builders saw no necessity to waste money on landscaping, high-quality construction, fine materials or niceties of design. Cuffe Parade might be judged an expensive slum, with a monotony similar to that of the most squalid public housing projects (figs. 234–36).

As it was described in one architectural journal, "The concrete jungle called the Backbay Reclamation scheme is like a pigeon hole without free air, a new hell for the nouveau riche to stew in their own juices. . . . Individual architectural endeavours, in most cases, are no more than moronic metaphors of simulated occidental design, each making a fitful attempt at doing something architectural, but eventually succumbing to motives of commercial greed."[18]

Because of their relatively slow pace in redevelopment, neither Calcutta nor Madras was subject to extensive high-rise development. In Calcutta, however, a few office towers began to break the skyline around the Maidan and Dalhousie Square,

Above and opposite
234. Apartment towers in Cuffe Parade.

235.
236.

237. Buildings facing the Maidan on Chowringhee Road, Calcutta.

renamed BBD Bag after independence, provoking protests against those who would "attempt to meet the problem of space by destroying old beautiful buildings and replacing them with ugly rectangular high-rises" (fig. 237).[19]

The years following independence reflected a gradual recognition of the architectural profession in India, as well as a noticeable expansion in professional training. In 1947, India had only two schools of architecture, and, to serve a population of 330 million, a total of 200 qualified architects, half of whom were in Bombay. By 1971, the number of architecture schools had risen to fifteen, and there were 5 thousand architects among a total population of 550 million. This provided one architect for every 110 thousand people, as compared to one for every 6 thousand in the United States, and one for every 3 thousand in the United Kingdom. In 1985, with a population of 750 million, India had fewer than 10 thousand registered architects.

After almost thirty years of discussion, the government created a system of national registration for architects through the formation of the Council of Architects in 1972. It was hoped thereby to provide recognition for the profession, and to prevent unqualified persons from representing themselves as architects. The council also served to establish minimum standards for architectural education.

In spite of improvements in numbers and status, architects continued to feel themselves handicapped as professionals. In 1967, the president of the Indian Institute of Architects declared that "the architectural profession in India today is facing a crisis of survival. The biggest obstacle to the profession is indifference to architecture, good or bad, both from the Government of India as well as the public. The architect is hardly accorded the same recognition as other specialists with an equally high education." Deploring the continuing dominance of engineers in public works departments, the president insisted that "architects in the Public Works and other government departments must be made completely independent of the government engineers, and be given full professional responsibility for design, construction and the supervision of projects under their control."[20]

A frequently voiced concern among architects was the absence of any enforceable scale of fees. Architects continued to undercut one another, and government agencies customarily required private architects to submit their fees to bid. Having achieved such a commission, the architect would presumably then supplement his fee through graft from the contractor. Work was frequently awarded on the basis of favoritism, and it was noted that "on grounds of caste loyalties, empires by way of practices have been built."[21]

Building construction was also complicated through confused systems of subcontracting and generally poor supervision. Materials were frequently unreliable and workmanship faulty. Although buildings might appear superficially "modern," they were often built by primitive and time-consuming methods. Discussing some of the problems of building in India, M. B. Achwal, an architect, observed in 1971 that "the simplest mechanical aids are unknown. Bricks are carried to the fifth floor by women workers in a basket on their heads. Human labour is cheap and a donkey or bullock is still the most economical mode of transport. . . . Material manufacturing, stock and supply [are] always uncertain. Time is of no importance since there is plenty of it. . . . There are no unified trade guilds or workers' unions." Once completed, buildings were often subject to rapid deterioration. In one architectural journal it was observed that "in few other countries are buildings—old or new—as badly maintained as in India. The dazzling speed with which new buildings are messed up is a performance in itself."[22]

In many ways, the Indian architect's lot was not a happy one, and as in other occupational fields, India was subject to a continual "brain drain." An editorial in *Design* commiserated with "young Indians who went abroad and returned to their country, with a fiery sense of purpose . . . only to leave, one by one, dispirited, disillusioned, discouraged. . . . The climate is without doubt hostile even to the normal working of the designer's profession, leave alone any great creative endeavor." In 1971, it was reported that 40 percent of the five hundred architects trained annually left the country, and by 1975 there were nearly three thousand Indian architects abroad as compared with five thousand in India. Of these, four hundred were in the Middle

East, seven hundred in Britain, and fifteen hundred in the United States. Meanwhile, those who remained in India, after studying abroad, were often reproached for their predilection for foreign ideas. It was pointed out that "architects educated abroad usually fail to integrate upon return and continue to maintain clichés and attitudes adopted abroad which are foreign to local conditions, life, climate and materials." Results might be better if students were to "study more of our climatic conditions, building materials and techniques, before they are sent to foreign countries."[23]

In addition to dissatisfaction with conditions of practice, there was also a certain unease regarding the social role of the architect. It has been in the nature of the architect's work that it frequently serves the moneyed and the powerful, and this has not been unique to India. The isolation of the architect within the urban elite, however, has been particularly dramatic in India. In a 1979 issue of *Design* it was observed that, "if the social role of any profession in this country is minimal in its impact on society, it is the architectural. . . . The architectural profession of this country is as divorced from the Indian reality as its 5-star hotels are from the stinking slums which abound within a few hundred yards of them."[24]

In India, as elsewhere, the work of high-art architects represents only a small volume of construction. Far more important in determining the nature of the city is the quality of ordinary building. An architectural journal pointed out in 1961 that "we worry about forming an Indian architecture. This is crazy. Without realizing it, we are building it right now. The architecture of the new housing colonies . . . will symbolize—at least as far as history is concerned—'Indian architecture in the mid-portion of the 20th century.'"[25]

In India, also as elsewhere, much of the environment was seen to be dependent on the general level of popular taste and the whims of speculative builders. In the case of Delhi, however, the most extensive body of construction was attributable to the Delhi Development Authority, which, with its control over the entire urban area, has been described as the world's largest real estate developer (figs. 238, 239). Although occasional DDA projects embodied distinctive design, much of its building attracted opprobrium in terms of both aesthetics and quality of construction. One critic noted that "every suburb in New Delhi looks like the other, the difference being, if any, that areas developed by Government agencies are meaner than those developed by housing societies." Observing an ensemble of middle-class housing, another writer declared that, "in private practice, with these results one would have to close down, but Civil Service gives a protection." Dwellings were characterized by "cheap colours, cheaper architectural motives—jallies and poor detailing that does not stand one monsoon. . . . The purchaser having received a house from a Government Agency presupposes it having been well constructed. When in point of fact, he finds it a jerry built structure held together with the formula of cheapness."[26]

In some instances, structural defects in DDA buildings were sufficient to cause complete collapse, leading to revelations of wide-spread negligence and corruption in the organization. Inquiries disclosed several instances in which cement was diluted and bad lime used together with inferior sand. It was noted that "the pilferage of DDA materials is so routine now, as is the case with the Municipal Corporation and the Central Public Works Department, they have acquired a brand image for themselves in the black market."[27]

238. Occasionally, the DDA engages outside architects to design housing. This ensemble was designed by Raj Rewal.

239. A middle-class DDA housing project in south Delhi.

Mechanical site planning and monotonous building characterize government projects in all the major cities, creating a dilapidated parody of the geometric formulas once promoted by European modernists. Like the skyscrapers, such ensembles appear to be yet another disastrous application of foreign concepts. According to the architect Ranjit Sabikhi, "this legacy of the draughtsman's mechanical layout came to us from the colonial period and still haunts us today" (figs. 240–42).[28] While it is hardly reasonable to blame the British for all monotonous design in present-day India, a prototype for the dispiriting layout of much low-cost housing can be found in the Improvement Trust chawls. Although largely superseded by other agencies, the Improvement Trusts continued to operate following independence, and, in spite of the derision that Trust housing attracted in the colonial era, no notable improvement in design standards has evolved.

Both Calcutta and Bombay were presented with challenging design opportunities in the development of Salt Lake City and New Bombay. These new settlements required large-scale site planning, including provision for a variety of industrial, commercial, governmental, and residential buildings. To anyone anticipating that a planned community might reflect a level of development superior to that produced by spontaneous accretion or commercial speculation, both are disappointing in terms of overall conception as well as detailed design.

Although the Salt Lake project was intended eventually to reflect a social and economic range, initial construction was keyed to the middle class, and the prevailing atmosphere has been similar to that produced in conventional suburbs. The plan is characterized by straight wide streets in grid formation. The allocation of park space is relatively generous, with small parks and playgrounds projected throughout the housing districts, together with a large central park area. If adequately maintained, such parks could provide a valuable amenity. Dwelling types include a mixture of freestanding houses and apartment blocks (figs. 243, 244). As in similar enclaves, the architecture appears essentially Western and "modern," with simple, boxlike building forms, occasionally enlivened with projecting balconies and fanciful decoration. Obviously, the planners of Salt Lake City were not seeking innovative design, and they may have correctly assumed that the inhabitants of the new settlement would be quite content with the environment of an ordinary middle-class housing estate.

New Bombay represents a highly ambitious undertaking, involving the coordination of a series of scattered settlements, including existing villages and towns as well as new urban centers. The project seems to have been so demanding in terms of large-scale planning that the quality of architectural design has received little consideration. Street patterns consist of crudely-scaled grids, and housing is dominated by large tracts of barrack-like workers' dwellings (fig. 245). Middle-class housing generally takes the form of uninspired terrace houses and apartments, with a few free-standing luxury dwellings on choice sites along the waterfront. Like much of the housing, commercial building is monotonous and coarsely detailed, lining broad streets that lack the attraction of even the poorest village bazaar (fig. 246). Landscaping, which might have mitigated the severity of the scene, has apparently been deemed an unnecessary luxury.

A strong proponent of New Bombay was the architect Charles Correa, and although his suggestions for large-scale planning were ignored, he succeeded in con-

240. *Public housing in Bombay.*

241. *Public housing in Calcutta.*

242. *Public housing in Madras.*

243–244. *Housing in Salt Lake City, Calcutta.*

245. *Housing in New Bombay constructed in 1986.*

246. *Commercial building under construction in 1986, Vashi, New Bombay.*

247. *Artists' village in Belapur, New Bombay, by Charles Correa, shown under construction in 1986.*

structing two housing projects there, one a middle-class apartment ensemble in Vashi, and the other a picturesque villagelike enclave of houses located in Belapur and intended for artists (figs. 247, 248). Houses are grouped around a sequence of spatial enclosures. In its evocation of traditional urbanism the artists' housing is similar to certain complexes in Delhi. Unlike the Delhi housing, however, it also attempts to recreate the style of vernacular building, employing tiled pitched roofs and shuttered windows. Although the complex has been well publicized, it seems destined to remain an isolated drop of whimsy in a sea of dullness.

Just as the architects most sensitive to tradition tend to be at the same time the most cosmopolitan, it is primarily among urbanized, "westernized" Indians that support for architectural preservation is encountered. Under the British, preservation activities had varied somewhat, according to vagaries of government patronage. Following independence, in 1959, the Ancient Monuments and Archaeological Sites and Remains Act was created. According to this act, any building more than one-hundred-years-old could be declared protected. It was also possible to regulate building activity in the vicinity of a monument. Preservation achievements, however, tended to be limited not only by financial resources but by general public apathy.

In India, it has been observed, those interested in "problems of preservation are considered eccentrics." An architectural journal in 1962 pointed to the paradox that while many new buildings had traditional motifs superficially applied to them, genuinely old buildings were allowed to deteriorate. The well-to-do, particularly, showed a

248. *Artists' village, New Bombay.*

consistent preference for new buildings, and it was observed that "whilst in some countries the highest premium is paid for an apartment in the oldest districts of the city, for example Paris and Rome, in India the very thought is considered too funny for words."[29]

The initial concern of preservationists had been for ancient Indian monuments. With the exception of Delhi, however, the major metropolises have no Indian monuments of significance, and it is British building that has come to embody the past. Many Indian preservationists deem colonial building to be part of India's architectural heritage, and they encourage its protection. The focus of interest has expanded, moreover, to encompass not only major buildings, but patterns of townscape. In India, as elsewhere, the forces of change erode the urban fabric, often obliterating the intimate scale of vernacular construction.

In the case of Delhi, preservationists have focused their attention on two disparate areas. They seek to maintain the compact townscape of Old Delhi, and at the same time to preserve the verdant spaces and low-rise character of New Delhi. The old city, over the years, had been periodically threatened with massive reconstruction by planners who tended to view its dense fabric as a slum. As the rest of the city sprawled amorphously, however, the visual richness of Old Delhi was increasingly appreciated. Many architects were becoming fascinated by traditional urban form, and Old Delhi, with its narrow streets, changing vistas and patterns of courtyard buildings, was subject to continual analysis. Of particular interest, from both a social and architectural point of view, has been the *katra* settlement, a formation in which a group of households inhabits buildings connected by passages and courtyards, sharing a common entrance.

Recognizing the historic and aesthetic values of the old city, the 1985 plan insisted that "the rebuilding/renovation of the buildings in the Walled City should be done sensitively, conserving the important monuments, and the architectural style,

249. Chandni Chowk.

skyline and street picture." Restoration was recommended for the remaining portions of the wall and gates. It was also suggested that the bazaar of Chandni Chowk "could be revamped by eliminating traffic of automobiles," and that it be restored "to the original state as far as possible." Although previous plans had often included the projection of wide streets through Old Delhi, the 1985 scheme recognized that "the road and street pattern in the Walled City is the spine of its urban character." Echoing the philosophy of Patrick Geddes, the plan recommended "conservative surgery as a planning tool" (figs. 249–51).[30]

The wording of the plan represented a statement of general intention, rather than a program of active preservation. The increasing commercial activity of the district, together with the high population densities, had led over the years to continual reconstruction of old buildings. Courtyards were partitioned, new stories and extensions constructed, and surfaces refaced. In the process, much of the architectural detail of buildings was removed or disguised. The enthusiasm for preservation shown by outsiders, moreover, was not necessarily shared by the inhabitants of the district. To illustrate the prevailing indifference, an architectural journal reported that "a trucking company owner who is also a prominent politician maintained that if he wished to pull down the narrow gateway to the courtyard of his ancestral *haveli,* no one could stop him. His new fleet of large trucks needed access to the parking area within."[31]

As the urbanized area of Delhi has spread, a number of existing settlements have been threatened with absorption. One such pocket of traditional townscape is the six-

250. *Old Delhi looking south from the Jama Masjid. High-rise buildings near Connaught Place can be seen in the distance.*

251. *Old Delhi.*

hundred-year-old Muslim settlement of Nizamuddin, situated in the rapidly evolving southern portion of Delhi. Because of its historic associations as well as the charm of its intimate urban fabric, Nizamuddin has become the focus of concerted efforts to preserve its unique physical and social identity (fig. 252).

Although Delhi, with its ancient heritage, would provide a natural focus for preservation efforts, other major cities also began to attract concern. The Save Bombay Committee was formed in 1972 through the instigation of an architect, Kisan Mehta. The organization sought to publicize preservation issues and bring pressure on public

252. Mosque in Nizamuddin.

officials dealing with environmental questions. A list of buildings of historical and cultural importance was created. As in Delhi, however, there was no effective legislation to insure conservation, and the longevity of most building has been left to the forces of economics.

Although some fear that skyscrapers may destroy the architectural harmony of the old business district in Bombay, the Back Bay landfill has provided a more tempting site for new commercial construction, sparing the old fort from pressures for intensive redevelopment. As a result, central Bombay has remained sufficiently preserved to inspire description as "the most thoroughly Victorian metropolis extant."[32] With the passage of time, the Gothic Revival has been critically rehabilitated, and the buildings that drew such scorn from Aldous Huxley in the 1920s now command affection. In contrast to Britain, where the bombs of the Second World War, together with the equally destructive forces of post-war renovation, obliterated much of the nineteenth-century urban fabric, Bombay stands relatively intact, embodying for certain British visitors a poignant reminder of all that has been lost at home (figs. 253–55). Indeed, a British writer, Gillian Tindall, noted that

nineteenth-century Manchester has been substantially destroyed: so have Liver-

253. *Looking toward the fort district of Bombay. Except for the Share Market, on the left, and the Reserve Bank of India, on the right, this district has escaped the intrusion of skyscrapers. The domed building on the left is the Prince of Wales Museum.*

254. *The Share Market and the old commercial vernacular.*

255. *"The most thoroughly Victorian metropolis extant." Looking from Flora Fountain toward Dadabhai Naoroji Marg.*

pool, Birmingham, Leeds, Halifax, Southampton and many other places: London itself has been altered in many parts out of recognition. . . . as you walk around . . . particularly at night when the narrow streets are empty of traffic and the large and terrible Bombay rats frisk in and out of the sewers through crumbling drainheads, it is not hard to believe that you are actually walking round a central district of London—the City of Holborn or Seven Dials, perhaps, in the time of Dickens. Here are the handcarts stacked on the pavements, and a few victorias parked near the Church with their drivers asleep on the leather cushions. Here are the great porticoed buildings that are the symbol of the power and prestige of money, and here the beggars and the homeless lie in wrapped sleep on the very granite steps. Here is India's present, and Britain's past.[33]

256. *A bank on B.B.D. Bag looms over the old governor's guard house in Calcutta.*

In Calcutta, a private effort to promote architectural conservation was reflected in the Society for the Preservation of Archival Materials and Monuments of Calcutta, formed in 1981. According to the society, "the city largely retained its character and beauty till the thirties of this century. It is now in a shambles." Particularly dramatic was the transformation of the quarters east of Chowringhee, where the predominant pattern of classical elegance was virtually obliterated through decay and reconstruction. The district around B.B.D. Bag (Dalhousie Square) was also succumbing to increasing pressure. A society report deplored the destruction of the Dalhousie Institute and its replacement by a high-rise building, pointing out that "continuing increase in the scale of commercial activities has turned the magnificent *Lal Dighi* into a hideous parking lot. Unless systematic steps are immediately taken to disperse Government and commercial offices from Dalhousie Square to other areas in or around the city, many other beautiful buildings, encrusted with historical associations, will soon be turned into rubble." It was urged that the square be declared a conservation area, "to retain its architectural character and integrity" (fig. 256).[34]

In India, as elsewhere, the longevity of a building is dependent on chance, and on its continued usefulness. Old mansions may be converted to commercial use or multiple occupancy, continuing to embellish with their faded dignity the clutter and tawdriness of deteriorating neighborhoods (figs. 257, 258). Calcutta, especially,

257. House in central Calcutta.

258. Mansion in north Calcutta, now used as an automobile repair shop.

abounds in romantic ruins, and to those who love to explore the urban jungle, discloses unexpected treasures. In the old British districts, decaying remnants of the classical era often lie concealed behind a screen of modern buildings. Wandering down a narrow lane in the old Indian districts of north Calcutta, one may suddenly confront a lofty portico gracefully ennobling some prosaic function. The evocation of the past, moreover, is not solely dependent on the survival of individual buildings. In spite of the attrition of aging structures, many of the old bazaar areas still perpetuate the image of the past through their dense building fabric and mazelike network of narrow streets. The sense of arrested time is supported not only by the built environment, but by patterns of activity that seem largely unaffected by the modern age. Propelled by the crowd, noting the boxlike shops and peddlers' stalls, dodging the hurrying porters and handcarts, one reflects that it must have been like this a hundred years ago. It must have been like this in Babylon.

At the national level, an attempt was begun to attract private support for preservation through the creation of Intach, the Indian National Trust for Art and Cultural Heritage in 1984. With its headquarters in Delhi, Intach announced its intention to act as a "culture bank," providing financial and technical assistance for preservation. Although the creation of Intach encouraged hopes that preservation might become a fashionable concern, doubts were raised as to its likely accomplishments. An architectural journal questioned Intach's effectiveness in "dealing with the forces which are really destroying our heritage. . . . Conservation, we cannot help thinking, will take second place to political considerations and personal whims."[35]

All in all, those who had anticipated a cultural renaissance to accompany Indian independence might view the past decades with disappointment. The architectural press has been full of criticism of contemporary buildings, and an Indian architect, Abu Nadeem, concluded in 1982 that India, "after attaining its independence more than thirty-three years ago, has hardly produced a single remarkable building which will stand the test of time. . . . It is ironical that a society which can produce exquisite pieces of art and handicrafts from people living in conditions of need, is unable to produce beautiful buildings! Let it be admitted that the privileged amongst us, who have had the opportunity of studying in well-known schools abroad, sometimes with acknowledged masters, have totally failed to produce something of lasting quality in the field of architecture."[36]

A variety of circumstances, including conditions of professional practice, economic and technical factors, and attitudes of clients, have tended to handicap architectural achievement. Charles Correa, arguing that Indians needed to develop a sense of concern for their environment, asked, "how can we reverse generations of apathy? The indifference of the urban Indian to his environment is truly metaphysical. The key ingredient in Mediterranean architecture—all the way back to the Greeks—is pleasure in environment. Architecture and urban planning are hedonistic arts, and there is a connection between Italian architecture, Italian food and Italian piazzas. But the Indian is no hedonist."[37] Correa's comparison of India with Italy is interesting, considering that India itself was once deemed the "Italy of Asia." India, we are often reminded, is a poor country. Italy, too, has known poverty, and the visual delight to be found in Italian cities has often coexisted with dirt, stench, pestilence, and a lack of potable water.

Correa's contention that Indians lack sufficient hedonism to produce a pleasurable environment is intriguing and provocative. And there is much to support his view. Even in instances where money does not seem to be the issue, even in luxury buildings, there is often neglect. Viewing Indian cities, one may infer Indians to possess, not merely an indifference, but a deep-seated hatred for the physical world. Buildings are often abused in ways that suggest a pent-up rage that might otherwise be unleashed in a frenzy of social destruction. There seems to be some force at work that is hard to explain. Yet the same Indians who appear in many ways indifferent to their physical surroundings flock to films that transport the viewer into a fantasy world of luxury and elegance. The escapism of films may, in fact, help to make the oppressive urban environment tolerable.

Beautiful townscape exists in India, but far from the affluent metropolises. Many old urban centers are characterized by building that is sensitive in scale, harmoniously composed, rich in detail, and decently maintained. Even rural villages frequently exhibit a canny sense of siting and building form. The small scale of an ancient provincial town, however, does not necessarily provide architectural guidelines for a modern metropolis. While admiring traditional design, architects remain uncertain as to its applicability to contemporary urbanism.

In India the question of dependence on foreign models continues to be debated. Many contend that in an age of rapid communication, contemporary building must be expected to reflect complex crosscurrents of international influence. While the old concept of a universal modern architecture has been rightly deemed a procrustean bed, the idea of a purely national architecture may be equally restrictive. The modern commercial metropolis has achieved a certain functional similarity throughout the world, and this has been reflected in the pattern of its building. In the view of Prime Minister Nehru, "this business of European or Indian or Iranian and American architecture has certainly some substance in it but not so much as is made out. . . . We cannot, obviously, even if we had the capacity, build Taj Mahals now."[38]

When Western classicism was introduced into India, its proponents were convinced that it was based on fundamental principles of order. The Gothic Revival embodied a message of craftsmanship and creative expression. The International Style and Art Deco carried associations of technical advancement and social progress. Each succeeding wave of influence had encompassed relatively consistent ideology and style. India achieved independence at a time when Western architecture was entering an era of ideological and stylistic confusion. To the dismay of some, the old certitudes that had infused the modern movement were being either ignored or actively challenged. Expanding technical virtuosity and formal permissiveness visibly reinforced Einstein's comment that "perfection of means and confusion of goals seem . . . to characterize our age."[39]

Against this background, India's position was one that might have militated for or against important achievement in design. Although the validity of monumental building was being questioned in the West, it might have had a legitimate role in India in providing institutional symbols. Lacking the "perfection of means" to support the architectural free-for-all seen in other parts of the world, Indian designers had the incentive to seek a truly unique form of expression, a type of building that would arise from Indian conditions and Indian needs. In 1968, Indira Gandhi observed, "in the past few decades, our architects have walked amongst international and indigenous idioms in search of an identity." Of the buildings that had been produced since independence, she maintained, only a few could "lay claim to being genuine architecture."[40] Defining national identity in terms of architecture is not easy, however, nor is the meaning of "genuine architecture" always clear.

Paradoxically, it is those Indian architects who seek links with the Indian past who are now most closely allied with the Western avant-garde. Postmodernist rhetoric embodies a respectful view of cultural differences, acknowledging the validity of historical symbolism. The relationship between past and present and the meaning of East and West in terms of the contemporary city, however, pose many unanswered questions. At present, the Indian metropolis seems destined to retain its hybrid form. It is, of course, not the "real" India. Nor is New York the "real" America, which lies, presumably, somewhere in rural Kansas. Cosmopolitan Paris is not the "real" France, nor is London the "real" England. The great city is by its nature oriented toward the world; it remains a place where cultures clash and meld. In all its cultural juxtaposition and confusion of image, it was the cosmopolitan metropolis that became the incubator of the new Indian nation.

Notes

Chapter 1.
Three Hybrid Cities

1 From "The Song of the Cities," *Collected Verse of R. Kipling* (New York: Doubleday, Page, 1907), 90–92.

2 George Viscount Valentia, *Voyages and Travels to India, Ceylon, the Red Sea, Abyssinia, and Egypt in the Years 1802, 1803, 1805, and 1806,* 3 vols. (London: William Miller, 1809), 1:390, and Eliza Fay, *Original Letters from India, 1779–1815,* repr. ed. (London: Hogarth Press, 1925), 163.

3 Quoted in Henry Davison Love, *Vestiges of Madras,* 3 vols. (London: John Murray, 1913), 2:73–74.

4 Mrs. Kindersley quoted ibid, 617.

5 Ibid., 77–78.

6 Quoted in Henry Dodwell, *The Nabobs of Madras* (London: Williams and Norgate, 1926), 167–68.

7 Valentia, *Voyages,* 389.

8 Fay, *Original Letters,* 163, and Steen Bille, quoted in *ITIHAS,* Journal of the Andhra Pradesh State Archives 7 (July–Dec. 1979): 41–42.

9 C. S. Srinivasachi, *History of the City of Madras* (Madras: P. Varadachary, 1939), 250–51.

10 Quoted in Krishnaswami Nayudu, *Old Madras* (Madras: Privately published, 1965), 69.

11 Val C. Princep, *Imperial India* (London: Chapman and Hall, 1879), 305.

12 Quoted in J. H. Furneaux, *Glimpses of India* (Bombay: Burrows, 1895), 16.

13 The quotations in this paragraph are taken from the *Imperial Gazetteer of India: Provincial Series, Madras* (Calcutta: Superintendent of Government Printing, 1908), 1:497–99 passim.

14 Sydney Low, *A Vision of India* (New York: Dutton, 1907), 236.

15 Quoted in Susan J. Lewandowski, "Urban Growth and Municipal Development in the Colonial City of Madras, 1860–1900," *Journal of Asian Studies* 34 (Feb. 1975): 345.

16 From "A Tale of Two Cities," *Departmental Ditties and Barrack-Room Ballads* (New York: Doubleday and McClure, 1899), 156–59.

17 Extract from the Chutanutte Diary and Consultation, Oct. 3, 1698, Factory Records, Calcutta, No. 3. Quoted by Pradip Sinha, *Calcutta in Urban History* (Calcutta: Firma KLM, 1978), 1.

18 Alexander Hamilton, *A New Account of the East Indies,* 1727, quoted in H. E. A. Cotton, *Calcutta Old and New* (Calcutta: Newman, 1907), 8.

19 Quoted in *Calcutta 200 Years: A Tollygunge Club Perspective* (Calcutta: Tollygunge Club, 1981), 29. The reference is taken from a court letter, Feb. 2, 1713.

20 Fanny Parks, *Wanderings of a Pilgrim in Search of the Picturesque* (London: Pelham Richardson, 1850), 30.

21 Fort William-India House correspondence, quoted in Suresh Chandra Ghosh, *The Social Conditions of the British Community in Bengal, 1757–1800* (Leiden: Brill, 1970), 96.

22 Valentia, *Voyages,* 236.

23 Fay, *Original Letters,* 171–72.

24 Quotations from Cotton, *Calcutta,* 69–70, and *Handbook to Calcutta* (Calcutta, Newman, 1892), 27–28.

25 Nemi Bose, ed., *Calcutta: People and Empire* (Calcutta: India Book Exchange, 1975), 10.

26 Valentia, *Voyages,* 236; Bose, *Calcutta,* 9; and *Handbook to Calcutta,* 96.

27 *Handbook,* 31.

28 Bose, *Calcutta,* 9.

29 Ibid., 126.

30 Ray, *Calcutta Keepsake,* 46, and Newman, *Handbook,* 27–28.

31 Bose, *Calcutta,* 222.

32 The public lottery was a popular means of selling property among the British, and in 1793 a lottery

had been administered by the Town Improvement Committee, of which 10 percent had been applied to public works. This set the precedent for employing a lottery as a regular means of financing municipal improvements.

33 Bose, *Calcutta,* 2.

34 "Anglo-Indian Architecture," *Bombay Builder,* May 5, 1866, 228–29.

35 Bose, *Calcutta,* 3–4.

36 Quoted in Rajat Ray, *Urban Roots of Indian Nationalism* (Delhi: Vikas, 1979), 13, n. 6.

37 Bose, *Calcutta,* 205–6.

38 Norman Macleod, *Peeps at the Far East* (London: Strahan, 1871), 195.

39 Edward Carpenter, *From Adam's Peak to Elephanta* (New York: Dutton, 1904), 231.

40 From "A Tale of Two Cities." See n. 16 above.

41 Excerpt from "The City of Bombay," 1894, in *Collected Verse of R. Kipling,* 94–95.

42 Quoted in Allister Macmillan, *Seaports of India and Ceylon* (London: Collingridge, 1928), 159.

43 Quoted from the *Asiatic Journal* of 1838, in *The Gazetteer of Bombay City and Island* (Bombay: Times Press, 1909), 2:147.

44 Parson, *Travels in Asia and America,* 1808, quoted in James McNabb Campbell, *Bombay Gazetteer, Materials Toward a Statistical Account of the Town and Island of Bombay,* 3 vols. (Bombay: Government Central Press, 1894), vol. 2, *Trade and Fortifications,* 216.

45 Company correspondence, 1756, in ibid., 447.

46 Walter Hamilton, *Description of Hindustan,* 1820, from R. P. Karkaria, ed., *The Charm of Bombay* (Bombay: Taraporavala, 1915), 528.

47 Committee Buildings Diary of 1787–93, quoted in Campbell, *Materials,* 494.

48 The Honourable Jonathan Duncan in a letter to the Court of Directors, quoted in *The Gazetteer of Bombay City and Island* (Bombay: Times Press, 1909), 494.

49 Bombay Town Committee Diary, quoted in Campbell, *Materials,* pp. 495–500.

50 *Asiatic Journal,* 1838, quoted in Edwardes, *The Rise of Bombay* (Bombay: Times of India Press, 1902), 33.

51 *A Guide to Bombay from the Bombay Times Calendar of 1855* (Bombay: Times Press, 1855), 78.

52 Forbes, *Oriental Memoirs,* quoted in *Guide to Bombay,* 487.

53 *Asiatic Journal,* quoted in the *Gazetteer,* 2:149.

54 Richard Bentley, *Life in Bombay* (London: Richard Bentley, 1852), 39.

55 Ibid., 261.

56 Grose's *Voyage to the East Indies,* quoted in the *Gazetteer,* 1:65.

57 Mrs. Elwood's *Narrative of an Overland Journey to India,* quoted in the *Gazetteer,* 1:10.

58 Emma Roberts, *Overland Journey to Bombay,* 1841, quoted in Karkaria, *Charm,* 317.

59 William Shepherd, *From Bombay to Bushire,* quoted in Karkaria, *Charm,* 326.

60 Quoted in the *Gazetteer,* 1:66.

61 Quotations taken from Edwardes, *Rise of Bombay,* 34; Macmillan, *Seaports,* 162, and *Gazetteer,* 1909, 154.

62 Quotations from ibid., 265, 275.

63 Quoted in Samuel Sheppard, *Bombay* (Bombay: Times of India Press, 1932), 76.

64 Quotations from Karkaria, *Charm,* 172, and Edwardes, *Rise of Bombay,* 294–95.

65 Edwardes, *Rise of Bombay,* 300.

66 Ibid., 325.

67 Sir Richard Temple, *A Bird's Eye View of Picturesque India,* 1898, 20–21, quoted in Karkaria, *Charm,* 537.

68 Sir Edwin Arnold, *India Revisited,* 1886, quoted in ibid., 76–77.

69 The Times quoted in ibid., 169.

70 Sydney Low, *A Vision of India* (London: Smith, Elder, 1907), 35.

71 Ibid., 34.

72 Furneaux, *Glimpses,* 198, and James Mackenzie Maclean, *A Guide to Bombay,* 12th ed. (Bombay: Bombay Gazette Steam Press, 1887), 173–74.

Chapter 2: The Architecture of Empire

1 Captain Alexander Hamilton, an Englishman who traveled in Asia between 1688 and 1723, visiting Calcutta around 1710, quoted in A. Ray, *Calcutta Keepsake* (Calcutta: RDDI–India, 1978), 61–62.

2 Jan Morris, *Stones of Empire: The Buildings of the Raj* (Oxford: Oxford University Press, 1985), 19.

3 Pasley quoted by Balwant Singh Saini, "Cantonment Architecture of India," *Design* 7 (March 1963): 17.

4 "Architecture in Bombay," *Bombay Builder* (Aug. 5, 1868), 63.

5 John Borthwick Gilchrist, *The General East India Guide and Vade Mecum* (London: Kingsbury, Parbury and Allen, 1825), 256. This book is based on *The East India Vade Mecum* by Thomas Williamson (London: Black, Parry and Kingsbury, 1810).

6 Julius George Medley, *India and Eastern Engineering* (London: Spon, 1873), 54, 59, 52.

7 Ibid., 62–63, 64.

8 "Modern Architecture in Western India," *The Building News* (June 3, 1870), 421.

9 Quoted by Margaret Martyn in "Georgian Architecture in Calcutta," *Country Life* (Dec. 3, 1948), 1174.

10 *The Builder,* Oct. 30, 1869, 857.

11 Quoted by Desmond Doig in *Calcutta: An Artist's Impression* (Calcutta: The Statesman, 1966). Pages not numbered.

12 Gilchrist, *East India Guide,* 240.

13 Fay, *Original Letters,* 175.

14 Mrs. Major Clemons, *The Manners and Customs of Society in India* (London: Smith, Elder and Son, 1841), 310.

15 Medley, *Engineering*, 80–81.

16 Macleod, *Peeps at the Far East*, 122.

17 Colesworthy Grant, *Anglo-Indian Domestic Life*, 2d ed. (Calcutta: Thacker, Spink, 1862), 29.

18 Macleod, *Peeps*, 117, and Fanny Parks, *Wanderings of a Pilgrim in Search of the Picturesque* (London: Pelham Richardson, 1850), 56–57.

19 Grant, *Anglo-Indian*, 14.

20 Reginald Heber, *Narrative of a Journey through the Upper Provinces of India: From Calcutta to Bombay, 1824–1826*, 3 vols. (London: John Murray, 1828), 1:24. Quoted in Suresh Chandra Ghosh, *The Social Condition of the British Community in Bengal, 1757–1800* (Leiden: Brill, 1970), 100.

21 Quoted in Edwardes, *Bound to Exile* (London: Sidgwick and Jackson, 1969), 22.

22 Richard Bentley, *Life in Bombay* London: Bentley, 1852), 13–15.

23 Ibid., 16.

24 Grant, *Anglo-Indian*, 13.

25 James Long, *Calcutta in the Olden Time: Its Localities and Its People* (Calcutta: Sanskrit Pustak Bhandar, 1974), 102.

26 Parks, *Wanderings*, 21.

27 Gilchrist, *East India Guide*, 352 and 340–41.

28 Quoted in Philip Davies, *Splendours of the Raj: British Architecture in India, 1660–1947* (London: John Murray, 1985), 35.

29 Marquis Curzon of Kedleston, *British Government in India* (London: Cassel, 1925), 1:41–42. Kedleston Hall had been built for Lord Curzon's great-great grandfather, the first Lord Scarsdale. According to Curzon, it was "the alleged correspondence between the two houses that first turned my attention, when a boy, to India, and planted in me the ambition, from an early age, to pass from a Kedleston in Derbyshire to a Kedleston in Bengal" (43).

30 Valentia, *Voyages*, 1:235–36.

31 "Life in Old Calcutta," reprinted from *The Englishman* in *Bengal, Past and Present* (July–Dec. 1924), 129.

32 Quoted by C. C. Dongerkery, *History of the University of Bombay, 1937–1957* (Bombay: University of Bombay, 1957), 62.

33 Macleod, *Peeps*, 205.

34 Sir Richard Temple, *India in 1880* (London: John Murray, 1881), 23.

35 James Mackenzie Maclean, *A Guide to Bombay* (Bombay: Steam Press, 1887), 197.

36 Sydney Low, *A Vision of India* (London: Smith, Elder, 1907), 10, and G. W. Forrest, *Cities of India* (London: Archibald Constable, 1903), 19.

37 Samuel Sheppard, *Bombay* (Bombay: Times of India Press, 1932), 116.

38 The citations in the paragraphs, in order are from: William Henry Adams, *India: Pictorial and Descriptive* (London: T. Nelson, 1888), 219; W. H. Carey, *The Good Old Days of the Honorable John Company* (Calcutta: Cambray, 1907), 454; and, the Rev. W. K. Firminger, *Thacker's Guide to Calcutta* (Calcutta: Thacker, Spink, 1906), 14.

39 Sir D. E. Wacha, *Shells from the Sands of Bombay, 1860–75* (Bombay: Bombay Chronicle Press, 1920), 314–19.

40 Sir J. R. Martin, *Notes on the Medical Topography of Calcutta*, 1837, 19–20, quoted in Pradip Sinha, *Calcutta in Urban History* (Calcutta: Firma KLM Private Ltd., 1978), 160.

41 Gilchrist, *East India Guide*, 191.

42 Macleod, *Peeps*, 170–71.

43 Quoted in Sinha, *Calcutta*, 19–20.

44 George Birdwood, *Handbook to the British Indian Section, Paris Universal Exposition, 1878* (London: Office of the Royal Commission, 1878), pages not numbered, and Edwardes, *Rise of Bombay*, 323.

45 Dr. Stanley Reed, quoted in Karkaria, *Charm*, 360; Mrs. Elwood, *Narrative of an Overland Journey*, 1830, quoted in *The Gazetteer of Bombay City and Island* (Bombay: Times Press, 1909), 195; and Edward Carpenter, *From Adam's Peak to Elephanta* (New York: Dutton, 1904), 294.

46 Low, *Vision*, 23–24.

47 Carpenter, *Adam's Peak*, 295.

48 Birdwood, *Handbook*, 76–77.

49 Parks, *Wanderings*, 382–83.

50 Rev. J. E. Padfield, *The Hindu at Home* (London: Hamilton Kent, 1908; reissued, Delhi: B. R. Publishing, 1975), 17–20.

51 John Martineau, *Life and Correspondence of Sir Bartle Frere* (London: John Murray, 1895), 1:461.

52 Heber, *Narrative*, 3:232.

53 Edwardes, *Rise of Bombay*, 55; Heber, *Narrative*, 3:234.

54 The title Kahn Bahadoor was created for Muslims and Parsees. The equivalent title for Hindus was Rao Bahadoor, and it was awarded to the engineer, Muckoond Ramchunder, who worked on the university senate hall and also executed sculpture on the university library.

55 Macleod, *Peeps*, 207, 209–10.

56 Begum Shaista Ikramullah, *From Purdah to Parliament* (London: Cresset Press, 1963), 17; quoted by Anthony King, "The Westernization of Domestic Architecture in India," *Art and Archaeology Research Papers* 11 (June 1977): 32–41. Dennis Kincaid, *British Social Life in India, 1606–1937* (London: Routledge and Sons, 1938), 220.

57 Rev. George Clutterbuck, *In India [the Land of Famine and of Plague] or Bombay the Beautiful* (London: Ideal Publishing Union, 1897), 32; Kincaid, *Social Life*, 242.

58 Wacha, *Shells*, 179–80.

59 Kylas Chunder Dutt [Tom Peep], *The Hindu Pioneer*, vol. 1, no. 7 (March 1836), reproduced in Ray, *Calcutta*, 160–64. The quotations in the following two paragraphs are also from this source.

Chapter 3. The Long Debate

1   William Henry Davenport Adams, *India, Pictorial and Descriptive* (London: T. Nelson, 1888), 208.
2   Major J. B. Keith, "Indian Stone Carving," *Journal of Indian Art and Industry* 1 (1886): 111, and Lord Curzon, address to the Asiatic Society in Bengal, Feb. 7, 1900, quoted in R. C. Majumdar, *The History and Culture of the Indian People: British Paramountcy and Indian Renaissance* (Bombay: Bharatiya Vidya Bhavan, 1965), 405.
3   Adams, *India*, 234.
4   James Fergusson, "On the Study of Indian Architecture," *Journal of the Society of Arts* 15 (Dec. 21, 1866): 71, 73, 75–76, and *History of Indian and Eastern Architecture* (London: John Murray, 1910), 2:324.
5   E. B. Havell, *Essays on Indian Art, Industry and Education* (Madras: Nateson and Co., 1912?).
6   Sir Bartle Frere, "Modern Architecture in Western India," *The Building News*, June 3, 1870, 421.
7   "Past Architecture and Present Building," *Bombay Builder*, Sept. 5, 1867, 92.
8   George Birdwood, "Want of Architecture in Bombay," *Bombay Builder*, Sept. 5, 1868, 105.
9   Julius George Medley, *India and Indian Engineering* (London: Spon, 1873), 23.
10 George Birdwood, *Handbook to the British Indian Section, Paris Universal Exposition, 1878* (London: Offices of the Royal Commission, 1878), 114.
11 An Anglo-Indian, *Indian Outfits and Establishments* (London: Upcott Gill, 1882), 60.
12 *Journal of Indian Art* 1 (Oct. 1886): i (Preface), and Alfred Chatterton, "Art Industries of Southern India," *Journal of Indian Art and Industries* 15: 44.
13 Quoted by John Lockwood Kipling in "Indian Architecture of Today," *Journal of Indian Art* 1 (1886): 3, and T. H. Hendley, "Decorative Art in Rajputana," *Journal of Indian Art and Industry* 3 (1888): 45.
14 John Lockwood Kipling, "The Industries of the Punjab," *Journal of Indian Art and Industries* 2 (1887): 25.
15 Kipling, "Indian Architecture of Today," 2.
16 E. B. Havell, "A Message of Hope for India," *The Nineteenth Century and After* 72 (Dec. 1912): 1278.
17 *Directory of Technical Institutes in India* (Poona: 1915), 39.
18 *Centenary—Government College of Art and Craft, Calcutta, 1864–1964* (Calcutta: Statesman Press, 1964), 8, 15.
19 Havell, *Essays in Indian Art, Industry and Education*, and *Centenary*, 22.
20 *Directory*, 39.
21 *Story of Sir J. J. School of Art* (Bombay: Government Central Press, 1957), 53.
22 Ibid., 67.
23 "The Indian Master Builder," *Royal Institute of British Architects Journal* 3d ser., 20 (Nov. 23, 1912): 59–

60. The article reproduces a portion of *The Annual Report on Architectural Work in India for 1912–1913* by John Begg, Consulting Architect to the Government of India.
24 F. O. Oertel, "Indian Architecture and Its Suitability," *East India Association Journal*, N.S., 4 (1913): 276–78 passim.
25 Frank Harriss, *Biography of J. N. Tata* (privately printed), 73.
26 Oertel, "Indian Architecture," 278.
27 E. B. Havell, *Indian Architecture* (London: John Murray, 1913), 230–31.
28 Marquis Curzon of Kedleston, *British Government in India*, 1:189. Heber, *Narrative*, 2:290.
29 Heber, *Narrative*, 2:285.
30 Macleod, *Peeps*, 312.
31 Clutterbuck, *In India*, 36.
32 Quoted in Narayani Gupta, *Delhi between Two Empires, 1803–1931* (Delhi: Oxford University Press, 1981), 26, and Jagmohan, *Rebuilding Sahjahanabad: The Walled City of Delhi* (Delhi: Vikas, 1975), 16.
33 Jagmohan, *Rebuilding*, 28.
34 Quoted in Gupta, *Delhi*, 30.
35 Preface to *Delhi Province: List of Muhammedan and Hindu Monuments, Part I, Shahjahanabad* (Calcutta: Superintendent, Government Printing, 1916), pages not numbered.
36 Ibid.
37 Quoted in Robert Grant Irving, *Indian Summer* (New Haven and London: Yale University Press, 1981), 29.
38 Havell, *Indian Architecture*, 247.
39 Quoted in E. B. Havell, *The Basis for Artistic and Industrial Revival in India* (Madras: Theosophist Office, 1912), 102.
40 Quoted by Christopher Hussey in *The Life of Sir Edwin Lutyens* (London: Country Life Ltd., and New York: Charles Scribner's Sons, 1950), 280, 277.
41 Quoted in Colin Amery, "The Contribution of Lutyens to Planning and Architecture," *The Future of New Delhi*, ed. E. F. N. Ribeiro and A. K. Jain (New Delhi: Delhi Development Authority, 1984), 10.
42 Hussey, *Lutyens*, 278, 279.
43 Ibid., 280.
44 Ibid., 270.
45 "The New Delhi," *Journal of the Royal Institute of British Architects* 3d ser., 19 (Oct. 19, 1912).
46 Robert Byron, "New Delhi I: The Architecture of the Viceroy's House," *Country Life* 69 (June 6, 1931): 708.
47 Robert Byron, "New Delhi," *Architectural Review* 69 (Jan. 1931): 18, 30.
48 Ibid., 14.
49 Claude Batley, "Modern Architecture in India," *Journal of the Indian Institute of Architects* 2 (April 1935): 119.
50 Quoted in Irving, *Indian Summer*, 136.
51 C. Northcote Parkinson, *Parkinson's Law* (Boston: Houghton Mifflin, 1957), 60–61.

52 Mahatma Gandhi, *The Story of My Experiments with Truth* (Navjivan, 1927–29), 2:106. A discussion of Ruskin's influence on Gandhi may be found in Takshmi V. Menon, *Ruskin and Gandhi* (Varanasi: Sarva Seva Sangh Prakaskan, 1965). *Unto This Last* first appeared in *Cornhill Magazine* (Sept.–Dec. 1860) and has been variously reissued.

Chapter 4. Modern Planning

1   E. B. Havell, "The Message of Hope for India," *The Nineteenth Century and After* 72 (Dec. 1912): 1277.
2   This citation and the ones that follow on pp. 114–15 are taken from Patrick Geddes, *Reports on the Towns in the Madras Presidency Visited by Professor Geddes* (1915), 5, 82, 86, 87, 86, 76.
3   H. V. Lanchester, *Town Planning in Madras* (London: Constable and Co., 1918), 99. Additional page references will be included in the text.
4   Quoted in Jaqueline Tyrwhitt, *Patrick Geddes in India* (London: Lund Humphries, 1947), 18.
5   Lanchester, *Town Planning*, 42, 49.
6   Ibid., 62–63.
7   Macmillan, *Seaports*, 267, 288, 274–75; *The Times—Special India Number* (Feb. 18, 1930), 177.
8   Rudyard Kipling, *The City of Dreadful Night* (Leipzig: Bernard Tauchnitz, 1900). Additional page references to this edition will be included in the text.
9   *Calcutta Sanitation: Being a Series of Editorial Articles Reprinted from the Indian Medical Record* (Calcutta: Record Press, 1896), 16–30 passim.
10 Quoted in Rajat Ray, *Urban Roots of Indian Nationalism* (New Delhi: Vikas Publishing House, 1979), 71.
11 Ibid.
12 E. P. Richards, *Report on the Condition, Improvement and Town Planning of the City of Calcutta and Contiguous Areas* (Calcutta: Calcutta Improvement Trust, 1914), 15. Additional page references will be included in the text.
13 Ray, *Urban Roots*, 73.
14 *Calcutta Illustrated* (Calcutta: Thacker, Spink, 1900), 52.
15 Patrick Geddes, *Barra Bazaar Improvement: A Report to the Corporation of Calcutta* (Calcutta: Corporation Press, 1919), 12.
16 Ibid., 29.
17 Macmillan, *Seaports*, 43, 47, 46.
18 *The Times: Special India Number*, 171–73.
19 Sydney Low, *A Vision of India* (London: Smith, Elder, 1907), 29.
20 Richards, *Report*, 385.
21 Discussion of chawls from A. R. Burnett-Hurst, *Labour and Housing in Bombay* (London: P. S. King and Son, 1925).
22 Ibid., 27.
23 H. B. Shivadasani, "City Improvement," a paper read before the Indian Institute of Architects, Oct. 20, 1938. *Journal of the Indian Institute of Architects* 6 (Jan. 1939): 86.
24 Quoted in the *Bombay Civic Journal* 30, no. 8 (Oct. 1983): 10.
25 W. R. Davidge, "The Development of Bombay," *Town Planning Review* 10 (Feb. 1924): 278.
26 Claude Batley, "Architectural Fables and Foibles," *Journal of the Indian Institute of Architects* 3 (Jan. 1937): 205; "The Architect's Sphere in Town Planning," *Journal of the Indian Institute of Architects* 10 (Nov. 1944): 23; and *Bombay's Houses and Homes* (Bombay: National Information and Publications, 1949), 8.
27 Macmillan, *Seaports*, 231.
28 *The Times*, special India number (Feb. 18, 1930), 159.
29 Delhi Town Planning Committee, *Final Report on the Town Planning of the New Imperial Capital* (London: H. M. Stationery Office, 1913), 2.
30 Quoted in Hume, *Report on the Relief of Congestion in Delhi* (Simla: Government of India Press, 1936).
31 Delhi Town Planning Committee, *Final Report*, 18.
32 *Report on the Relif of Congestion in Delhi*, 18.
33 Quoted in Irving, *Indian Summer*, 78.
34 Delhi Town Planning Committee, *Final Report*, 15.
35 Cecil Beaton, *Far East* (London: B. T. Batsford, 1945), 8–9.
36 Walter George, "The Roadside Planting of Lutyens' New Delhi," *Urban and Rural Planning Thought* 1 (Jan. 1958): 79.
37 Sir Reginald Craddock quoted in Irving, *Indian Summer*, 88, 79.
38 "The New Capital City at Delhi," *Town Planning Review* 4 (Oct. 1913): 186.
39 *The Times*, special India number, 161, and George, "Roadside Planting," 79.
40 Percival and Margaret Spear, *India Remembered* (Delhi: Orient Longman, 1981), preface, and Beaton, *Far East*, 9.
41 Delhi Town Planning Committee, *Final Report*, 2.
42 D. Natarajan, *Census of India, 1971: Indian Census Through a Hundred Years* (New Delhi: Office of the Registrar General, 1971), 432, and Census of India 1941, 1:26. Quoted in Ashish Bose and Jatinder Bhatia, *India's Urbanization, 1901–2001* (New Delhi: Tata McGraw-Hill, 1978), 75.

Chapter 5. The Modern Movement

1   Aldous Huxley, *Jesting Pilate* (New York: George Doran, 1926), 17–18.
2   A. G. Shoosmith, "Present Day Architecture in India," *The Nineteenth Century and After* 123 (Feb. 1938): 209.

3 Walter George quoted in Patwant Singh, "The Architecture of Walter George," *Design* 4 (Sept. 1960): 22.

4 This quotation and those in the next two paragraphs are from ibid., 16–25 passim.

5 Kate Platt, *The Home and Health in India* (London: Balliere, Tindall and Cox, 1923), 16–17.

6 Editorial, *Journal of the Indian Institute of Architects* 4 (Jan. 1937): 1.

7 Mrs. Hansa Mehta, "Domestic Architecture in India," *Journal of the Indian Institute of Architecture* 3 (April 1936): 116.

8 Dennis Kincaid, *British Social Life in India 1606–1937* (London: Routledge and Sons, 1938), 288.

9 James Mackenzie Maclean, *A Guide to Bombay* (Bombay: Bombay Gazette Steam Press, 1875), 166, and Robert Cable, "The Architectural Treatment of Reinforced Concrete," *Indian Institute of Architects Yearbook 1925–26*, 38.

10 Cable, ibid., 31–32, 36.

11 Quoted in H. J. Billimoria, "The Origin and Growth of the Indian Institute of Architects," *Journal of the Indian Institute of Architects* 9 (Jan. 1942): 203.

12 Correspondence, *Journal of the Indian Institute of Architects* 2 (Oct. 1935): 49.

13 Billimoria, "Origin and Growth," 210.

14 Editorial, *Journal of the Indian Institute of Architects* 6 (July 1940): 1.

15 Patrick Geddes, *Report on the Re-planning of Six Towns in the Bombay Presidency, 1915* (Bombay: Government Printing and Stationery Office, 1965), 13.

16 Claude Batley, Inaugural Address, *Bombay Architectural Association Yearbook 1925–26*, 16–17.

17 Editorial, *Bombay Architectural Association Yearbook 1925–26*, 5.

18 Chatterjee and Corbett quotations from *Modern Indian Architecture—The Work of Sris Chandra Chatterjee, Architect, Calcutta* (Calcutta: Modern Art Press, 1935), 3–6.

19 Paul Schultze-Naumburg quoted in Barbara Miller Lane, *Architecture and Politics in Germany 1919–1945* (Cambridge: Harvard University Press, 1968), 135.

20 Claude Batley, "This New Architecture," *Journal of the Indian Institute of Architects* 2 (Jan. 1935): 103–04.

21 Ibid.

22 R. S. Despande, *Modern Ideal Homes for India* (Poona: United Book Corporation, 1939), 78, 80. Further page references will be included in the text.

23 H. J. Billimoria, "Interior Decoration," *Journal of the Indian Institute of Architects* 8 (Oct. 1941): 186.

24 A. G. Shoosmith, "Present-Day Architecture," 211.

25 A. R. Burnett-Hurst, *Labour and Housing in Bombay* (London: P. S. King and sons, 1925), 91.

26 K. H. Vakil, "Architecture as a Social Necessity," *Journal of the Indian Institute of Architects* 3 (Feb. 1936): 79.

27 Perviz N. Peerozshaw Dubash, *Hindu Art in Its Social Setting* (Madras: National Literature Publishing, 1934), 254–55.

28 Shoosmith, "Present-Day Architecture," 204–05, 210–11.

29 Claude Batley, "Architectural Education in India," *Journal of the Indian Institute of Architects* 6 (Jan. 1940): 83, and "This Question of Tradition," *Journal of the Indian Institute of Architects,* 7 (Jan. 1941): 77.

30 Bernard Matthews, "The Evolution of Architecture in Calcutta," *Journal of the Indian Institute of Architects* 8 (Jan. 1942): 230–32; L. M. Chitale, "Architecture in India," *Journal of the Indian Institute of Architects* 12 (April 1946): 58; and Janardan Shastri, "Traditional Domestic Architecture of Bombay," *Journal of the Indian Institute of Architects* 6 (April 1939): 140.

31 H. G. Rawlinson, *British Achievement in India* (London: William Hodge, 1948), 240.

32 John Summerson, "The Mischievous Analogy," an essay read before the Architectural Association in 1941, and included in *Heavenly Mansions* (New York: W. W. Norton, 1963), 205.

Chapter 6. The Post-Independence City

1 Jawaharlal Nehru, *Speeches, 1963–64* (New Delhi: Ministry of Information and Broadcasting, 1968), 5:100.

2 Ashish Bose assisted by Jatinder Bhatia, *India's Urbanization 1901–2001* (New Delhi: Tata McGraw Hill, 1978), 29.

3 *Report of the Delhi Improvement Trust Enquiry Committee* (Delhi: 1951), 1:3.

4 The Ford Foundation team included Albert Mayer, Gerald Breese, Edward G. Echeverria, Walter Hedden, Bert F. Hoselitz, Arch Dotson, Britton Harris, and George Goetschius. In addition, the Ford Foundation engaged the British architect Gordon Cullen as a consultant. He had become noted for his visual analyses of British townscapes and he produced a series of architectural studies for selected areas of Delhi. These were published in a book entitled *The Ninth Delhi* (New Delhi: Government of India Press, 1961).

5 Delhi Development Authority, *Master Plan for Delhi* (Delhi, 1962), 1.

6 "Delhi 2001," *Vikas Varta* 2 (a house journal of the Delhi Development Authority, special issue; 1985): 10.

7 "Development of New Delhi," *The Indian Architect* 23 (May 1981): 103.

8 Inder Malhotra, "Rebuilding Lutyens's Delhi," *Indian Institute of Architects Journal* 43 (Oct.–Dec. 1977): 10.

9   Delhi Development Authority, *Draft Master Plan for Delhi* (Delhi, 1960), 1:59.

10 "Delhi 2001," 15.

11 Ibid., 42.

12 "Inner City Problems of Bombay," *The Indian Architect,* May 1980, 83, and R. K. Wishwakarma and Gangadhar Jha, "Employment and Function of New Delhi: A Model of Growth Structure," in *The Future of New Delhi,* 127.

13 Ashok Mitra, *Delhi Capital City* (Delhi: CFPI Reprography Unit, 1968), 14.

14 Ibid., 49.

15 "Calcutta: The Basic Development Plan," *Royal Institute of Architects Journal* 74 (March 1967): 111.

16 Calcutta Metropolitan Planning Organisation, *Basic Development Plan for the Calcutta Metropolitan District, 1966–1980* (Calcutta: Government of West Bengal, 1966), 86–87.

17 Quoted in ibid., ix.

18 Quoted in Allen G. Noble and Ashok K. Dutt, *Indian Urbanization and Planning* (New Delhi: Tata McGraw Hill, 1977), 261–62. Among the foreign planners involved in the Calcutta Development Plan were Edward Echeverria, Gordon Colin, Brian Berry, Norton Ginsberg, Ian Burton, Jac. P. Thijsse, Leo Jakobson, and the consulting firms of Wilbur Smith, and Metcalf and Eddy.

19 Calcutta Metropolitan Planning Organisation, *Basic Plan,* 1.

20 Ibid., 5.

21 Ibid., 35.

22 Ibid., 60.

23 Noble and Dutt, *Indian Urbanization,* 271.

24 Ashok Mitra, *Calcutta: India's City* (Calcutta: New Age, 1963), 39.

25 Bombay City and Suburbs Post-War Development Committee, *Preliminary Report of the Development of Suburbs and Town Planning Panel* (Bombay: Government Central Press, 1946), 10.

26 *Journal of the Indian Institute of Architects* 12 (July 1945): 2.

27 *The Greater Bombay Scheme: Report of the Housing Panel* (Bombay: Municipal Printing Press, 1946), 67.

28 N. V. Modak and Albert Mayer, *An Outline of the Master Plan for Greater Bombay* (Bombay: Municipal Printing Press, 1948), 8, 3.

29 *Report on the Development Plan for Greater Bombay* (Bombay: Government Central Press, 1964), lx.

30 Ibid., 50.

31 Ibid., 50, 86.

32 S. Muthiah, *Madras Discovered* (Madras: Affiliated East-West Press, 1981), 163.

33 The Madras metropolitan area was defined in 1965 in the Interim Development Plan created by the Tamil Nadu Directorate of Town Planning. It comprised an area of 725 square miles. The Madras urban agglomeration, of 330 square miles, included the city and a series of urbanized villages located on the periphery of the city and along transportation corridors leading to the city.

34 "Madras: A Planning Study," *Urban and Rural Planning Thought* 3 (April 1960): 74.

35 *Madras Metropolitan Plan, 1971–1991* (Government of Tamil Nadu, 1971), preface.

36 Ibid., 34.

37 *Structure Plan for Madras Metropolitan Area,* vol. 2, *Guidelines for Growth* (Madras Metropolitan Development Authority, June 1980), 15. The structure plan comprised three volumes. Volume 1, *The Existing Situation,* was written jointly by the MMDA team and the British consultants. Volume 2 was written by the consultants and presented in the form of policy recommendations to the MMDA. Volume 3, *Working Papers,* consisted of a series of technical papers produced in the course of the study. In addition to Alan Turner, the consulting team included David Pinnock, Richard Wetmacott, Alan Proudlove, Kenneth Wren, and Roy Brockman. They worked together with an eleven-member study team from the Metropolitan Development Authority.

38 Patwant Singh, "On the Technical Failure of India," *Design* 13 (Aug. 1969): 11, and "Delhi, Past, Present and Future," *Design* 14 (March 1970): 26, 27.

39 Charles Correa quoted in "New Bombay," *Architectural Review* 150 (Dec. 1971): 337.

40 Vic Tapner, "Culture Clash," *Indian Institute of Architects Journal* 45 (July–Sept. 1979): 13.

41 Bose, *India's Urbanization,* 29.

42 Ibid.

Chapter 7. The Architecture of Independence

1   "Royal Gold Medalists, 1848–1984," *RIBA Journal* 91 (May 1984): 143.

2   V. R. Talvalkar, "Future of Indian Traditional Style," notes from a paper given to the Indian Institute of Architects, Aug. 28, 1947, *Indian Institute of Architects Journal* 15 (Jan. 1948): 51, 3. "Modernism in India," editorial, *Design* 23 (Jan. 1979): 17.

3   "Indianness in Artistic Expression," *Design* 15 (June 1971): 15.

4   G. H. Franklin, "Towards an Indigenous Architecture," *Design* 1 (Nov. 1957): 5, and "Without Comment," *Design* 2 (Jan. 1958): 1.

5   S. K. Saraswati, *Indian Art at the Crossroads* (Calcutta: Pilgrim Publications, 1973), 25.

6   Ranjeet Sabikhi, "Outdoor Space in the Indian Context," *Techniques et Architecture* 3 (Aug.–Sept. 1985): 133.

7   All three quotations are from "The Sixties: A P/A Symposium on the State of Architecture," *Progressive Architecture* 42 (March 1961): 122–33.

8   Patwant Singh, "Contemporary Classicism," *Design* 3 (July 1959): 49, 50, 51.

9   S. H. Parelkar, "The Present Day Architect," *The Indian Architect* 3 (Nov. 1961): 18.

10 Editorial, *Journal of the Indian Institute of Architects* 27 (Jan.–March 1961): 1. The editors at this time were architects Vina Mody and Charles Correa.

11 Ranjit Sabikhi, "Outdoor Space in the Indian Context," *Techniques et Architecture* 3 (Aug.–Sept. 1985): 138.

12 William Curtis, *Modern Architecture since 1900* (Englewood Cliffs, N.J.: Prentice Hall, 1987), 397, 398.

13 Editorial, *Indian Architect* 4 (Aug. 1962): 5.

14 Reproduced in the *Indian Architect* 4 (Sept. 1962): 18–19.

15 "The Tale of Two Cities," *The Indian Architect* 23 (Jan. 1981): 7.

16 Patwant Singh, "The Nine Delhis," *Design* 15 (March 1971): 13.

17 Editorial, "A Capital of Quality," *Design* 28 (Jan.–March 1984): 21.

18 Sudhir Diwan and Kannaiya Vakhariya, "Big Money and Political Power Have Made Bombay's Backbay Scheme India's Biggest Urban Fraud," *Design* 24 (Jan.–March 1980): 25.

19 Society for the Preservation of Archival Materials and Monuments of Calcutta, *Calcutta: Save Its Past to Save Its Future* (Calcutta: n.d.). No page numbers.

20 J. R. Bhalla, "The Role of the Architect in India Today," *Royal Institute of Architects Journal* 74 (March 1967): 102.

21 Editorial, *Indian Architect* 15 (Feb. 1973): 134.

22 M. B. Achwal, "Low-Cost Housing," *The Architectural Review* 158 (Dec. 1971): 367, and Editorial, *Design* 8 (Feb. 1964): 13.

23 Editorial, *Design* 8 (May 1964): 13, and Parelkar, "Present Day Architect," 19.

24 Editorial, "The Architect's Role in Society," *Design* 23 (Feb. 1979): 17–18.

25 Editorial, *Journal of the Indian Institute of Architects* (Jan.–March 1961): 1.

26 "Housing the Middle Class—Delhi Development Authority Way," *The Indian Architect* 22 (Nov. 1980): 202.

27 B. M. Sinha, "The Damaging Record of the Delhi Development Authority: From the Dubious to the Disgraceful," *Design* 27 (April–June 1983): 50.

28 Sabikhi, "Outdoor Space," 134.

29 "Time to Establish a National Trust for Historic Buildings," *Design* 19 (March 1975): 17, and Editorial, *Design* 6 (Aug. 1962): 15.

30 "Delhi 2001," 44, 18.

31 "Saving Delhi from Becoming the Private Preserve of a Few," *Design* 26 (Oct.–Dec. 1982): 21.

32 William Wurster, "Indian Vernacular Architecture: Wai and Cochin," *Perspecta* 5 (1959): 38.

33 Gillian Tindall, *City of Gold* (London: Temple Smith, 1982), 26, 210.

34 Society for the Preservation of Archival Materials and Monuments, *Calcutta* (pages not numbered).

35 "Intach and the Indian Culture," *Design* 28 (Oct.–Dec. 1984): 19.

36 Nadeem, "How Form Follows Fiasco," 39–40.

37 Charles Correa, "Programmes and Priorities," *Architectural Review* 150 (Dec. 1971): 329, 331.

38 "Mr Nehru on Architecture," *Urban and Rural Planning Thought* 5 (April 1959): 49.

39 Albert Einstein, *Out of My Later Years* (London: Thames and Hudson, 1950), quoted in *Morrow's International Dictionary of Quotations,* compiled by Jonathan Green (New York: Morrow, 1982), 19.

40 Indira Gandhi, letter to the *Journal of the Indian Institute of Architects* 34 (Feb. 12, 1968).

Selected Bibliography

Architecture

The Colonial Period

"Anglo-Indian Architecture." 1866. *Bombay Builder*, May 5, 228–29.

An Anglo-Indian. 1882. *Indian Outfits and Establishments*. London: Upcott Gill.

Archer, Mildred. 1966. "Aspects of Classicism in India." *Country Life* 140 (Nov. 3): 1142–46.

Archer, William. 1917. *India and the Future*. London: Hutchinson.

"Architects in India." 1866. *Bombay Builder,* Dec. 5, 121.

"Architectural Development in Bombay during the Last 25 Years." 1940. *IIA Journal* 6 (Jan.): 87–88.

"Architectural Education: The Growing Demand." 1940. *IIA Journal* 6 (July): 3–4.

"Architecture in Bombay." 1868. *Bombay Builder*, Aug. 5, 62–63.

Atkinson, George Franklin. 1911. *Curry and Rice on Forty Plates*. 5th ed. London: W. Thacker.

Batley, Claude. 1934. "Architects' Commission and Salaries." *IIA Journal* 1 (April): 14.

———. 1935a. "Modern Architecture in India." *IIA Journal* 1 (April): 118–19.

———. 1935b. "Presidential Address for the Session 1935–36," *IIA Journal* 2 (Oct.): 47–49.

———. 1936. "The Engineer and the Architect in India: A Plea for Co-operation rather than Competition." IIA Journal 3 (April): 117–23.

———. 1937a. "Architectural Fables and Foibles." *IIA Journal* 3 (Jan.): 204–5.

———. 1937b. "This New Architecture." *IIA Journal* 1 (Jan.): 103–4.

———. 1940a. "Architectural Education in India." *IIA Journal* 6 (Jan.): 82–85.

———. 1940b. "The Making of an Architect in India." *IIA Journal* 6 (Oct.): 57–58.

———. 1942. "The Prospect for Architectural Education in India." *IIA Journal* 8 (Jan.): 212–15.

———. 1946. *Architecture*. Oxford: Oxford University Press.

Begg, John. 1920. "Architecture in India." *RIBA Journal*, 3d ser., 27 (April): 333–49.

Begg, John, and Crouch, Henry. 1910–21. *Annual Report on Architectural Work in India*. India: Office of the Consulting Architect. Calcutta: Department of Industries and Labour, Public Works Branch.

Bence-Jones, Mark. 1970. "An English Mansion in Bengal." *Country Life* 147 (Feb. 5): 328–29.

———. 1973. *Palaces of the Raj*. London: Allen and Unwin.

Billimoria, H. J. 1941. "Interior Decoration." *IIA Journal* 8 (Oct.): 184–87.

———. 1942. "The Origin and Growth of the Indian Institute of Architects." *IIA Journal* 8 (Jan): 203–4.

Birdwood, George. 1868. "Want of Architecture in Bombay." *Bombay Builder*, Sept. 5, 105–6.

———. 1878. *Handbook to the British Indian Section, Paris Universal Exposition*. London: Office of the Royal Commission.

Bombay Architectural Association Year Book. 1925–26.

"Bombay Blackwood Furniture." 1867. *Bombay Builder*, Dec. 5, 208–9.

Book of the Madras Exhibition, 1915–1916, The. 1916. Madras: Government Press.

Brown, Hilton. 1948. *The Sahibs*. London: William Hodge.

"A Building Act for Bombay." 1865. *Bombay Builder*, Aug. 5, 24–25.

Butler, Arthur Stanley George. 1950. *The Architecture of Sir Edwin Lutyens*. Vol. 2. New York: Charles Scribner's Sons.

Cameron, Roderick. 1958. *Shadows From India.* London: Heinemann.

Centenary: Government College of Art and Craft, Calcutta, 1864–1964. Calcutta: Statesman Press. (no date)

Chatterton, Alfred. 1911. "Art Industries of Southern India." *Journal of Indian Art and Industries* 15: 42–49.

Chitale, L. M. 1946. "Architecture in India." *IIA Journal* 12 (April): 57–59.

Clarke, C. Purdon. 1884. "Street Architecture of India." *Journal of the Society of Arts* 32 (July 4): 650, 779–90.

Clemons, Mrs. Major. 1841. *The Manners and Customs of Society in India.* London: Smith, Elder and Son.

Concrete Association of India. 1946. *Sixty Designs for Your New Home.* Bombay.

Curzon, George N., Marquis of Kedleston. 1925. *British Government in India.* 2 vols. London: Cassell.

Davies, Philip. 1985. *Splendours of the Raj: British Architecture in India, 1660–1947.* London: John Murray.

Despande, R. S. 1931. *Residential Buildings Suited to India.* Poona: Privately published.

————. 1939. *Modern Ideal Homes for India.* Poona: United Book Corporation.

————. 1969. *Cheap and Healthy Homes for the Middle Classes in India.* 2d. ed. Poona: United Book Corporation.

Ditchburn, D. W. 1940. "Presidential Address." *IIA Journal* 6 (July): 5–10.

Dongerkery, Kamala S. 1973. *Interior Decoration in India.* Bombay: Taraporavala.

Doyley, Charles, and Williamson, Captain Thomas. 1813. *The European in India.* London: Blagdon.

Dutton, Major the Honorable C. 1882. *Life in India.* London: W. H. Allen.

Edwardes, Michael. 1967. *British India, 1772–1947.* New York: Taplinger.

————. 1969. *Bound to Exile.* London: Sidgwick and Jackson.

————. 1971. *East-West Passage.* New York: Taplinger.

Edwards, Ralph, and Codrington, K. de B. 1935. "The Indian Period of European Furniture." *Apollo* 21 (Feb.): 67–71; (March): 130–34; (April): 187–92; (June): 335–38; and 22 (July): 13–18.

————. 1937. "India and the West; Reflections upon a Recent Controversy." *Apollo* 26 (Nov.): 267–70.

"Exhibition of Architectural Work." 1940. *IIA Journal* 6 (July): 11–14; 7 (Oct.): 51–54.

Fay, Mrs. Eliza. 1925. *Original Letters from India, 1779–1815.* London: Hogarth Press.

Fergusson, James. 1866. "On the Study of Indian Architecture." *Journal of the Society of Arts* 15 (Dec. 21): 71–80.

————. 1910. *History of Indian and Eastern Architecture.* London: John Murray.

Frazer, R. W. 1896. *British India.* London: Fisher Unwin.

"First Impressions of Art and Architecture in Bombay." 1865. *Bombay Builder,* July 5, 4–6, and Aug. 5, 25–26.

Frere, Sir Bartle E. 1870. "Modern Architecture in Western India." *Building News* 18 (June): 421–22.

Gerrard, C. R. 1942. "Tradition and the Modern Architect," *IIA Journal* 8 (Jan.): 252–55.

Gilchrist, J. B. 1825. *The General East India Guide and Vade Mecum* (Digest of the work of the late Thomas Williamson). London: Kingsbury, Parbury and Allen.

Golant, William. 1975. *The Long Afternoon: British India, 1601–1947.* London: Hamish Hamilton.

Greenberger, Allen J. 1969. *The British Image of India.* Oxford: Oxford University Press.

Griffiths, Percival. 1952. *The British Impact on India.* London: Macdonald.

Havell, E. B. 1906. *Stone Carving in Bengal.* Calcutta: Bengal Secretariat.

————. 1912a. *The Basis for Artistic and Industrial Revival in India.* Madras: Theosophist Office.

————. 1912b. *Essays on Indian Art, Industry and Education.* Madras: Nateson and Co.

————. 1912c. "A Message of Hope for India." *The Nineteenth Century and After* 72 (Dec.): 1274–82.

————. 1913. *Indian Architecture.* London: John Murray.

Heber, Reginald. 1828. *Narrative of a Journey through the Upper Provinces of India: From Calcutta to Bombay 1824–1826.* 3 vols. London: John Murray.

Hendley, T. H. 1888. "Decorative Art in Rajputana." *Journal of Indian Art and Industries* 2:43–49.

"The High Court, Calcutta: Public Works of India." 1869. *The Builder* 27 (Oct. 30): 857–66.

Hitchins, Francis. 1967. *The Illusion of Permanence: British Imperialism in India.* Princeton: Princeton University Press.

Hull, Edmund C. P. 1878. *The European in India, or the Anglo-Indian's Vade Mecum*; and with Mair, R. S. *A Medical Guide for Anglo-Indians.* London: Kegan Paul.

Huxley, Aldous. 1926. *Jesting Pilate.* New York: George Doran.

"The Ideal Home Exhibition." 1938. *IIA Journal* 4 (Jan): 319–25.

"Indian Institute of Architects 25th Year." 1942. *RIBA Journal* 3d ser. 49:151.

Indian Institute of Architects Yearbook. 1923–24. Bombay.

"The Indian Master Builder." 1912. *RIBA Journal,* 3d ser., 20 (Nov): 59–60.

"The Institute and the Profession." 1943. *IIA Journal* 10 (Oct.): 27–29.

James, Sir Evan. 1915–16. "Wood Carving in Gujerat." *Journal of Indian Art and Industry* 18:55–76.

Kapadia, P. P. 1936. "Indian Institute of Architects Presidential Address." *IIA Journal* 3 (July): 149–50.

Keith, Major J. B. 1886. "Indian Stone Carving." *Journal of Indian Art and Industry* 1:110–12.

Kincaid, Dennis. 1938. *British Social Life in India, 1606–1937.* London: Routledge and Sons.

King, Anthony. 1977. "The Westernization of Domestic Architecture in India." *Art and Archaeology Research Papers* 11 (June): 32–41.

———. 1984. *The Bungalow.* London: Routledge and Kegan Paul.

Kipling, John Lockwood. 1886a. "The Brass and Copper Ware of the Punjab and Cashmere." *Journal of Indian Art and Industry* 1:5–8.

———. 1886b. "Indian Architecture of Today." *Journal of Indian Art* 1:25–42.

———. 1887. "The Industries of the Punjab." *Journal of Indian Art and Industry* 2:25–42, 57–63.

Kshirasagar, G. B. 1939. "Architecture and Architectural Education." *IIA Journal* 6 (July): 7–9.

Lanchester, H. V. 1942. "Architecture and Housing in India." *Architectural Design and Construction* 12 (May): 94–101.

Majumdar, R. C., ed. 1965. *British Paramountcy and Indian Renaissance.* bombay: Bharatuja Vidya Bhavan.

Martyn, Margaret. 1948. "Georgian Architecture in Calcutta." *Country Life* 104 (Dec. 3): 1174–1177.

Matthews, Bernard. 1942. "The Evolution of Architecture in Calcutta." *IIA Journal* 8 (Jan.): 229–32.

Mayhew, Arthur. 1926. *The Education of India.* London: Faber and Gwyer.

Medley, Julius George. 1873. *India and Indian Engineering.* London: E. and F. N. Spon.

Mehta, Mrs. Hansa. 1936. "Domestic Architecture in India." *IIA Journal* 2 (April): 115–16.

Mhatre, G. B. 1937. "Flats on Back-Bay Reclamation." *IIA Journal* 3 (July): 270–71.

Mistri, M. J. P., and Billimoria, A. 1942. "Architectural Development in Bombay during the Last Twenty-Five Years." *IIA Journal* 8 (Jan.): 216–23.

Mitchell, George. 1977. "Neo-Classicism in Bengali Temple Architecture." *Art and Archaeology Research Papers* 11 (June): 28–31.

———. 1980. "Neo-Classical Hindu Temples in Bengal." *Lotus International* 26 (June): 95–100.

"Modern Architecture in India." 1870. *The Builder,* Aug. 27, 680–82. (Summary of a lecture given by Lord Napier.)

"Modern Architecture in India." 1937. *IIA Journal* 3 (Jan.): 199.

Morris, Jan, with Winchester, Simon. 1983. *Stones of Empire: The Buildings of the Raj.* Oxford: Oxford University Press.

Murzban, Muyban Muncherji. 1915. *Leaves from the Life of Kahn Bahudur Muncherji Cowasji Murzban, C.I.E.* Bombay: Marzban.

Nilsson, Sten. 1968. *European Architecture in India, 1750–1850.* London: Faber and Faber.

Oertel, F. O. 1913. "Indian Architecture and Its Suitability for Modern Requirements." *East India Association Journal,* N.S. 4:276–78.

Ormerod, H. E. 1935. "A Layman's Views on Building Design." *IIA Journal* 2 (Oct.): 53–58.

Padfield, Rev. J. E. 1908. *The Hindu at Home.* London: Hamilton Kent.

Parks, Fanny. 1850. *Wanderings of a Pilgrim in Search of the Picturesque.* 2 vols. London: Pelham Richardson; repr. Oxford: Oxford University Press, 1975.

"Past Architecture and Present Building." 1867. *Bombay Builder,* Sept. 5, 91–92. Response, Oct. 5, 154–55. Response to response, Nov. 5, 180–81.

Pieper, Jan. 1980. "European Tombs in the Moghul Style." *Lotus International* 26:90–93.

Platt, Kate. 1923. *The Home and Health in India.* London: Balliere, Tindall and Cox.

Princep, V. C. 1879. *Imperial India.* London: Chapman and Hall.

"The Question of Tradition." 1941. *IIA Journal* 7 (Jan.): 77–78.

Rawlinson, H. G. 1948. *The British Achievement in India.* London: William Hodge.

Report of the Second Indian Industrial Conference, held at Calcutta, 1906. 1907. Calcutta: Mazumdar Press.

Roberts, Emma. 1837. *Scenes and Characteristics of Hindustan.* London: Allen and Co.

Rowe, Rev. A. D. 1881. *Every Day Life in India.* New York: American Tract Society.

Saini, Balwant Singh. 1963. "Cantonment Architecture of India." *Design* 7 (March): 15–18.

Sanderson, Gordon, with Hasan, Maulvi Zafar, and Gupte, Y. R. 1916. *Delhi Province. List of Muhammedan and Hindu Monuments.* Part I. Shahjahanabad. Calcutta: Superintendent of Government Printing.

Sastu, Pandit Natesa. 1888. "The Decline of South Indian Arts." *Journal of Indian Art and Industry* 3, nos. 25–32: 23–24, 28–32.

"Sir Bartle Frere." 1867. *Bombay Builder,* Feb. 5, 171–72, 175.

Smith, T. Roger. 1873. "Architectural Art in India." *Journal of the Society of the Arts* 21 (March 7), 278–87.

Spear, Percival and Margaret. 1981. *India Remembered.* Delhi: Orient Longman.

Spear, T. G. P. 1932. *The Nabobs: A Study of the Social Life of the English in 18th-Century India.* Oxford: Oxford University Press.

Stamp, Gavin. 1976. "Indian Summer (Two British Architects Who Worked in India Earlier This Century)." *Architectural Review* 159 (June): 365–72.

————. 1978. "Marble Palace." *Architectural Design* 35 (Oct.): 161–66.

————. 1981. "British Architecture in India, 1857–1947." *Royal Society for the Encouragement of Arts, Manufactures and Commerce. Proceedings* 129 (May): 357–79. Also printed in *Design* 25 (Oct.–Dec. 1981): 25–40.

The Story of the Sir J. J. School of Art, 1857–1957. [1957/58?]. Bombay: Government of Maharashtra.

"Send-off to Professor Claude Batley." 1944. *IIA Journal* 10 (Jan.): 61–66.

Shoosmith, A. G. 1938. "Present-Day Architecture in India." *The Nineteenth Century and After* 123 (Feb.): 204–13.

Tarapor, Mahrukh. 1980. "John Lockwood Kipling and British Art Education in India." *Victorian Studies* 24:53–81.

————. 1982. "Growse in Bulandshahr." *Architectural Review* 172 (Sept.): 44–52.

Temple, Captain R. C. 1886. "A Study of Modern Indian Architecture as Displayed in a British Cantonment." *Journal of Indian Art* 1:57–60.

Temple, Sir Richard. 1881. *India in 1880.* London: John Murray.

Trevelyan, G. O. 1864. *The Competition Wallah.* London and Cambridge: Macmillan.

Vakil, K. H. 1936. "Architecture as a Social Necessity." *IIA Journal* 2 (Feb.): 79.

Valentia, George, Viscount. 1809. *Voyages and Travels to India, Ceylon, the Red Sea, Abyssinia, and Egypt in the Years 1802, 1803, 1805, and 1806.* 3 vols. London: William Miller.

Williamson, Thomas. 1810. *East India Vade Mecum.* 2 vols. London: Black, Parry and Kingsbury.

————. 1813. *The European in India.* London: Blagdon.

The Growth and Planning of Bombay, Madras, Calcutta, and Delhi

The Colonial Period

Adams, William Henry. 1888. *India: Pictorial and Descriptive.* London: T. Nelson.

Ahuja, Sarayu. 1979. "Indian Settlement Patterns and House Designs." *Art and Archaeology Research Papers* 15 (June): 33–38.

Ansari, Jamal. 1977. "Evolution of Town Planning Practice and System of Urban Government in India." *Urban and Rural Planning Thought* 20 (Jan.–Mar.): 9–23.

Back Bay Enquiry Committee. 1926. *Evidence Oral and Documentary.* 2 vols. London: H. M. Stationery Office.

Bagchi, P. C. 1939. *Calcutta, Past and Present.* Calcutta: Calcutta University.

Barlow, Glyn. 1921. *The Story of Madras.* London: Humphrey Milford.

Barry, John. 1940. *Calcutta 1940.* Calcutta: Central Press.

Batley, Claude. 1934. "Bombay Looks Ahead." *IIA Journal* 1 (April): 11–13.

————. 1944. "The Architect's Sphere in Town Planning." *IIA Journal* 11 (Nov.): 21–24.

————. 1945. "The Housing of Labour." *IIA Journal* 12 (Oct.): 18–21.

————. 1946. "Post-War Housing in Bombay." *IIA Journal* 13 (Oct.): 23–25.

————. 1949. *Bombay's Houses and Homes.* Bombay: National Information and Publications Ltd.

Bentley, Richard. 1852. *Life in Bombay.* London: Richard Bentley.

Blechynden, Kathleen. 1978. *Calcutta, Past and Present.* Calcutta: General Printers and Publishers.

Bombay City and Suburbs Post-War Development Committee. 1946. *Preliminary Report of the Development of Suburbs and Town Planning Panel.* Bombay: Government Central Press.

"The Bombay Flats." 1866. *Bombay Builder*, Sept. 5, 47–48.

Bombay Joint Town Planning Committee. 1939. "Report for the Period Ending 31 December 1938." *IIA Journal* 6 (Oct.): 56–59.

Bombay: Past and Present. 1919. Bombay: The Times Press.

Bombay Port Trust. 1973. *The Port of Bombay: A Brief History.* Bombay: Bombay Port Trust.

Bombay Presidency Development Committee. 1914. *Report of the Bombay Development Committee.* Bombay.

"Bombay Town Planning Act, 1915." 1916. *Town Planning Review* 6 (April): 250–51.

Bose, Nemi. 1975. *Calcutta: People and Empire.* Calcutta: India Book Exchange.

Burnett-Hurst, A. R. 1925. *Labour and Housing in Bombay.* London: P. S. King and Sons.

Busteed, H. E. 1897. *Echoes from Old Calcutta.* Calcutta: Thacker, Spink and Co.

Byron, Robert. 1931. "New Delhi." *Architectural Review* 69 (Jan.): 1–30.

The Calcutta Improvement Act, 1911, and Allied Matters. Calcutta: Calcutta Improvement Trust.

Calcutta Improvement Trust. 1914–67. *Annual Reports.* Calcutta: Calcutta Metropolitan Development Authority. 1981.

Calcutta Port Trust. 1920. *The Calcutta Port Trust: A Brief History of Fifty Years' Work, 1870–1920.* Calcutta: Thacker, Spink and Co.

Calcutta Sanitation: Being a Series of Editorial Articles Reprinted from the Indian Medical Record. 1896. Calcutta: Record Press.

Calcutta: The City of Palaces. 1931. Calcutta: Times of India Press.

Calcutta 200 Years: A Tollygunge Club Perspective. 1981. Calcutta: Tollygunge Club, Ltd.

Cameron, Roderick. 1958. *Time of the Mango Flowers*. London: Heinemann.

Campbell, James McNabb, 1894. *Materials toward a Statistical Account of the Town and Island of Bombay*. 3 vols. *Bombay Gazetteer*, 26 (District Gazetteer Series). Bombay: Government Central Press.

Carey, W. H. 1907. *The Good Old Days of the Honorable John Company*. Calcutta: R. Cambray.

Carpenter, Edward. 1904. *From Adam's Peak to Elephanta*. 2d ed. New York: Dutton and Co.

Centenary: Government College of Art and Craft, Calcutta, 1864–1964. Calcutta: Statesman Press.

Centenary Souvenir: University of Bombay, 1857–1957. Bombay.

Chander, Tertius, and Fox, Gerald. 1974. *3,000 Years of Urban Growth*. New York and London: Academic Press.

"City without a Soul." 1946. *IIA Journal* 12 (Jan.): 34–36.

Clutterbuck, Rev. George. 1897. *In India (the Land of Famine and of Plague), or Bombay the Beautiful*. London: Ideal Publishing Union.

Committee on Greater Bombay Scheme, Communications (Traffic and Railways). 1945. *The Greater Bombay Scheme: Preliminary Report*. Bombay Government.

Condon, Captain J. K. 1900. *The Bombay Plague*. Bombay: Education Society.

Cotton, H. E. A. 1907. *Calcutta: Old and New*. Calcutta: Newman and Co. Reissued, Calcutta: Surajit Das, 1980.

Curtis, Sir George. 1921. "The Development of Bombay." *Journal of the Royal Society of Arts* 69: 560–77.

Dandekar, G. P. 1942. "The Problems of Housing and Slum-Clearance in Bombay." *IIA Journal* 8 (Jan.): 261–62.

Davidge, W. R. 1924. "The Development of Bombay." *Town Planning Review* 10:275–79.

Deb, Raja Binaya Krishna. 1905. *The Early History and Growth of Calcutta*. Calcutta: Romesh Ghose. Reissued, Calcutta: RDDI, 1977.

Delhi Town Planning Committee. 1913. *First, Second and Final Reports of the Delhi Town Planning Committee*. London: H. M. Stationery Office.

Dobbin, Christine. 1972. *Urban Leadership in Western India: Politics and Communities in Bombay City, 1840–1885*. Oxford: Oxford University Press.

Dodwell, Henry. 1926. *Nabobs of Madras*. London: Williams and Norgate.

Dongerkery, C. S. 1957. *History of the University of Bombay*. Bombay: University of Bombay.

Douglas, James. 1886. *Round about Bombay*. Bombay: Bombay Gazette Steam Press.

———. 1893. *Bombay and Western India*. 2 vols. London: Sampson Low, Marston and Co.

———. 1900. *Glimpses of Old Bombay*. London: Sampson Low, Marstan and Co.

Dutt, Ashok, and Dhussa, Ramesh. 1976. "The Contrasting Image and Landscape of Calcutta

through Literature." *Proceedings of the Association of American Geographers* 8:102–06.

Edwardes, Stephen Meredyth. 1902. *The Rise of Bombay*. Bombay: Times of India Press.

———. 1912. *By-Ways of Bombay*. Bombay: Taraporavala.

Fanshawe, H. C. 1902. *Shah Jahan's Delhi: Past and Present*. London: John Murray.

Firminger, Rev. W. K. 1906. *Thacker's Guide to Calcutta*. Calcutta: Thacker, Spink and Co.

Forrest, G. W. 1903. *Cities of India*. London: Archibald Constable and Co.

Fraser, Lovat. 1911. *Old and New Bombay: An Historical and Descriptive Account of Bombay and Its Environs*. Bombay: Claridge.

Furneaux, J. H. 1895. *Glimpses of India and Ceylon*. Bombay: Burrows.

Gatacre, W. F. (brig-general and chairman, Plague Committee). 1897. *Report on the Bubonic Plague in Bombay 1896–97*. Bombay.

Gazetteer of Bombay City and Island, The. 1909. 3 vols. Bombay: Times Press. Reprinted by the Government of Maharashtra in 1977–78.

Geddes, Patrick. 1915. *Reports on the Towns in the Madras Presidency Visited by Professor Geddes, 1915*. Tamil Nadu State Archive.

———. 1919. *The Bara Bazaar Improvement. A Report to the Corporation of Calcutta*. Calcutta: The Corporation Press.

———. 1965. *Report on the Re-Planning of Six Towns in the Bombay Presidency, 1915*. Bombay: Government Printing and Stationery Office.

George, Walter. 1958. "The Roadside Planting of Lutyens' New Delhi." *Urban and Rural Planning Thought* 1:78–90.

Ghosh, Suresh Chandra. 1970. *The Social Conditions of the British Community in Bengal, 1757–1800*. Leiden: Brill.

Goodfriend, Douglas. 1982a. "The Tyranny of the Right Angle: Colonial and Post-Colonial Urban Development in Delhi, 1857–1957." *Design* 26 (April–June): 54–58.

———. 1982b. "A Chronology of Delhi's Development, 1803–1952." *Design* 26 (Oct.–Dec.): 36–50.

Grant, Colesworthy. 1862. *Anglo-Indian Domestic Life*. 2d ed., revised and enlarged. Calcutta: Thacker, Spink and Co.

"Greater Bombay—Across the Harbour." 1945. *IIA Journal* 13 (July): 1–3.

"The Greater Bombay Scheme—Review." 1945. *IIA Journal* 12 (Oct.): 27–28.

Griffiths, Sir P. J. 1945. *Better Towns: A Study of Urban Reconstruction in India*. Allahabad.

Guide to Bombay—From the Bombay Times Calendar of 1855, A. 1855. Bombay: Times Press.

Gupta, Narayani. 1981a. "Historical Growth of New Delhi up to 1911." *Indian Architect* 23 (Jan.): 18–24.

———. 1981b. *Delhi between Two Empires, 1803–1931*. Delhi: Oxford University Press.

Handbook to Calcutta. 1892. Calcutta: Newman and Co.

Harriss, Frank. n.d. *Biography of J. N. Tata.* Bombay.

Havell, E. B. 1912. *The Building of the New Delhi.* Guildford.

———. 1913. "The Building of the New Delhi." *East India Association Journal,* N.S., 4:1–30.

Hume, A. P. 1936. *Report on the Relief of Congestion in Delhi.* Simla: Government of India Press.

Hussey, Christopher. 1950. *The Life of Sir Edwin Lutyens.* New York: Charles Scribner's Sons.

Irving, Robert Grant. 1981. *Indian Summer: Lutyens, Baker and Imperial Delhi.* New Haven and London: Yale University Press.

Kapadia, P. P. 1934–35. "Bombay Municipal Building Regulations—Their Evolution—Their Defects—A Few Suggestions." *IIA Journal* 1 (April 1934): 29–32; (July 1934): 53–56; (Jan. 1935): 89–91; (April 1935): 136–42.

———. 1939. "Concrete Castles in the Air—Master Plan for the Town of Bombay." *IIA Journal* 6 (July): 10–11.

Karkaria, R. P. 1915. *The Charm of Bombay.* Bombay: Taraporevala.

King, Anthony. 1976. *Colonial Urban Development.* London: Routledge and Kegan Paul.

———. 1977–78. "Exporting 'Planning': The Colonial and Neo-Colonial Experience." *Urbanism, Past and Present* 5 (Winter): 12–22.

Kotraiah, C. T. M. 1979. *Indo-European Architecture in Madras.* Reprinted from ITIHĀS 7 (July–Dec.): 1–45.

Lanchester, Henry Vaughan. 1914. "Calcutta Improvement Trust: Precis of Mr E. P. Richards' Report on the City of Calcutta." *Town Planning Review* 5:114–130, 214–224.

———. 1915. "Notes on the Calcutta Report of Mr E. P. Richards." *Town Planning Review* 6:27–30.

———. 1918. *Town Planning in Madras.* London: Constable and Co.

———. 1942. "Indian Cities and Their Improvement." *Architectural Design and Construction* 12 (June): 116–20.

Landon, Percival. 1906. *Under the Sun: Impressions of Indian Cities.* London: Hurst and Blackett.

Lawson, Sir Charles. 1905. *Memories of Madras.* London: Swan Sonnenschein and Co.

Lewandowski, Susan. 1975. "Urban Growth and Municipal Development in the Colonial City of Madras, 1860–1900." *Journal of Asian Studies* 34:341–60.

———. 1980. *Migration and Ethnicity in Urban India: Kerala Migrants in the City of Madras, 1870–1970.* Delhi: Manohar.

"Life in Old Calcutta." 1924. *Bengal, Past and Present* 28 (July–Dec.): 129–41. (Reprinted from *The Englishman.*)

Long, Rev. James. 1974. *Calcutta and Its Neighborhood: A History of Calcutta and Its People from 1690–1857.* Calcutta: Indian Publications.

(Reproduces articles from *The Calcutta Review,* Dec. 1852 and Sept. 1860.)

Lovat, Fraser. 1911. *Old and New Bombay.* Bombay: Claridge.

Love, Henry Davison. 1913. *Vestiges of Old Madras.* 4 vols. London: John Murray.

Low, Sydney. 1907. *A Vision of India.* London: Smith, Elder and Co.

Maclean, James Mackenzie. 1875. *Guide to Bombay.* Bombay: Gazette Steam Press. Several editions were produced.

Macleod, Norman. 1871. *Peeps at the Far East.* London: Strahan and Co.

Macmillan, Allister. 1928. *Seaports of India and Ceylon.* London: Collingridge.

Maden, James, and Shrosbree, Albert de Bois. 1913. *Calcutta Improvement Trust: City and Suburban Main Road Projects.* Calcutta.

Madras Chamber of Commerce. 1936. *Centenary Handbook, 1836–1936.* Madras.

The Madras Tercentenary Commemorative Volume. 1939. Oxford: Oxford University Press.

MARG 18 (June 1965). Special issue on Bombay.

"A Market for Bombay: Responsibility versus Efficiency." 1866. *Bombay Builder,* May 5, 230–32.

Martineau, John. 1895. *Life and Correspondence of Sir Bartle Frere.* 2 vols. London: John Murray.

Massey, Montague. 1918. *Recollections of Calcutta for over Half a Century.* Calcutta: Thacker, Spink and Co.

Matthews, Bernard. 1942. "The Evolution of Architecture in Calcutta." *IIA Journal* 8 (Jan.): 229–32.

Mehta, Pravina, and Monroy, Antonio. 1980. "Bombay: The Making of a Centre from 1850–1950." *Lotus International* 26:73–83.

Meller, Helen. 1977. "Patrick Geddes and His Contribution to Modern Town Planning." *Urban and Rural Planning Thought* 20:1–8.

———. 1979. "Urbanisation and the Introduction of Modern Town Planning Ideas in India." *Economy and Society: Essays in Indian Economic and Social History.* Ed. K. N. Chaudhuri and C. J. Dewey. Delhi and New York: Oxford University Press.

Mukherjee, S. N. 1977. *Calcutta: Myths and History.* Calcutta: Subarnarekha.

Murray, John. 1920. *Handbook of India, Burma and Ceylon.* London: John Murray.

———. 1949. *A Handbook for Travellers in India and Pakistan, Burma and Ceylon.* London: John Murray.

Murray's Handbook to the Bombay Presidency. 1881. London: Murray.

Muthiah, S. 1981. *Madras Discovered.* Madras: Affiliated East-West Press.

Natarajan, D. 1971. *Indian Census through a Hundred Years.* 2 vols. New Delhi: Office of the Registrar General.

"New Capital City at Delhi, The." 1913. *Town Planning Review* 4:185–87.

"New Delhi, The." 1912. *RIBA Journal* 3d ser. 19:758–59.

"Nine Delhis, The." 1971. *Design* 15 (March): 11–13.

Noe, Samuel. 1982. "Old Lahore and Old Delhi." *Design* 26 (July–Sept.): 39–51.

Nayudu, W. S. Krishnaswami. 1965. *Old Madras.* Madras: W. S. Krishnaswami Nayudu.

Orr, James Peter. 1911. *The Bombay City Improvement Trust from 1898 to 1909.* Bombay: Times Press.

Pearson, R. 1933. *Eastern Interlude: A Social History of the European Community in Calcutta.* Calcutta: Thacker, Spink and Co.

The Port of Bombay. C. 1973. Bombay: Trustees of the Port of Bombay to Mark the First Centenary of the Bombay Port Trust (1873–1973).

Ray, Alok, ed. 1978. *Calcutta Keepsake.* Calcutta: RDDI–India.

Ray, A. K. 1982. *A Short History of Calcutta* (reproduced from the *Census of India* 1901, vol. 7, part 1). Calcutta: RDDI–India.

Ray, Rajat. 1979. *Urban Roots of Indian Nationalism.* New Delhi: Vikas Publishing House.

Report of the Bombay Plague Committee 1897–1898. 1898. Bombay.

"Report of the Housing Panel—Greater Bombay Scheme." 1946. *IIA Journal* 12 (April): 50–53.

Richards, E. P. 1914. *Report on the Condition, Improvement and Town Planning of the City of Calcutta and Contiguous Areas.* Calcutta: Improvement Trust.

Rivett-Carnac, Mrs. M. 1886. "An Afternoon's Ramble in an Indian Bazaar." *Journal of Indian Art* 1:6–8. (Reprinted from *The Calcutta Englishman.*)

Roy, B. V. 1946. *Old Calcutta Cameos.* Calcutta: Asoka Library.

Sandemon, Hugh David, ed. 1869. *Selections from the Calcutta Gazette in the Years 1816–1823.* Calcutta: Calcutta Central Press Co.

"Sanitation in Bombay." 1868. *Bombay Builder,* Jan. 6, 245–47.

Shastri, Janordan. 1939. "Traditional Domestic Architecture of Bombay." *IIA Journal* 5 (Jan.): 93–98, and (April): 136–41.

Sheppard, Samuel. 1917. *Bombay Place Names and Street Names.* Bombay: Times Press.

———. 1932. *Bombay.* Bombay: Times of India Press.

Silan, S. L. 1940. "Slum Service in the City." *IIA Journal* 6 (April): 115–19.

Singh, Pradip. 1970. "The City as a Physical Entity—Calcutta, 1750–1850." *Bengal, Past and Present* 89:264–76.

———. 1978. *Calcutta in Urban History.* Calcutta: Firma KLM Private, Ltd.

Shivadasani, H. B. 1939. "City Improvement." *IIA Journal* 5 (Jan.): 84–86.

Srinivasachari, C. S. 1939. *History of the City of Madras.* Madras: P. Varadachary and Co.

Stamp, Gavin. 1977. "Victorian Bombay: Urbs Prima in India." *Art and Archaeology Research Papers* 11 (June): 22–27.

Symons, N. V. H. 1935. *The Story of Government House.* Alipore: Bengal Government Press.

Times, The. 1930. *India,* a reprint of the special India number of *The Times,* Feb. 18. London: Times Publishing Co.

Tindall, Gillian. 1982. *City of Gold.* London: Temple Smith.

Town Planning Panel. 1946. *Bombay City and Suburbs, Post-War Development Committee.* Bombay: Government Central Press.

Tyrwhitt, Jacqueline. 1947. *Patrick Geddes in India.* London: Lund Humphries.

Wacha, Sir D. E. 1920. *Shells from the Sands of Bombay, Being My Recollections and Reminiscences 1860–1875.* Bombay: Bombay Chronicle Press.

Wheeler, J. Talboys. 1861–62. *Madras in the Olden Time.* 2 vols. Madras: Higgenbotham and Co.

———. 1972. *A History of British Settlements in India.* New ed. Delhi: Vishal.

The Post-Independence City

Ahuja, Sarayu. 1982. "The Changing Street Scene." *Design* 26 (Oct.–Dec.): 51–54.

Ambedekar, V. N. 1948. "Master Plan for Greater Bombay." *IIA Journal* 15 (Oct.–Dec.): 27–29.

Anklesaria, Shaknaz. 1984. "Lost in the Concrete Jungle." *Design* 28 (July–Sept.): 31–35.

Ansari, Jamal. 1977. "Evolution of Town Planning Practice and System of Urban Government in India." *Urban and Rural Planning Thought* 20 (Jan.–March): 9–23.

"An Appeal to Mrs Indira Gandhi, Prime Minister." 1983. *Indian Architect* 25 (Jan.): 56–57.

Bharat, Sevak Samaj. 1958. *Slums of Old Delhi.* Delhi: Atma Ram and Sons.

Bhardwaj, R. K. 1979. *Urban Development in India.* Delhi: National Publishing House.

Bhattacharya, Sri M. 1967. "Some Administrative Aspects of Calcutta's Basic Development Plan." *ITPI Journal* 50 (June): 20–26.

Birla, G. D., chair. 1951. *Report of the Delhi Improvement Trust Enquiry Committee.* Delhi: Government of India Press.

Boman-Behram, B. K., and Confectioner, A. N. 1969. *The Decline of Bombay.* Bombay: Boman-Behram.

"Bombay Building Ordinance." 1948. *IIA Journal* 14 (April): 81–85.

Bombay Civic Trust. 1970. *Bombay's Development and Master Plan: A 20 Year's Perspective.*

Bombay Metropolitan Regional Planning Board. 1974. *Regional Plan for Bombay Metropolitan Region: 1970–91.*

"Bombay's Multi-Storey Growth without a Plan."
1975. *Indian Architect* 17 (June): 85–86.

Bopegamage, A. 1957. *Delhi: A Study in Urban Sociology.* Bombay: University of Bombay.

Bose, Nirmal Kumar. 1965. "Calcutta: A Premature Metropolis." *Scientific American* 213:90–105.

Bose, Ashish, assisted by Bhatia, Jatinder. 1978. *India's Urbanization, 1901–2001.* New Delhi: Tata McGraw-Hill.

Buch, M. N. 1980a. "Oliver Asks for More: A Cry for a Place in the Sun for Urban India." *Design* 24 (July–Sept.): 47–51.

———. 1980b. "Rationalizing the Management of Urban India." *Design* 24 (Oct.–Dec.): 53–56.

———. 1981. "The Neglect of Urban India." *Design* 25 (April–June): 33–35.

"Calcutta: A City Returns from the Brink." 1984. *Urban Edge* 8:3–6.

"Calcutta: The Basic Development Plan." 1967. *RIBA Journal* 74 (March): 111–12.

Calcutta Metropolitan Planning Organisation. 1965. *Calcutta's Problems—Calcutta's Future.* Calcutta: Government of West Bengal.

———. 1966. *Basic Development Plan, Calcutta Metropolitan District, 1966–1980.* Calcutta: Government of West Bengal.

———. 1967a. *Challenge for Calcutta: Recommendations for the Basic Development Plan for Calcutta Metropolitan Region.* Calcutta: Government of West Bengal.

———. 1967b. *Howrah Area Development Plan, 1966–1986.* Calcutta: Government of West Bengal.

———. 1967c. *Traffic and Transportation Plan for the Calcutta Metropolitan Region.* Calcutta: Government of West Bengal.

"A Capital of Quality." 1984. *Design* 28 (Jan.–March): 20–22.

Chakrabartty, Syamal. 1958. *Housing Conditions in Calcutta.* Calcutta: Bookland.

Chaterjee, A. K. 1977. *Contemporary Urban Architecture: A Design Approach. A Study of Bombay.* Delhi: Macmillan.

Chatterjee, Siris Chandra. 1949. *India and New Order.* Calcutta: University of Calcutta.

Chokravorty, Samir K. 1985. "Land Conversion for Urban Development in East Calcutta: Process—Pattern Relationships." *ITPI Journal* 4 (June–Sept.): 4–16.

Choudhary, B. R., and Jhaj, G. 1978. "The Second Plan for Delhi." *Urban and Rural Planning Thought* 21:102–17.

Correa, Charles. 1970. "New Bombay: Model for India's Urban Future." *ITPI Journal* 64 (Sept.): 14–20.

———. 1971. "New Bombay." *RIBA Journal* 150 (Dec.): 335–38.

———. 1985. *The New Landscape.* Bombay: Book Society of India.

Cullen, Gordon. 1960. "IXth Delhi." *Architectural Review* 127 (Feb.): 110–17.

———. 1961. *The Ninth Delhi.* New Delhi: Ministry of Health, Town Planning Organisation.

———. 1971. "The Steamroller and the Flower." *Architectural Review* 150 (Dec.): 376–79.

Datta, Abhijit. 1967. "Some Fiscal Aspects of Calcutta's Basic Development Plan." *ITPI Journal* 50 (June): 27–32.

Davej, J. M. 1978. "The Environmental Pollution Problems of Indian Urban Settlements." *Urban and Rural Planning Thought* 21:79–86.

Davar, S. K. 1962. "Shopping Facilities and Trends in Delhi." *ITPI Journal* 29–30 (Jan.–April): 89–93.

"Defense Colony, New Delhi, and Its Lessons." 1962. *Indian Architect* 4 (Sept.): 20–23; (Oct.): 26–31.

Delhi Development Authority. 1960. *Draft Master Plan for Delhi.* 2 vols. Delhi.

———. 1961. "Some Salient Features of the Draft Master Plan for Delhi." *ITPI Journal* 25–26 (Jan.–April): 104–10.

———. 1962. *Master Plan for Delhi.* Delhi.

———. 1984. *The Future of New Delhi.* Delhi.

Delhi Improvement Trust Enquiry Committee. *Report 1951.* 2 vols. Delhi.

"Delhi 2001?" 1982. *Design* 26 (Jan.–March): 21–24.

"Delhi 2001." 1985. *Vikas Varita* 2. Special issue of a house publication of the Delhi Development Authority.

Delhi Urban Art Commission. *Fourth Report, 1979–80.* Delhi: Lok Nyak Bhawan.

Desai, S. V. 1970. "Restructuring Bombay." *Urban and Rural Planning Thought* 13:152–62.

Desai, Saravashir S. V., and Godambe, B. B. 1960. "Greater Bombay Takes Up Preparation of Development Plan." *ITPI Journal* 21–22 (Jan.–April): 40–44.

"Development of New Delhi—Halting and Timid Proposals by Study Group." 1981. *Indian Architect* 23 (May): 101–03.

Dhar, D. N. 1983. "Development of New Delhi." *Indian Architect* 25 (Dec.): 259–64.

D'Monte, Darryl. 1978. "Saving Bombay from Chaos: No Easy Options." *IIA Journal* 44:16–18.

Diwan, Sudhir, and Vakhariya, Kamnaiya. 1980. "Big Money and Political Power Have Made Bombay's Backbay Scheme India's Biggest Urban Fraud." *Design* 24 (Jan.–March): 25–36.

Doig, Desmond. 1966. *Calcutta: An Artist's Impression.* Calcutta: The Statesman.

D'Souza, J. B. 1975. "Urban Planning and Our Housing Problem." *Urban and Rural Planning Thought* 18:15–22.

Fernandes, B. G. 1970. "Review of Mass Transportation Systems in Metropolitan Cities of India." *Urban and Rural Planning Thought* 13:226–42.

Fonseca, Rory. 1969. "The Walled City of Old Delhi." *Landscape* 18 (Fall): 12–25.

Gandhi, N. K. 1973. *Study of Town and Country Planning in India.* Bombay: Ashok Press.

Ghosh, Bijit. 1962. "Central Vista, New Delhi." *ITPI Journal* 31 (July): 18–23.

———. 1970. "Oh Calcutta!" *ITPI Journal* 64 (Sept.): 3–13.

Ghosh, Marari, Dutta, Alok, and Ray, Biswanath. 1972. *Calcutta: A Study in Urban Growth Dynamics.* Calcutta: Mukhopadhyay.

Goodfriend, Douglas. 1981. "Old Delhi: Modern Lessons from Traditional Architecture." *Design* 26 (Jan.–March): 45–51.

Gonsalves, Colin. 1981. *Bombay: A City under Siege.* Bombay: Institute of Social Research and Education.

Gujaral, I. K. 1984. "Has Delhi a Future?" *Design* 28 (Jan.–March): 23–26.

Gupta, Devendra. 1985. *Urban Housing in India.* Washington, D.C.: World Bank.

"Housing the Middle Class—Delhi Development Authority Way." 1980. *Indian Architect* 22 (May): 202–04.

Howland, Marie. 1977. "Delhi's Large-Scale Land Acquisition, Development and Disposal Policy." *ITCC Review* 6:53–83.

Indian Chamber of Commerce. 1978. *Calcutta 2000: Some Imperatives for Action Now.* Calcutta: Indian Chamber of Commerce.

"Inner City Problems of Bombay." 1980. *Indian Architect* 22 (May): 84–86.

"Inner City Problems of Delhi." 1984. *Indian Architect* 26 (Jan.): 23–24.

ITPI Journal 57 (Dec.): 1968. Special issue devoted to the Seventeenth Annual Town and Country Planning Seminar on the theme "National Capital—Planning and Development."

ITPI Journal 58 (March): 1969. Special issue containing selected papers from the Seventeenth Annual Town and Country Planning Seminar.

ITPI Journal 88–89 (Dec.–March): 1975/76. Special issue based on the Twenty-fourth Town and Country Planning Seminar focusing on Bombay. Consists of "Technical Papers: Bombay Seminar."

ITPI Journal 96–97 (Oct.–Jan.): 1977/78. Special issue with title "Towards a Second Development Plan for Delhi."

Jagmohan. 1975. *Rebuilding Shajahanabad: The Walled City of Delhi.* Delhi: Vikas.

Jain, A. K. 1983. "Planning the Old City: The Case of Delhi." *ITPI Journal* 2:7–15.

———. 1987. "Delhi through History." *Design* 31 (July–Sept.): 23–29.

"Janpath Must Be Saved from Destruction." 1969. *Design* 13 (March): 11–17.

Jha, Gangadhar. 1975. "The Future of Delhi's Walled City: Problems and Prospects." *Design* 19 (June): 27–30.

Khambatta, Shri R. S. 1960. "Some Thoughts on Bombay Plan." *ITPI Journal* 21–22 (Jan.–April): 44–45.

"Kotla Mubarakpur—An Urban Village." 1958. *Urban and Rural Planning Thought* 1:41–54.

Kumar, E. R. Ram. 1978. " 'New Bombay' Turns into a Nightmare." *IIA Journal* 44 (Oct.–Dec.): 18–19.

Malhotra, Inder. 1977. "Rebuilding Lutyens' Delhi: Harsh Truth about Urban Housing." *IIA Journal* 43 (Oct.–Dec.): 10–11.

Mira, Girish, and Gupta, Rakesh. 1981. *Resettlement Policies in Delhi.* Delhi: Indian Institute of Public Administration.

Mitra, Ashok. 1963. *Calcutta, India's City.* Calcutta: New Age.

———. 1970. *Delhi: Capital City.* New Delhi: Thompson Press.

"Madras City: A Planning Study." 1960. *Urban and Rural Planning Thought* 3:51–98.

Madras Metropolitan Development Authority. 1980. *Structure Plan for Madras Metropolitan Area.* 3 vols. Madras.

Madras Metropolitan Plan, 1971–1991. 1971. Madras: Government of Tamil Nadu, Rural Development and Local Administration Department.

Manickam, T. J. 1960. "Indian City Patterns." *Urban and Rural Planning Thought* 3:110–29.

Modak, N. V., and Meyer, Albert. 1948. *Outline of the Master Plan for Greater Bombay.* Bombay: Municipal Printing Press.

Moorhouse, Geoffrey. 1971. *Calcutta.* London: Weidenfeld and Nicolson.

Mukhopadhyay, Shri Sunil Chandra. 1960. "Development Plan for Calcutta City Extension—North Salt Lake Area." *ITPI Journal* 21–22 (Jan.–April): 73–77.

———. 1962. "Planning for Community Facilities in Land Development and Housing Schemes in and around Calcutta." *ITPI Journal* 29–30 (Jan.–April): 94–109.

Mullick, Sri U. P. 1962. "Planning for Utilities, Services and Community Facilities in the Master Plan for Greater Calcutta." *ITPI Journal* 29–30 (Jan.–April): 110–49.

New Bombay: Draft Development Plan. 1973. Bombay: CIDCO.

Noble, Allen G. 1977. *Indian Urbanization and Planning.* New Delhi: Tata McGraw-Hill.

Oak, S. C. 1949. *A Handbook of Town Planning.* Bombay: Hind Kitabs.

Papers from the Seminar on Urbanization in India, University of California, Berkeley, June 26–July 2, 1960. 1962. Berkeley: University of California Press.

Problems of Urban Housing. 1960. Bombay: Indian Institute of Public Administration. Popular Book Depot.

"Projet de restructuration du quartier central d'affaires de Delhi." 1968. *Architecture d'aujourd'hui* 140 (Oct.–Nov.): 48–49.

Rai, P. B. 1971. "Functional Integration of 'Old and New' in Delhi." *ITPI Journal* 69 (Dec.): 22–27.

Ramade, Arun. 1976. "What Has Gone Wrong at Back Bay?" *IIA Journal* 42 (Oct.–Dec.): 14–18.

Ransal, Bharar Kumar. 1971. "Delhi: Disasters and Opportunities." *Architectural Review* 150 (Dec.): 384–86.

Rao, D. V. R. 1972. "Rehousing Squatters—A Case Study in Delhi." *Urban and Rural Planning Thought* 15 (Oct.): 1–47.

—————. 1973. "Housing of Squatters in Delhi—Search for a Solution." *Urban and Rural Planning Thought* 16 (April): 51–81.

Rao, D. V. R., and Bahri, H. P. 1972. "An Urban Renewal Study of Motia Khan, Delhi." *Urban and Rural Planning Thought* 15 (Oct.): 48–92.

Rao, G. B. Krishna. 1978. "The Town Planning Legislation in India: Problems and Prospects." *Urban and Rural Planning Thought* 21 (Jan.–June): 55–59.

Rao, V. K. R. V., and Desai, P. B. 1965. *Greater Delhi: A Study in Urbanisation, 1940–1957.* Bombay: Asia Publishing House.

"Redevelopment of the Turkman Gate Area." 1977. *Design* 21 (Oct.): 23–28.

Report of the Ad Hoc Committee on the Revision of the Lay Out for the Backbay Reclamation Scheme. Bombay, 1975.

Ribeiro, E. F. N., and Jain, A. K., eds. 1984. *The Future of New Delhi: Proceedings of a Seminar Organized by the Delhi Development Authority.* New Delhi.

"Road Structure of Nariman Point, Bombay." 1983. *Indian Architect* 25 (June): 156–57; (July–Aug.): 183–87.

Roy, Shri Kamalendu. 1961. "The Central Area of Calcutta: Its Growth and Development." *ITPI Journal* 25–26 (Jan.–April): 74–77.

"Sabotaging and Urban Arts Commission." 1977. *Design* 21 (Aug.): 17–18.

Saini, Bahwant Singh. 1973. "Slum Improvement and Squatters Rehabilitation: The Calcutta and Bombay Experience." *Design* 17 (Aug.): 27–31.

Salubris [pseud.]. 1980. "Is Delhi a Safe City to Live In?" *Design* 24 (July–Sept.): 61–68.

Samaddar, Sivaprasad. 1978. *Calcutta Is.* Calcutta: Corporation of Calcutta.

Sarkar, Shri Syamal Kumar De. 1961. "Calcutta: A Problem Metropolis." *ITPI Journal* 25–26 (Jan.–April): 63–73.

Satellite Towns for Madras. 1972. Madras: Government of Tamil Nadu, Directorate of Town Planning.

"Saving Delhi from Becoming the Private Preserve of a Few." 1982. *Design* 26 (Oct.–Dec.): 21–22.

"Seminar on the Development of Connaught Circus as the Metropolitan City Centre of Delhi." 1971. *ITPI Journal* 68 (Sept.): 1–10.

Sen, S. N. 1958. *The City of Calcutta: A Socio-Economic Survey, 1954–55 to 1957–58.* Calcutta: Bookland.

Seth, P. N. 1978. "Bombay's Jeevan Bima Nagar." *IIA Journal* 44 (April–June): 8–12.

Shafi, Sayed S. 1961. "Population Growth and Change in Densities in Delhi." *ITPI Journal* 27 (July): 29–37.

—————. 1980. "Traditional Indian Communities—Shahjehanabad: Improving the Quality of Life." *IIC Quarterly* 7:75–85.

—————. 1986. "Delhi 2001—Problems and Perspectives." *Nagarlok* 18 (Jan.–March): 64–74.

—————. 1987. "Retrospect Seminar on Calcutta's Development." *Design* 31 (April–June): 36–40.

Shrivastav, P. P. 1974. "A New Deal for the Delhi Slum-Dweller." *ITPI Journal* 82 (Sept.): 11–23.

Singh, Patwant. 1977. "Between Distorted Priorities and Deliberate Neglect." *Design* 21 (July): 27–29.

Sinha, B. M. 1983. "The Damaging Record of the Delhi Development Authority: From the Dubious to the Disgraceful." *Design* 27 (April–June): 46–51.

"Site Planning of Multi-Storied Flats in the Tropics. (As Applied to Back Bay Reclamation Bombay)." 1960–61. *Indian Architect* 2–3 (Dec. 1960): 22–24; (Feb. 1961): 14–17.

"The Tale of Two Cities—New Delhi, Chandigarh." 1981. *Indian Architect* 23 (Jan.): 4–10.

Town Planning Organisation, New Delhi. 1957. *Interim General Plan for Greater Delhi.* Delhi: Government of India.

—————. 1959. "Future Industrialisation of Delhi." *ITPI Journal* 17–18 (Jan.–April) 61–65.

—————. 1975. *Redevelopment of Shahjahanabad: The Walled City of Delhi.* Delhi: Government of India Ministry of Works and Housing.

Trivedi, Harshad. 1975. "A Study of Katra Settlements in Old Delhi." *Urban and Rural Planning Thought* 18:127–37.

—————. 1976. *Urbanism: A New Outlook.* Delhi: Atma Ram.

—————. 1980. *Housing and Community in Old Delhi: The Katra Form of Urban Settlements.* Delhi: Atma Press.

Urban and Rural Planning Thought 13 (1970). Special number: "Seminar on Traffic and Transportation in Metropolitan Cities."

Vaidya, Shanta A. 1978. *Industrial Worker in Bombay: A Socio-Economic Profile.* Bombay: Mill Mazdoor Sabha.

Wasi, Jehanara and Muriel, eds. 1980. "The Successive Delhi's: From the Sensuous Architecture of the Past to the Insignificance and Inappropriateness of the Present." *Design* 24 (Jul.–Sept.): 25–36.

"What Has Gone Wrong at Back Bay?" 1976. *IIA Journal* 42 (Oct.–Dec.): 14–18.

"What Is Wrong with Nehru Place, New Delhi?" 1980. *Indian Architect* 22 (Dec.): 119–21.

"The Whys and Whatfors of Western Urbanologists in Asia." 1977. *Design* 21 (July): 23–26.

Wood, Jack. 1959. *Town Planning in India: Status and Education.* Delhi: Ministry of Scientific Research and Cultural Affairs.

Post-Independence Architecture

"About Technology: Appropriate, Intermediate or Otherwise." 1977. *Design* 21 (Oct.) 21–22.

Achwal, M. B. 1971. "Low-Cost Housing." *Architectural Review* 150 (Dec.): 367–69.

————. "New Lamps for Old: Evolving New Strategies for Mass Housing." 1977. *IIA Journal* 43 (July–Sept.): 13–18.

Anand, Mulk Raj. 1980. "Postscript to Contemporary Architecture in India." *Design* 24 (Jan.–March): 48–54.

Architectural Review. 1971. 150 (Dec.). Issue on India.

Architecture d'aujourd'hui. 1968. 140 (Oct.–Nov.). Issue on Third World (pages 24–75 on India).

"Asian Games Housing, Delhi." 1983. *Mimar* 7:2–8.

Autar, Ram. 1980. "Postal and Telecon Buildings in Bombay." *IIA Journal* 45 (Oct.–Dec.): 17–21.

Bhalla, J. R. 1967. "The Role of the Architect in India Today." *RIBA Journal* 74 (March): 102.

————. 1968. "Architects' Registration Bill." *IIA Journal* 34 (Oct.–Dec.): 25–27.

————. 1971. "The State of the Profession." *RIBA Journal* 150 (Dec.): 344.

Batti, S. S. 1978. "Architecture: A Case against Pseudo-Modernism." *IIA Journal* 44 (July–Sept.): 19–21.

"Beginnings of an Architectural Brain Drain, The." 1975. *Design* 19 (Jan.): 21–22.

Chatterjee, A. K. 1977. *Contemporary Urban Architecture.* Bombay: Macmillan.

Chatterjee, Sris Chandra. 1948. *The Architect and Architecture Then and Now: An Essay on Human Planning.* Calcutta: University of Calcutta.

Cement Marketing Company of India. 1950. *80 Designs of Buildings for Every Purpose.* Bombay: Cement Marketing Company.

Concrete Association of India. 1955. *Conrete Structures in India.* Bombay.

————. N.d. *40 Designs for Low-Cost Houses.* Bombay.

"Charles Correa." 1984. *RIBA Journal* 91 (Feb.): 16–18.

Charles Correa. 1984 and 1987. Singapore: Concept Media.

Correa, Charles. 1971. "Programmes and Priorities." *Architectural Review* 150 (Dec.): 329–32.

"Debate on Architecture, The." 1959. *Design* 3 (May): 12–19.

"Degredation of the Architectural Profession in India, A Disgraceful Story of Anti-Professionalism, The." 1968. *Design* 12 (Aug.): 21–23.

Despande, R. S. 1964. *Build Your Own Home.* 4th ed. Poona: United Book Corporation.

"Embassy for the Belgians, An." 1984. *Design* 32 (April–June): 23–31.

"Five-Star Cult and the Indian Reality, The." 1981. *Design* 25 (Oct.–Dec.): 25–35.

"4 Schemes for the Tajmahal Intercontinental Hotel, Bombay." 1969. *Design* 13 (Oct.): 15–23.

Franklin, G. H. 1957. "Towards an Indigenous Architecture." *Design* 1 (Nov.): 4–5, 24.

George, Walter. "Indian Institute of Architects Presidential Address." *IIA Journal* 16 (July–Sept.): 40–42, 64.

————. 1951. "Indian Architecture: The Prospect Before Us." *IIA Journal* 17 (Jan.–March): 3–4.

Grover, Satish. 1971. "Conservation Problems." *Architectural Review* 150 (Dec.): 380–83.

Gupta, D. N., and Datta, A. K. 1971. "The Architects' Registration Bill." *Design* 15 (March): 19–22.

"Housing and Post-War Reconstruction." 1947. *IIA Journal* 14 (July): 2–3.

"Imitation and the Myth, The" 1955. *ITPI Journal* 4 (Oct.): 1–2.

"In New Delhi and Montreal: Cellular Solutions for High-Density Living." 1965. *Architectural Forum* 123 (July): 68–69.

India. Ministry of Works, Housing and Supply. 1967. *Building Materials and Housing in India.* Delhi: National Buildings Organisation.

————. 1972. *India Builds.* Delhi: Ministry of Works and Housing.

Indian Institute of Architects. 1972a. *The Architect and His Work.* Bombay: Architectural Publishing Corporation.

————. 1972b. *Code of Professional Conduct.* Bombay: Architectural Publishing Corporation of India.

————. 1972c. *Conditions of Engagement and Scale of Professional Fees and Charges.* Bombay: Architectural Publishing Corporation of India.

Indian Institute of Public Administration. *Problems of Urban Housing.* 1960. Bombay: Popular Book Depot.

"Indian Trend." 1967. *RIBA Journal* 74 (March): 113–15.

"Indianness in Artistic Expression." 1971. *Design* 15 (June): 15–16.

"Intach and the Indian Culture." 1984. *Design* 28 (Oct.–Dec.): 19–22.

Krathan, Allen. 1972. "The Problems and Prospects of Indian Architecture." *AIA Journal* 57 (Feb.): 35–39.

Kukreja, C. P. 1978. *Tropical Architecture.* New Delhi: Tata McGraw-Hill.

"Mr Nehru on Architecture." 1959. *Urban and Rural Planning Thought* 2 (April): 46–49.

"Modernism in India." 1979. *Design* 23 (Jan.): 17–18.

Nadeem, Abu. 1982. "How Form Follows Fiasco: An American Writer Unwittingly Mirrors the Ongoing Fiasco in India." *Design* 26 (Jan.–March): 39–42.

National Buildings Organisation. 1963. *Low Cost House Design.* Delhi.

"New Building in India." 1971. *Architectural Review* 150 (Dec.): 345–65.

"New Municipal Office Building for the Capital, A" 1985. *Design* 29 (July–Sept.): 24–28.

"Olympic Village, New Delhi." 1982. *Design* 26 (April–June): 26–38.

Parelkar, S. H. 1958. "Architectural Education in India." *IIA Journal* 24 (Oct.–Dec.): 8–15.

———. 1961. "The Present-Day Architect." *Indian Architect* 3:17–20.

Patel, Suryakant. 1973. "A Reappraisal of the Cities We Build and the Construction Materials We Use is Overdue." *Design* 17 (Aug.): 32–36.

Reuben, S. S. 1968. "Architectural Education in India." *IIA Journal* 34. Golden Jubilee Number.

Rewatkar, K. P., and Anantha Krishna, K. S. 1984. "Architects' Image in Society." *Indian Architect* 26 (March): 75–77.

Paul, S. 1973. "Housing Policy: A Case of Subsidising the Rich?" *Urban and Rural Planning Thought* 16:34–49.

Rao, B. Bhaskara. 1975. "Housing 2000 A.D.: A Long-Range Perspective for India." *Urban and Rural Planning Thought* 18:1–14.

"Reserve Bank of India." 1981. *IIA Journal* 46 (July–Sept.): 10–14.

Rewal, Raj. 1985. "Complexity of Community Housing Spaces." *Techniques et Architecture* 3 (Aug.–Sept.): 69–71.

RIBA Journal 1967. 74 (March). Special issue on India.

"Role of the Architect in India Today, The." 1967. *RIBA Journal* 74 (March): 102.

Sabikhi, Ranjeet. 1985. "Outdoor Space in the Indian Context." *Techniques et Architecture* 3 (Aug.–Sept.): 133–41.

Saraswati, S. K. 1973. *Indian Art at the Crossroads.* Calcutta: Pilgrim Publishers.

Seminar on Architecture. 1959. Delhi: Lalit Kala Akademi.

Serenyi, Peter. 1985. "From Lutyens to Young Indian Architecture: Sixty Years of Housing in New Delhi." *Techniques et Architecture* 3 (Aug.–Sept.): 55–63.

Singh, Patwant. 1959. "Contemporary Classicism." *Design* 3 (July): 49–52.

———. 1973. "Delhi: The Changing Skyline." *Design* 17 (April): 32–38.

"Sixty Years of Gregson, Batley and King." 1977. *IIA Journal* 43 (July–Sept.): 21.

Society for the Preservation of Archival Materials and Monumenta in Calcutta. N.d. *Calcutta: Save Its Past to Save Its Future.*

"Taj Intercontinental, The." 1973. *IIA Journal* 39 (April–June): 21–24.

Talvalkar, V. R. 1948. "Future of Indian Traditional Style." *IIA Journal* 14 (Jan.): 51–54, 56.

Tapner, Vic. 1979. "Culture Clash." *IIA Journal* 45 (July–Sept.): 13–14.

Techniques et Architecture. 1985. 3 (Aug.–Sept.). Issue on India.

"Time to Establish a National Trust for Historic Buildings." 1975. *Design* 19 (March): 17–18.

"Training Indian Architects for Indian Conditions." 1975. *Design* 19 (Aug.): 121–22.

"Weathering of Buildings in the Tropics." 1981. *Indian Architect* 23 (Aug.): 158–60.

"Where Are We?" 1976. *IIA Journal* 42 (Oct.–Dec.): 14–17.

Index

Photographic Credits

All photographs are by the author unless otherwise indicated. Sources cited in short form can be found in full in the bibliography.

1. Victoria Memorial, Calcutta

2. India Office, London

3. Bodleian Library, Oxford, Gough maps 41 (0), fols. 76–77

4. India Office, London

6. Furneaux 1895

7. Murray, *Handbook,* 1859 ed.

8. India Office, London

9. Macmillan 1928

10. Macmillan 1928

11. Macmillan 1928

13. Victoria Memorial, Calcutta

14. Victoria Memorial, Calcutta

15. India Office, London

16. India Office, London

17. India Office, London

18. India Office, London

19. India Office, London

20. Victoria Memorial, Calcutta

21. Richards 1914

22. Maden and Shrosbree 1913

23. Forrest 1903

26. Victoria Memorial, Calcutta

27. Douglas 1893

28. India Office, London

29. Campbell 1894

30. India Office, London

31. Furneaux 1895

32. *Journal of Indian Art* 1 (1885)

33. India Office, London

34. India Office, London

35. India Office, London

36. Randolph Langenbach

37. Randolph Langenbach

46. *Journal of Indian Art* 2 (Oct. 1888)

49. Grant 1862

50. Grant 1862

51. Victoria Memorial, Calcutta

52. Macleod 1871

54. Victoria Memorial, Calcutta

62. India Office, London

63. India Office, London

65. Delhi Archive

76. Tata Industries

77. Daniell, *Oriental Scenery*

78. *Journal of Indian Art* (1889)

89. India Office, London

90. India Office, London

91. Delhi Archive

93. The Delhi Development Authority Draft Master Plan, vol. 1, 1960

103. Randolph Langenbach

105. Macmillan 1928

106. Macmillan 1928

108. Lanchester 1918

110. Furneaux 1895

111. Furneaux 1895

112. India Office, London

113. Furneaux 1895

114. Richards 1914

115. Richards 1914

116. Richards 1914

117. Richards 1914

118. Richards 1914

119. Richards 1914

120. Richards 1914

122. Calcutta Improvement Trust Annual Report, 1934–35; photograph from the RIBA Library

123. Calcutta Improvement Trust Annual Report, 1934–35; photograph from the RIBA Library

128. India Office, London

129. India Office, London

131. Randolph Langenbach

132. Jagdish Mistry

135. *The Builder* 124 (1923)

139. Hussey 1950

140. The Delhi Archives

151. Despande 1935

152. Despande 1935

153. *Indian Institute of Architects Journal* 4 (Jan. 1938).

164. *Journal of the Indian Institute of Architects* 10 (April 1946)

165. Melvin Webber

175. Melvin Webber

179. Melvin Webber

180. Melvin Webber

181. Melvin Webber

183. Melvin Webber

185. Melvin Webber

186. Melvin Webber

188. Melvin Webber

189. Melvin Webber

200. *New Bombay: Draft Development Plan* 1973

210. Melvin Webber

215. Rondal Partridge

240. *Times of India*

241. Melvin Webber